Southern League

ALSO BY LARRY COLTON

Goat Brothers

*Counting Coup: A True Story of Basketball and
Honor on the Little Big Horn*

*No Ordinary Joes: The Extraordinary True Story of
Four Submariners in War and Love and Life*

Southern League

A TRUE STORY OF BASEBALL, CIVIL RIGHTS, AND THE DEEP SOUTH'S MOST COMPELLING PENNANT RACE

LARRY COLTON

GRAND CENTRAL
PUBLISHING

NEW YORK   BOSTON

Grand Central Publishing
Hachette Book Group
237 Park Avenue
New York, NY 10017

www.HachetteBookGroup.com

Printed in the United States of America

RRD-C

First Edition: May 2013
10 9 8 7 6 5 4 3 2 1

Grand Central Publishing is a division of Hachette Book Group, Inc.
The Grand Central Publishing name and logo is a trademark of Hachette Book Group, Inc.

The Hachette Speakers Bureau provides a wide range of authors for speaking events. To find out more, go to www.hachettespeakersbureau.com or call (866) 376-6591.

The publisher is not responsible for websites (or their content) that are not owned by the publisher.

Library of Congress Cataloging-in-Publication Data

Colton, Larry.
  Southern League : a true story of baseball, civil rights, and the deep South's most compelling pennant race / Larry Colton.
      pages cm
  Includes index.
    ISBN 978-1-4555-1188-4 (hardcover) — ISBN 978-1-4789-7727-8 (audiobook) —
ISBN 978-1-4555-1187-7 (ebook)
  1. Birmingham Barons (Baseball team)   2. Southern League (Baseball league)—
History.   3. Minor league baseball—Alabama—Birmingham.   4. Baseball—Alabama—
Birmingham—History.   5. Discrimination in sports—United States—History.   I. Title.
  GV875.B57C65 2013
  796.357'640976—dc23
                                                                      2012051309

To Barbara Colton Juelson
The best sister and everlasting backstop the game has ever known

Birmingham is probably the most thoroughly segregated city in the United States. Its ugly record of brutality is widely known. Negroes have experienced unjust treatment in the courts. There have been more unsolved bombings of Negro homes and churches in Birmingham than in any other city in the nation. These are the hard, brutal facts of the case.

—Dr. Martin Luther King Jr.
"Letter from Birmingham Jail"

CONTENTS

Southern League

"Are You Trying to Be a Smart-Ass?"

When nineteen-year-old Johnny "Blue Moon" Odom saw the flashing lights of a Birmingham police car reflected in his rearview mirror, he eased off the accelerator in his brand-new candy-apple-red Ford Galaxy, hoping the cop would speed around him.

It was midnight on June 18, 1964. Odom—nicknamed Blue Moon by a school chum for his dark oval face and his sometimes forlorn demeanor—was savoring the sweet taste of success. Two weeks earlier, he'd signed for the largest bonus—$75,000—ever offered to a black athlete. Charlie Finley, the wealthy and controversial owner of the Kansas City A's, had personally come to his small duplex in the projects of Macon, Georgia, to sign Odom while Florine Odom, a domestic worker and the widowed mother of John and his three siblings, proudly looked on. To seal the deal, Finley helped cook dinner—fried chicken, okra, corn bread, and black-eyed peas. He also arranged for the purchase of Blue Moon's new four-on-the-floor Galaxy. Blue Moon had installed a one-of-a-kind, custom-built 45-record player on the dash.

Baseball experts were proclaiming Blue Moon and his extraordinary talent as the beacon to the future of the lowly A's. In high school, he had pitched eight no-hitters and lettered in four sports. Scouts from every major-league team had pursued him. To start his pro career, the A's had assigned him to the Class AA Birmingham Barons of the Southern League, but everybody assumed it was just a brief stopover and he'd be called up to The Show faster than a Birmingham fire hose could knock the bark off a tree.

Checking his mirror again, Blue Moon watched the police car pull closer, its lights still whirling. He'd only been in Birmingham a few days, but he knew enough to understand that a young black man shouldn't be running from the infamous Birmingham police. He'd seen the televised images from the previous spring, when young black demonstrators were knocked to the ground by the blasts of fire hoses and attacked by snarling police dogs. He knew that four

1

little black girls had been murdered a few months earlier, when thugs with the Ku Klux Klan had ignited 122 sticks of dynamite at the nearby 16th Street Baptist Church.

Blue Moon eased to the curb.

Growing up in the heart of Dixie, Blue Moon was no stranger to the ways of Jim Crow. In school, he'd never had a white kid in any of his classes; at his summer job scraping food off dishes at the Dempsey Hotel in Macon, he wasn't allowed to walk through the lobby; on city sidewalks, he had to step off the curb so as not to stand taller than a white. When he signed his big contract, Mr. Finley warned him that Birmingham could be even worse. Martin Luther King Jr. had declared it "the most segregated city in America," and the *New York Times* described it as "a place where fear stalks the streets."

But Blue Moon wasn't a civil rights activist. On occasion, he could be a bit of a hothead, but he had never been in big trouble. He didn't drink alcohol or chase after white women. He was a ballplayer, just one week into his pro career—he didn't even know the names of all his teammates yet, or that he was playing on the first-ever integrated team of any sport in Alabama. For the first time in his life, he was away from home, on his own, with a wad of money in his pocket, a hot new car, and not only white teammates, but three Latin players, too, dark-skinned like himself yet cultural strangers. Back in Macon, he had a pretty girlfriend—they'd even talked about getting married—but she still had a year left of high school. For his temporary accommodations in Birmingham, a city with *rigidly enforced* legally segregated neighborhoods, the ball club had found him a room to rent a few blocks from the ballpark in the upstairs of a house owned by an elderly black woman. She sometimes fixed him meals, but so far he usually just grabbed a milk shake and a few burgers at White Castle after games.

For him, national racial issues were just background chatter. He was focused on what was in front of him, such as whether his new manager, Haywood Sullivan, who'd grown up in Dothan, Alabama, and had kinfolks who'd witnessed lynchings in the town square, was a racist redneck...or rather someone who could teach him how to throw a good changeup.

Shutting off his engine, Blue Moon watched a big, burly cop get out of his patrol car. In Birmingham, there were no black police officers.

"Let me see your driver's license," demanded the cop, shining his flashlight on Blue Moon's face.

"Sir, what did I do wrong?" asked Blue Moon.

"I said, let me see your driver's license."

Blue Moon fumbled for his license.

"Do you even have a license?"

"Yes, sir," replied Blue Moon, pulling out his wallet.

"Well, let me see it."

"Yes, sir, but can you please tell me what I did wrong?"

"Shut up."

"Yes, sir," said Blue Moon, handing him his license.

Like most blacks in the South, Blue Moon had been raised to address whites with *yes-sir, no-sir.* In high school, he had never sassed his teachers, popped off to his coaches, or back-talked his mother. That's not to say that he didn't have a temper or a fierce competitive streak. The day he joined the Barons, he told Sullivan that he'd knock down his own mother if she tried to dig in on him.

The cop took his license, then surveyed the new car. "Is this yours?" he asked.

"Yes, sir."

"Why do you have it?"

"Whattya mean?"

"Do you understand English, boy? Why...do...you...have...this...car?"

Blue Moon squinted into the glare of the flashlight. "Because I like it," he answered.

"How'd you get it?"

"I bought it."

"Where?"

Blue Moon paused, feeling his anger rising. On the day he signed his pro contract, he told Mr. Finley what kind of car he wanted, and Mr. Finley had arranged for it to be delivered to him at the ballpark in Birmingham. The payment—$2,400—was deducted from Blue Moon's bonus check.

"I don't know where it was purchased...it was delivered to me."

"Do I look stupid?" said the cop. "You telling me this brand-new car is yours but you don't know where it come from?"

"Yes, sir."

The cop opened the driver's-side door. "Step out of the car," he ordered.

Blue Moon did as instructed.

The officer glanced at Blue Moon's license. "This says you're from Georgia. Whattya doing in Birmingham?"

"I play for the Barons."

"Huh?"

"I...play...for...the...Barons."

"Are you trying to be a smart-ass? Because if you are, it's a bad idea."

"Yes, sir."

The cop shone his flashlight on the license. "Johnny Lee Odom...is that you?"

"Yes, sir."

The cop paused, contemplating the name. Suddenly, a light went on. "Are you that new bonus baby pitcher I read about?"

"Yes, sir."

"The newspaper said they gave you loads of money. That true?"

"Guess so."

"Boy, what's a nigger like you gonna do with all that money?"

Blue Moon ignored the question. "Sir, can I ask you what I did wrong to make you pull me over?"

The cop hesitated, and then replied. "When you turned onto 14th, you didn't signal far enough in advance."

"There weren't no cars."

"Don't matter."

"I won't do it again."

"Well, Johnny Lee Odom, this is your lucky day. I'm going to let you go."

"Thank you, sir. Thank you."

"But let me give you some advice."

"What's that, sir?"

"This is Birmingham, Alabama. It's real important you stay in the nigger part of town."

Introduction

Southern League and Me

In 1966, two years after this story takes place, I was a twenty-three-year-old pitcher for the Macon Peaches in the Southern League, a California boy experiencing the South for the first time. The idea of becoming a writer, let alone writing this book, never occurred to me then, not for a nanosecond. I was a ballplayer. That's it. Baseball defined who I was.

I could easily decouple baseball from the civil rights movement. I was not in Macon to observe the onerous habits of Jim Crow; my job was to blow the ball by any sonuvabitch who carried a Louisville Slugger into the batter's box. Like the players in this book, I was singular in purpose: have a good season and get to the major leagues.

I played against some of the players written about in this book, including Blue Moon. I am now almost forty years removed from the game, but instinctively and emotionally, once you've lived in the land of baseball, you're a permanent resident.

As a player in the Southern League, I never took notes or recorded my thoughts into a tape recorder—I would've been laughed out of the locker room. But over the years, a few distinct memories have stuck stubbornly in my mind. Details of specific games are long gone. The memories I do carry, however, were the seeds from which this book would emerge four decades later. And each of those memories had to do with race.

The first seed was planted on our initial road trip of the season, a visit to Montgomery, Alabama, to play the Rebels, a Detroit farm team. After the series opener at Paterson Field, the twenty-two Macon players and our manager, Andy Seminick, climbed onto our bus—nicknamed the Coffin—for the ride back to the hotel. I was sharing a seat with Leroy "Cat" Reams, an outfielder from Oakland, California. Leroy and I had played together on a semi-pro team

5

in the Bay Area prior to launching our pro careers in the Phillie organization. This was his second year in the Southern League, my first.

Several blocks from the team hotel, the bus pulled to the curb and Leroy and the two other black players on the team got up and started down the aisle toward the door. "Hey, Cat," I said. "Wanna go grab a bite to eat?"

He whirled around and looked at me as if I'd lost my skull. "Not unless you have a death wish." He turned and got off the bus and disappeared into the Alabama night.

Okay, I was in *that* Montgomery, the city where Rosa Parks had started the bus boycott a decade earlier and where George Wallace sat as governor. It didn't matter that the Civil Rights Act had been passed two years earlier—most hotels and restaurants in Alabama still didn't serve blacks, and hooded members of the Ku Klux Klan were as common as grits.

I played that whole season and never knew where Leroy and the others went after the games. I never asked. I saw them only on the bus and at the ballpark.

A second memory is of a team picnic, a chance for us to gather socially with our families on a rare day off and to share some brews and barbecued burgers. I brought my wife, Denise; she was eight months pregnant. She had been an art major at Berkeley, and had just finished a haunting charcoal portrait of the four young black girls who had been murdered in the bombing of the Birmingham church. It hung in the living room of our small Macon apartment right next to another one of her paintings—Mickey Mantle sliding into third. (In our divorce several years later, I got the Mantle painting.)

We arrived at the park at the same time as Cat and John Lucas, who was Hank Aaron's cousin. Together, we headed into the park, searching for our teammates. As we walked deeper into a wooded area, the path led us toward an opening and a very large white tent. Suddenly, Cat and John spun around and started sprinting back toward the street, looking like they'd seen seven ghosts.

"What's wrong?"

They pointed back toward the tent. Standing there were half a dozen hooded Ku Klux Klan members, squinting through the slits of their hoods.

It was one thing to have seen newsreel footage of KKK cross burnings, but an altogether different experience to peer into those hard, angry eyes. Our picnic was canceled.

Perhaps my most vivid memory of my season in the Southern League springs from a road trip to Mobile. Somewhere along US 31 between Montgomery and Mobile, the Coffin stopped for lunch at a small greasy spoon café nestled in a clump of pine trees. I took a seat at the counter. A heavyset waitress wearing a hairnet served me a glass of water in a plastic tumbler. Watching the rest of the team straggle in, she spotted Cat.

"Niggers have to eat out back," she instructed.

Andy Seminick, an old-school, barrel-chested, tobacco-chewing native of West Virginia who once caught a World Series game with a broken wrist, and was the Phillie catcher the day Jackie Robinson broke into the major leagues, glared at her.

"Then you don't serve none of us," he said, signaling the team to head back to the bus.

His response surprised me. I'd never thought of him as a champion of civil rights, yet when I thought more about it, his stance was consistent with his constant preaching about the importance of being a team. "We're in this together," he repeatedly said. "We got to jump on 'em, both feet."

Back on the bus, we all returned to our seats, nobody trying to analyze what had just happened. The card games, chewing, and spitting continued. We were a team of twenty-year-olds from all over the country, not Freedom Riders. Neither Cat nor the other black players said anything.

But Seminick's declaration of the unifying principle of team above all else never left me. The four other books I've written have all had a common theme of team, seen not just as wins and losses, but as stories illuminating how people function and interact under pressure—whether it's a championship NBA team; a college fraternity; a high school girls' basketball team on an Indian reservation; or submariners facing the ultimate test in World War II. In dissecting each of those teams, I learned that the subjects' relationships to time and place, as well as to each other, are what shape the narrative.

Four decades passed before the seeds that had been planted in memories of the Southern League's red Georgia clay began to take root as a story. Long after I was out of baseball, I began to think of the sport in its broader context. I was no longer obsessed with my own trajectory in the game—that arc had led to a crash landing. Instead, I puzzled over baseball's place in American culture—both the good and the bad—and its assigned role in our country's evolution. Since its inception, baseball has been a way to connect us, to transcend the boundaries of time and place, to bind generations, and to offer us a unique sense of community, a dialogue among strangers. In *Southern League*, baseball brings blacks and whites together in a place where it had never happened before.

I am constantly reminded of how, to many, baseball is a religion. I played in only one big-league game in 1968, and yet I still get a steady stream of letters requesting an autograph on my Topps rookie baseball card. I have been a writer for over three decades, but it's a rare day when I receive a copy of one of my books in the mail with a request to sign it.

It is this fascination with baseball's place in the cosmos that ultimately drew me to the 1964 Birmingham Barons, a story that somehow seemed to fit the notion that baseball is a perfect companion to our history, and even at times an augur of politics, as in the marvelous chronicle of Jackie Robinson. This seemed like just such a story.

More than the home runs and suicides squeezes, what drew me in were the backstories of the players—twenty-two young men as diverse as America—and the way they intertwined (or didn't) with the turmoil that was Birmingham, the epicenter of the civil rights movement in 1964. I was looking for glimpses into the nobility of the sport and its recurrent sagas of success and failure... and, occasionally, perhaps, redemption.

To tell this narrative, I chose to focus on four players—two black, John Odom and Tommie Reynolds; and two white, Hoss Bowlin and Paul Lindblad—along with their manager, Haywood Sullivan, a man whose roots in the South were as deep as those of the trees used for lynchings in the town square where he was raised.

Along the way, I talked to the players, their wives (or ex-wives), and, in one case, a player's widow. I wasn't exactly sure what I was looking for, but I was hoping it would be a story where baseball and the real world collided... and baseball won.

Baseball is reassuring. It makes me feel as if the world is not going to blow up.

—Sharon Olds, poet

PART I

SPRING TRAINING

CHAPTER I

Tommie Reynolds

Asleep at the Wheel

Tommie Reynolds, twenty-two, felt his eyes getting heavy. It was February 1964, and as he drove east along the Gulf Coast on his way to spring training, he yawned, trying to keep alert.

This was the start of Reynolds's second year in pro ball, and he was on the fast track to the big leagues. In his first year at Burlington in the Class A Midwest League, he led the league in batting average (.326) and home runs (27), and was so impressive that he'd gotten called up to Kansas City for the last month of the season, a rare feat for a player from A ball. And now he was heading to the big-league training camp in Bradenton, Florida. Pretty heady stuff, especially for a guy the scouts had ignored when he played outfield at Lincoln High in baseball-rich San Diego.

Spotting a Holiday Inn sign, he didn't even think about stopping. This was 1964, and motels across America weren't an option for blacks, certainly not in the Deep South. Having slept in his car for three nights, he was a bit discombobulated.

Ahead, he eyed a highway sign announcing a rest stop in five miles.

Even though he'd grown up in the relative racial calm of San Diego, Reynolds understood the reality of America's racial divide. His parents were from Louisiana and had shared stories of the Jim Crow way of life where they'd grown up. In his early years, he'd lived in the projects of San Diego, and although he didn't have to drink out of separate drinking fountains, the city's rigid redlining had kept neighborhoods segregated. And during his two years in the army, either at Fort Leonard Wood in Missouri or at the base in Augsburg, Germany, he knew that certain places were off-limits to blacks, and that many of his white comrades dismissed him simply because of the color of his skin.

Nearing the rest stop, he felt his head nod forward, and then jerk back,

11

snapping him back to the task at hand. Ending up in a ditch would be a lousy outcome for many reasons, including the damage it would surely do to his new '64 Chevy Malibu Super Sport, with its wire rims, aqua-green custom paint job, and front-seat console. It was his first car.

To his dismay, the rest area was closed for construction. But it was late at night and he was dead tired. To keep going would be foolish, so after survey-ing the scene and figuring it was safe, he steered his Super Sport off to the side of the construction site, turned off the engine, and leaned back his seat. He checked to make sure his .45-caliber service revolver was within easy reach beneath his seat, and then fell fast asleep.

The Early Years

Born in Louisiana in 1941, Tommie Reynolds migrated to San Diego with his family when he was one. The third of seven siblings, he first lived with his family in Frontier Housing, a government project for defense workers in the low-income Midway area of San Diego, on the north end of Point Loma. His dad, J. D. Reynolds, had moved west in the hope of finding a good wartime job, joining thousands of other families lured from around the country by San Diego's military support industry (78 percent of income in the area was derived from defense spending). Mr. Reynolds landed a job working on the assembly line with Convair, helping build the B-36 strategic bombers. But with seven kids to feed, he also worked a second job, busing dishes at Oscar's, a popular drive-in restaurant. He had little time to play catch with his sons.

Minnie Reynolds was a housewife, staying home to take care of their seven kids, doing laundry and fixing meals. The family always ate dinner together, and she arose early every day to make them breakfast and pack lunches. A tough disciplinarian, she demanded that her kids buckle down in school. Tom-mie didn't dare sass a teacher or blow off his homework, and Mom wasn't shy about coming to school to check up on him. She was the one to take out the belt, with Dad stepping in only as a last resort. Her response to misbehavior was always the same: "God don't like ugly," she'd say.

Eventually, Mr. Reynolds quit his job at Convair to take a higher-paying job with the San Diego Sanitation Department as a garbage man. His goal was to move the family out of Frontier Housing.

When the Reynolds family moved west and away from Jim Crow in Loui-siana, a friend had told them black people could live anyplace they wanted in California, as long as they had the money. But they quickly learned that wasn't true. Jim Crow was subtler in San Diego—there were no separate drinking fountains, no overt discrimination at lunch counters—but the explicit restrictions on real estate sales to blacks, practiced by banks and local Realtors and known as redlining, kept the city segregated. The fear was that the arrival of minorities would drive down property values. Once, north of San Diego, the Reynoldses passed a sign posted alongside Highway 395 just outside Escondido that read: STAY OUT NIGGERS. NO NEED TO STOP IN ESCONDIDO.

But slowly, as white families began a flight to the suburbs, black families started moving to southeast San Diego and into neighborhoods historically populated by white families. When Tommie was in junior high, his family purchased a home in Logan Heights. Built in the postwar boom of the late 1940s, the house was a modest, three-bedroom, one-bath California wood-frame with a patio, fenced backyard, and two-car garage, although the family had only one car, a big black Chrysler Imperial with the new push-button drive and fins almost as big as Escondido. The Reynoldses were one of the first black families to move onto their block. Tommie earned his fifty-cents-a-week allowance mowing the lawn. He never shirked his duty. Disobeying was not part of his character.

The Sound of Shattering Glass

The sound of breaking glass jarred Tommie from his sleep. Groggily, he looked around, and quickly saw that the passenger window of his Super Sport was shattered, shards of glass spread across the passenger seat as if somebody had taken a hammer and smashed it.

Tommie reached under his seat for his gun, and then straightened in his seat, looking around. He didn't see anyone. Without bothering to get out and investigate or clean the glass off the seat, he started the car and quickly drove away.

But thirty miles down the road, he was sleepy again. Maybe he was in Alabama now, maybe the Florida panhandle. He rolled down his window, trying to let the cool February air keep him alert. It was past midnight. If he could find another rest stop, he reckoned, he'd sleep until daylight and then drive all the way to Bradenton...and big-league training camp. No more having to sleep in his car and worry about getting attacked.

He didn't hear the sound of gravel under his wheels as he started to drift off the highway.

CHAPTER 2

Hoss Bowlin

Every Slide but One

It was the fourth day of the Kansas City A's minor-league spring training camp in Daytona Beach. Gathered around the sawdust pit, thirty players, all wearing baggy wool uniforms, waited restlessly for sliding instruction to begin. A few shielded their eyes from the relentless Florida sun; others dabbed at the zinc oxide they'd smeared on their noses and necks.

"Hoss, step up here," ordered Haywood Sullivan, the first-year manager of the Birmingham Barons. "You can help show how it's done."

Second baseman Weldon "Hoss" Bowlin stepped forward and smiled. At five foot seven, he was one of the shortest of the two hundred players in camp. This was the start of his sixth year in pro ball, none above A ball . . . not exactly the express lane for making it to the big leagues. Standing next to the towering six-foot-four Sullivan, he felt dwarfed.

He liked it that Sullivan had called his name—a good sign. But more than that, he was thrilled just to be in spring training and to have a shot at making the Double A Barons. It had been only two months since that dreadful December day in Memphis when his oncologist told him he wasn't sure if the surgery had gotten all the cancer, and even if it had, baseball would be out of the question.

"Let's start with the hook slide to the right," said Sullivan, motioning Hoss toward the end of the runway leading to the pit.

Hoss took off running toward the pit, and when he got to a few feet in front of it he launched himself airborne, horizontal to the ground, his right leg extended, his left leg bent at the knee . . . a textbook hook slide.

"Perfect," said Sullivan, patting him on the rump as Hoss hustled back to the head of the runway. "Now show 'em how to do it from the left side."

And Hoss did that one, too. And then he demonstrated the fadeaway, the pop-up, and the break-up-the-double-play slides.

"Okay, one more," said Sullivan, glancing at Hoss. "Let's show 'em the headfirst."

Hoss returned the glance, and shrugged his shoulders. "I think I better not try that one yet," he said.

"I understand," replied Sullivan. "No need to take any unnecessary chances."

A Bad Hop to the Testicles

Hoss had spent the previous season at Lewiston, Idaho, in the Northwest League, enjoying his best year. With a week to go, he was hitting .285, on his way to being named to the All-Star team, leading the league in doubles. But then he suffered every infielder's worst nightmare—a bad hop to the balls.

He limped off the field, but in the dugout he started turning green and throwing up. As a precaution, he sat out the final few games with ice bags on his groin, and then returned home to Paragould, Arkansas, with his wife, Madelyn, and their three-year-old son, Parrish. The pain subsided—the only time it bothered him was during orgasm—and when the A's invited him to the Florida Instructional League in Bradenton (two months of extended work for promising players), he jumped at the chance. It was decent money—$500 a month—and with Madelyn attending classes full-time at Arkansas State in Jonesboro to become a teacher, it was better pay than he'd made the previous off-season driving a milk truck for predawn deliveries to schools all over Green County. Instructional League was where he'd first met Sullivan, and when they first shook hands Hoss thought Sullivan had the biggest hands he'd ever seen. Sullivan appreciated Hoss's gritty approach to the game, always hustling and always fundamentally sound.

After returning to Arkansas after Instructional League, Hoss was lying on the couch one evening when Parrish accidentally hit him in the left testicle with a plastic golf club. He doubled over in pain, and a day later when his left testicle was swollen to twice its normal size and the pain persisted, he went to a doctor, who found a suspicious lump. The diagnosis was bad—he had testicular cancer. On December 10, 1963, he traveled to a hospital in Memphis, where doctors removed his testicle and a malignant tumor. Worried that the cancer could spread, the doctor removed all the lymph nodes from his waistline to his sternum, leaving him with a twenty-inch scar up his chest. The doctor couldn't guarantee that the cancer wouldn't return.

For two weeks, Hoss was confined to his bed in the Memphis hospital, the incision in his chest stitched together with surgical wire, twisted at the ends and protruding from his skin so that he could only lie on his back. Desperately wanting to get home to be with Madelyn and Parrish for Christmas, he persuaded the doctor to release him. But first the nurse had to take a pair of clippers and cut off the twisted ends of the wire. That pain was nothing compared with when the doctor took a pair of needle-nose pliers to pull out the wire—with no medication. It hurt so bad that Hoss wet himself.

On Christmas Eve, a blizzard swept through the region and the police weren't letting cars cross the bridges in and out of Memphis. But Hoss's older brother Jimmy pleaded with a state trooper, telling him that he needed to get to the hospital to pick up his brother, who had cancer. so that he could come home and spend what might possibly be his last Christmas with his wife and son. The trooper consented, and when Jimmy finally walked into the hospital room, Hoss teared up, overcome by not only his brother's determination to drive through a blizzard but by the words his doctor had just told him: "Your baseball career is over."

It took Hoss and his brother five hours to slip and slide the seventy miles back home through the blizzard, but he got his wish to spend the holiday with his family. In the weeks ahead, he began to feel better. There was still a tightness in his chest from the surgery, but as the days passed he started to have thoughts of proving the doctor wrong and resuming his career.

"You need to just rest and relax," insisted Madelyn.

But that had never been his style. In mid-January, he started working out, nothing too strenuous, just some simple stretching and walking. His biggest problem was that he'd lost thirty pounds, and it had zapped him of his strength.

At first, Madelyn was dubious about Hoss going to spring training, especially after he tripped on the front porch and was in such pain that he couldn't get up without her help. But as he slowly recuperated, and the stretching and walking turned into running and jumping jacks, she could see his determination and knew it was hopeless to try to talk him out of it.

"What the hell else am I going to do with my life?" he argued.

She also gave him support when he got pissed off at the Kansas City organization shortly before leaving for spring training. He had forwarded an unpaid hospital bill for $1,500 to them, and they refused to pay it, maintaining it wasn't baseball-related. With little bargaining power, he had no choice but to accept their counteroffer of a $50-a-month raise, which they maintained he could use to pay off the bill.

Screw Charlie Finley, he thought.

CHAPTER 3

John Blue Moon Odom

Tell Mama the News

Blue Moon Odom, eighteen, sat on the front stoop of his duplex in Macon, Georgia, waiting for his mother to come home. He couldn't wait to tell her the news. He'd just pitched another no-hitter, the sixth of his already legendary high school career at Ballard-Hudson High...and he still had six weeks left in the season. Two more scouts had given him their cards, so fourteen out of Major League Baseball's sixteen teams had now contacted him.

His future looked as bright as sunshine on the sea.

It was March 1964. In Florida, spring training for the Birmingham Barons had just begun, but Blue Moon still had the prom and graduation to think about. Not to mention what he and his girlfriend, Perrie Washington, were going to do that weekend. In the very segregated city of Macon, their options were limited, especially since he didn't have a car. His mother didn't, either. But maybe Perrie could talk her father into letting her use his car, and they could drive down and park along the bank of the Ocmulgee River.

He walked to the end of the block to see if he could spot his mother, Florine Odom, getting off the bus. She was late. Six days a week she worked as a domestic for a wealthy white family, cleaning floors, washing clothes, fixing meals, and wiping the runny nose of the couple's five-year-old daughter. Usually, Florine rode the bus home, always sitting in the back, even if the law—thanks to Rosa Parks and Martin Luther King—said she could now ride up front. ("It's safer in back," she explained.)

The youngest of four children—he had two sisters and a brother—Blue Moon was the man of the household. His father had died of lung cancer when he was only five, his two sisters were now married and out of the house, and his brother was in the army. He and his mom lived in a two-bedroom, one-story red-brick duplex in the projects on the west side of town in a black neighborhood that some called "The Alphabet." (Its streets were A, B, C, D, and so on.) It was home to Blue Moon, a lot better than the previous shack where he and his mom had lived, which didn't have indoor plumbing. Macon, located seventy-five miles south of Atlanta, was the only place he'd ever lived.

Although Macon had not been hit by the violence that had made national news in other cities in the South, it certainly knew the cruel bite of Jim Crow and the activism of the civil rights movement. Recently, fifteen hundred marchers had blocked the entrance to City Hall, demanding justice in the shooting death of an unarmed black man by Macon police.

Blue Moon had heard friends at school talk about that case, as well as about the church bombing in Birmingham that killed the four young girls. He'd also heard his mom talk about a lynching that had happened on the outskirts of Macon in the 1950s. But he was focused on being a high school athlete, spending his days in classrooms, getting mostly C's and waiting impatiently for the final bell to let him out so he could go practice or play a game. He would be the first student at Ballard-Hudson to letter all four years in baseball, football, basketball, and track.

Like all blacks in Macon, he knew there were places he wasn't allowed—the lunch counter at Woolworth's, the lobby of the Dempsey Hotel, all the other high schools in town. He accepted it as just part of life in the South. What choice did he have?

With darkness descending, he eyed a sleek Buick Roadmaster slowing in front of the duplex. The right rear door opened and his mother wearily unfurled, her gray domestic's uniform bearing the patina of her labor. Usually, she rode the bus, but on this evening Mrs. Blanchard, the woman she cooked for and whose house she kept spotless, had driven her home. Bette, the blond, curly-haired five-year-old daughter, sat in the front seat.

"Bye, Florine," said Bette.

"Bye-bye, Miss Bette," Florine replied. "See y'all tomorrow."

As the Roadmaster pulled away, Florine slowly walked up to the porch. Blue Moon stood to greet her, wearing a frown.

"How'd your game go today?"

Blue Moon didn't respond.

"What's wrong with you?" she asked.

"Nothing."

It had never really registered that every morning his mother trudged off to work, scrubbing floors, cooking meals, and spending more time with Bette than she did with him. Like so many other things in Blue Moon's world, that was just the way it was.

But on this day, something about what he'd witnessed struck him as fundamentally wrong. He knew it was a way of life for blacks to *never* call whites by their first names—it was "Yes, sir," or "No, ma'am," or "Thank you, Mrs. Blanchard," or "Good-bye, Miss Bette." But why did that little girl get to call his mom by her first name, while she had to address "Miss Bette" as if she were some sort of cornpone royalty?

"So, John, I'll ask you again," said Florine. "How'd the game go?"

"Ya know," he replied, "when I'm a big-league ballplayer, you ain't gonna have to work no more. I promise you that."

Already a Georgia Legend

There were two outs in the bottom of the seventh, the last chance for the Ballard-Hudson Maroon Tigers, trailing 5–3. With the bases loaded, Blue Moon dug in at the plate. On this sunny Georgia afternoon two days after his sixth no-hitter, he was playing shortstop and batting cleanup, as he did every game when he wasn't pitching.

The first pitch was a ball, low and away. In his previous three at-bats, he had a double, a single, and a walk. To go along with his undefeated record on the mound, his six no-hitters, and his fifteen strikeouts per seven-inning game, his batting average on the season was .526.

Seated in the rickety bleachers along the first-base side was Jack Sanford, an ex–first baseman with the Washington Senators and head regional scout in the South for the Kansas City A's. He'd seen Blue Moon pitch several games. His report to the front office was simple and succinct: "Best I've scouted."

Baseball scouts were always easy to spot. White, deeply tanned, dressed in slacks, alpaca sweaters, and a hat, often a fedora, the scouts carried the tools of their trade (in the days before radar guns and laptops) with just a hint of ostentation. A notebook, some business cards, and a stopwatch let everyone know they were not just casual spectators. Most were, like Sanford, leathery-skinned former players, baseball lifers, putting thousands of miles on their cars and calluses on their butts from sitting for endless hours on hard bleachers. Scouts were the gatekeepers to an amateur player's dream palace. The scouts had dreams, too, hoping that around the next bend they'd discover another Stan Musial. Scouting wasn't a lucrative job, but it kept these men connected to the game. Sitting on the hard slats at amateur ballparks, they talked endless baseball, and if by chance one of the players they signed made it to The Show, there was a bonus in it for them.

The second pitch to Blue Moon was also a ball, this one even farther outside. He stepped out of the box and glared at the pitcher, his eyes saying, *Come on, chickenshit, give me something to hit.*

Although he was arguably the best high school hitter in Georgia, it was his pitching that the scouts loved. He threw hard, very hard, too fast for all but a few high school hitters to do anything more than get the bats off their shoulders. He also had a good curve, wicked enough to buckle batters' knees, although some scouts thought it was too flat, and if he was going to be successful in the pros, he would need to come more overhand to make it break downward rather than sideways. All the scouts agreed, however, that it was the movement on Blue Moon's fastball that made him such a good prospect. Pitchers who threw hard were not all that uncommon; pitchers who threw hard and had great movement were the ones with a chance. Blue Moon had a naturally sinking fastball, one that got to the plate in a hurry and then exploded downward. Sometimes it moved so much that his catcher couldn't handle it.

The third pitch was low and outside again, not even close to the strike zone. Once more, Blue Moon stepped out and glared toward the mound. Was this puss-arm really going to walk him intentionally with the bases loaded?

Another thing the scouts all agreed on was Blue Moon's competitive ferocity. In the long history of the game, there had been boatloads of players oozing natural talent, guys able to throw the ball through a wall or hit it into the stratosphere, and yet when it mattered, they somehow couldn't perform, didn't live up to the promise. The baseball graveyards were filled with these phantom prospects. Maybe they were too soft inside, or maybe they didn't push themselves hard enough, or maybe they simply couldn't handle the pressure and choked. Then there were the guys who had a fire burning inside them, the ones who did whatever it took to milk every last ounce of their natural ability. These were the guys who outworked everybody on the team and took every pitch, every at-bat personally. To them, the game was more than just a newspaper clipping or a meal ticket. It was their life. Blue Moon radiated this singular passion.

Blue Moon wasn't interested in shaking hands with the opposition or apologizing if he hit somebody in the back. Baseball was his ticket to a better universe…and nothing was going to get in his way, not even the teenage temptations of girls. His motivation wasn't just money and fame. He loved competing…and winning…and the respect he earned for being the best player on the field. He knew enough about life in Macon to understand that there weren't many ways for a black man to gain this respect. That's what baseball could do for him. From an early age, he'd told his aunt Elena that he was going to become one of two things when he grew up—a professional singer or a baseball player. (Two graduates of Ballard-Hudson, Otis Redding and Little Richard, were making names for themselves in the music biz.) So far, the only singing John had done was in the shower or while washing dishes at the Dempsey Hotel.

With the count 3–0, he moved up in the box, crowding the plate. If this pussy out there on the bump was going to walk him on purpose, then the guy damn well better throw that fourth ball so far outside that he couldn't reach it with his hand-me-down fishing pole.

The pitcher went into his windup and delivered. Blue Moon's eyes got as big as a Dempsey dinner plate, the ball coming in waist-high and about six inches outside. With a vicious swing, Blue Moon put the bat on the ball in perfect harmony. The ball rocketed over the second baseman's head and headed into the gap in right-center. Before the outfielders could even reach second gear, it was past them, on its way toward yet another inscription for the monument of Georgia's newest legend.

A Hard Choice

Singing along to "Heat Wave" on the radio by Martha and the Vandellas, Blue Moon eyed the clock. Forty more minutes and he'd be off work at his weekend job scraping dishes at the Dempsey—just in time to join his buddies to go fishing down on the banks of the Ocmulgee River. Fishing was one of his escapes, along with hunting quail and playing pool.

Up until the start of his senior year, Blue Moon hadn't been much of a ladies' man. Consumed with sports, he was satisfied with an occasional fishing or hunting adventure. Until, that was, he'd met Perrie. She was a year behind him, quiet, courteous, and as far as he was concerned the prettiest girl at Ballard-Hudson. And on top of that, she sometimes had access to her daddy's car. Opportunity, it seemed, was just around the corner.

This wouldn't be Blue Moon's first time fishing from the banks of the Ocmulgee, which rolled lazily past the edge of downtown, less than a mile from Luther Williams Field, home of the Macon Peaches, a member of the newly formed Southern League. John had been to the ballpark a few times as a kid and sat in the segregated bleachers to watch, among others, a young Pete Rose on his way to the big leagues.

On this day's adventure to the Ocmulgee—or the "Old Muddy" as locals sometimes called it—he would be fishing for channel catfish, bluegill, and bass using the red wigglers he'd bought out of the dollar-an-hour pay he earned at the Dempsey.

His boss approached. "Moon, you've got a visitor out back," he said. "Make it quick."

Blue Moon offered a puzzled look. Who could be visiting him at work? Whoever it was, he knew this person had to be black. The Dempsey didn't allow blacks to even walk through the lobby or dining room, let alone stay there. Blue Moon and the other black help had to use the back entrance.

Blue Moon opened the screen door to the alley behind the Dempsey. Standing there, looking pretty as always, was Perrie.

"I've got my daddy's car for a few hours," she said temptingly.

Blue Moon liked her enthusiasm. He paused, weighing this sudden new moral dilemma. He could go with Perrie and enjoy all the possibilities of that opportunity, or he could stick to his promise to go fishing with the guys.

His instinct and his heart told him to pick Perrie. Fishing would always be there; her daddy's car wouldn't. On the other hand, he heard his mother's voice preaching in his ear: "Be a man of your word."

"I promised the guys I'd go with them."

"But..."

"You wouldn't want me breaking my word with you, would ya?"

With a long face, Perrie turned and exited the screen door, heading to her daddy's car. Blue Moon returned to washing dishes and checking the clock.

CHAPTER 4

Tommie Reynolds

Waking in a Ditch

Opening his eyes, Tommie struggled to get his bearings.

Slowly, he put it together—he'd fallen asleep at the wheel and run off the road, his prized Super Sport landing in a ditch, just short of a marsh. He imagined alligators and snakes lurking nearby, assessing his nutritional potential.

He glanced to his left, startled to see something ominous on his driver's-side window—somebody had drawn a target, with the bull's-eye right where his head had been resting.

Cautiously, holding tight to his .45, he opened the door to survey the damage to his car... and whether he would be able to back it out of the mess. If he couldn't, the chances of getting a tow truck to come out in the middle of the night were slim, even if he could find a phone booth... or even if he was white. This was a highway in the Deep South, not the Pacific Coast Highway running through La Jolla. A black guy standing on the side of the road in the dead of night, trying to flag down a car, had no chance.

But luck was with Tommie Reynolds. He was able to jockey the car out of the gunk with only minor damage and to continue on the road to Florida and spring training.

The High School Years

When he was still in high school in San Diego at Lincoln High—a school with a 10 percent minority population—Tommie was the only black player on the baseball team. He paid for his equipment with money from his part-time job busing tables at Del Mar Racetrack... but he never saved enough to buy a letterman's jacket, and with seven kids in the family, it wasn't in his parents' budget. On the football team, where he played tight end and defensive back, he was one of a dozen blacks, including his best friend, Kenny Tucker, a straight-A student who gave Reynolds rides to school every morning in his customized '38 Chevy. Tommie was notorious for his helmet-rattling hits on defense.

He didn't have a steady girl. In the classroom, he was a B student, taking all college prep classes. His favorite class was social studies with Mr. Nelson, partly because Mr. Nelson's no-nonsense approach echoed his own family's style. Tommie appreciated a clear sense of rules, whether it was on the ball field or in the classroom. In Mr. Nelson's class, he read about civil rights events in the South—the beating death of Emmett Till; President Eisenhower calling out the federal troops to integrate Central High in Little Rock; the lunch-counter sit-ins in North Carolina; the bitter resistance to *Brown vs. Board of Education*. But being seventeen and far removed from the Deep South, Reynolds regarded those struggles as distant and detached from his life at Lincoln High. Although students segregated themselves into separate groups in the cafeteria, the jocks at least were trying to do their part for integration, black and white athletes eating lunch and hanging out together every day on an outside patio.

Traditionally, the football team chose the homecoming queen, and in 1958 they selected Evelyn Elston, who was smart, beautiful... and black. This didn't sit well with a group of white parents, who complained to the principal, who persuaded the football coach to ask the team to reconsider its choice. Tommie and his buddy Kenny were having nothing of it, and lobbied their teammates not to back down. In the end, the team voted unanimously for Evelyn to keep her crown. Reluctantly, the administration accepted the vote, but decreed that future votes for queen would be by the whole student body, not just the football team. It would be two decades before Lincoln selected its second black queen.

Welcome to Spring Training

After twenty-five hundred miles, Tommie finally arrived in Bradenton. It had been a rough trip—no shower, fitful sleep, gas station junk food, a torn-up front fender, a broken passenger-side window, and a target drawn on the driver's side. He was relieved he'd made it.

Realistically, his chances of making the big club (or as the players called it, "going north") were a long shot. From the '63 Burlington club, he and pitcher Ron Tompkins, also of San Diego, were the only two players promoted to the forty-man big-league roster. In his brief stint with the A's at the end of the year, he hadn't exactly torn it up, getting only two hits in nineteen at-bats. Defensively, he still needed a lot of work, and although he could hit the ball a mile, he still didn't know the strike zone, striking out almost one in every four at-bats his first year in A ball.

The chances were more likely that he would end up either in Dallas, the A's Triple A farm team, or with Birmingham in Double A. He didn't want to go to either place, but he definitely didn't want to go to Birmingham. He'd read about the bombing of the 16th Street Baptist Church that killed those four innocent girls, and knew enough about the racial violence that he didn't want to play there.

Tommie was looking forward to the $15-per-diem paid to players on the big-league roster during spring training. That would be $450 a month, which was $50 more than he made his first year in Burlington. (Players' salaries didn't begin until the beginning of the regular season.) And it wasn't as if he had wads of cash stashed away from a big bonus. He'd gotten a measly $500 bonus to sign, plus a new Wilson A2000 glove. He'd been able to scrape by during his first off-season, spending three months playing in the Florida Instructional League for $500 a month, and then surviving December and January by living at home with his parents back in San Diego.

But as much as anything else in spring training, he was looking forward to seeing Penny Preston again. They had met the previous spring in Daytona Beach while he was at minor-league training camp. She was a sophomore English major at Bethune-Cookman, a prestigious black college in Daytona. He'd come to a cafeteria to eat, and she was there selling tickets to a play. He didn't buy a ticket—"I can't afford it," he said—but he did get her phone number. She made him work for it, however. With his close-cropped hair and youthful appearance, she pegged him to be only seventeen or eighteen. She was twenty, and there was no way she'd date a guy younger than her. When he told her he was twenty-one, she demanded to see his ID. ("I carded him," she later said.) Not only was he old enough, but his California driver's license made him seem almost worldly. They went out several times before he had to leave to go play ball in Iowa. She thought he was quiet, mature, and very much the gentleman. He thought she was beautiful and smart.

While he was in Burlington, they wrote letters, talked on the phone, and professed their love. Tommie had no doubt she was the one for him, even though they'd spent less than thirty hours together. When he returned to Florida in the fall for Instructional League in Bradenton, she did something very bold and daring for a nice college girl in 1963—she rode a Greyhound bus across the state and visited him in Bradenton for a few days. This was borderline scandalous, although her mother back in Georgia didn't know about it. And now, if all went according to Tommie's spring training plan, she'd travel across the state again, only this time she'd get to see him in a big-league uniform.

Pulling his Super Sport into the hotel parking lot, he saw its neon sign proclaiming that it was THE SPRING TRAINING HEADQUARTERS OF THE KANSAS CITY

A's. (The players called the hotel the "Big Pink" because of the way it glowed in the late afternoon sunshine.) Tommie smiled, grabbed his one suitcase, and headed for the lobby. The woman at the front desk furrowed her brow.

"I'm Tommie Reynolds with the A's," he said.

"Oh, I'm sorry," she replied. "We don't accept Negroes here."

CHAPTER 5

Paul Lindblad

Crybaby

Lying in bed, twenty-two-year-old Paul Lindblad stared at the ceiling of his efficiency apartment in Daytona Beach, trying to ignore the crying two-month-old baby girl across the room. It was 3 a.m., just nine hours before he was scheduled to make his first spring training start for the Birmingham Barons, his first test of the sore elbow that had derailed his promising initial year in pro ball at Burlington, Iowa. The injury had sent him to the Mayo Clinic in Minnesota and raised serious doubts about his baseball future.

As the baby continued to cry, he slowly swung himself to the edge of the bed.

"No, you stay in bed," whispered his wife, Kathy, twenty-one.

Ignoring her offer, he picked up his daughter Paula and paced the room, holding the child close to his chest. In the crib at the foot of the bed, his and Kathy's other child, nineteen-month-old Cindy, continued to sleep.

This was the fourth night in a row the young father had been up in the middle of the night. Still, he was glad he'd brought his family to spring training. Not many minor leaguers did. In fact, some organizations only allowed players in the big-league camp to bring their wives.

After finally rocking Paula to sleep, Paul lay back down and closed his eyes, imagining starting off the first hitter tomorrow with a slider, his best pitch... and the one most likely to test his injured arm.

Secrets of the Heartland

Arriving at the park for his spring training debut, Paul felt surprisingly calm. He kissed Kathy and the kids good-bye.

"I'll pick you up after the game," said Kathy.

Paul and Kathy had met in 1959 when he was seventeen and a senior at

Chanute High in southeastern Kansas. A three-year letterman for the Blue Comets in basketball and a state champion in the javelin (in 1959, Kansas did not have high school baseball), he was the oldest of five brothers and lived a few miles out of town. His dad worked for the railroad and spent more time in Kansas City, a hundred miles away, than he did with the family. Kathy was a year younger, a shapely, brown-haired, blue-eyed cheerleader, a regular in the church choir, a member of Future Homemakers of America, and—despite her cheerleading—very shy. Paul was also shy, especially with girls, or so Kathy thought.

As is often the case in a small town, where people seem to know each other's business, secrets abounded. Paul Lindblad, the star athlete, and Kathy Overby, the cute cheerleader, both held tight to family secrets…secrets so deeply rooted that even after they married, they were reluctant to reveal them.

Paul Lindblad…the Teen Years

It wasn't just Paul's athletic grace and nice smile that first attracted Kathy. When he was gliding up and down the basketball court, she couldn't help checking out his broad shoulders, long legs, and dark, thick, tousled, Elvis-like hair. Her friends had told her that he was soft-spoken, modest, and polite to his teachers. That was a good thing—she wasn't interested in the guys who were too slick or rowdy.

In addition to his good looks and athletic grace, he also had the coolest car, a turquoise '49 Plymouth convertible with the name he'd given it—Red River Rock—pin-striped on the front fender. On weekends he worked at Tommy Anderson's gas station, pumping gas and washing windshields. Once, Kathy had been sitting in the backseat when her stepdad pulled in for a couple bucks' worth of gas, but she'd been too shy to say hello or even smile. If Paul spotted her, he didn't let on. Besides, she and her three sisters were convinced their stepdad, a former used-car salesman and then co-owner of a motel in town with Kathy's mother, was a bad person. When he died in a boating accident after her junior year, she didn't shed any tears.

Paul was a decent enough student at Chanute High, especially in math and drafting, but sports were his passion. In basketball, he wasn't the best player on the team, but he relentlessly hustled, often slamming into the wrestling mats hung behind the baskets to protect players from crashing into the brick walls. As a cheerleader, Kathy could barely keep her eyes off him. Although the cheerleaders didn't go to track meets, sometimes after school she'd go to the track and retrieve the javelin for him.

Like most teenage boys in Chanute, Paul liked to cruise Main Street. On

Saturday night, he'd pick up Kathy and head for Barker's Dairy Bar, where they'd share the house specialty, a large scoop of chili in a sugar cone. Or he'd take her to a John Wayne movie at the Guild, or for a soda at Cardinal Drug Store. During the summer, he'd bring her to his American Legion games.

When he'd pull up in front of her house in his Red River Rock, she never knew what to expect, like the time he took off his cap and smiled sheepishly. He'd shaved his head…a look not exactly fashionable to Chanute in 1960. He'd done it in response to his teammates on the track team razzing him about always brushing back his ample hair.

Or there was the time he led her blindfolded to his car and told her he had another surprise for her. Because he was always tinkering with that car, she figured maybe he'd painted it blue and gold, the school colors, or hopped up the engine, but when he took off her blindfold and opened the passenger door, she discovered he'd removed the front bench seat and replaced it with two unanchored folding chairs, his precursor to bucket seats. As they cruised down Main Street on that freezing winter night, with the top down, wobbling in their seats, she held on for dear life.

In truth, she just loved being with him. She'd gone fishing with him down at the Neosho River, even though she didn't fish; she'd gone quail hunting with him, even though she'd just sit in the car and freeze.

Chanute, population ten thousand, was the center of their universe. Surrounded by cornfields and with the oldest soda fountain in the Midwest, it had the look of a town in a Norman Rockwell painting. It was not, however, at the cutting edge of the civil rights movement. There were a few black kids at the high school, but none on the basketball team with Paul or on his summer American Legion teams.

The Kansas of Paul's youth was the state where Oliver Brown of Topeka had tried to enroll his third-grade daughter in an all-white elementary school, and when she was refused admittance, Brown joined with the NAACP and took the Topeka Board of Education to court, eventually winning the 1954 landmark *Brown vs. Board of Education* decision that decreed, "Segregation of white and colored children in public schools has a detrimental effect upon the colored children." It was a decision that would have dramatic consequences on Birmingham, the city where Paul hoped to play in 1964.

Warming Up for the Big Test

As Kathy dropped off Paul at the ballpark in Daytona for his spring training debut, he wasn't thinking about *Brown vs. Board of Education*. He was zeroed in on his three-inning stint, anxious for the day to unfold.

The morning dragged by. For Paul, it was fielding bunts, pickoff moves to first, and backing up third and home on hits to the outfield. With each new drill, he went full speed. In high school, he was always the last one to leave practice.

Finally, it was time to head to the bullpen to start warming up for his big test.

"Nervous?" Hoss asked.

"No," he lied.

CHAPTER 6

Hoss Bowlin

A Boy Named Lois

Slowly regaining his strength following his cancer surgery, Hoss felt frustrated after the first week of spring training in Daytona. He tired easily, and at the plate his bat speed was glacial, making it hard to pull the ball. He was frustrated enough that if he didn't make the Birmingham club and had to go back to A ball, he was considering quitting and heading home to Arkansas and his wife and son...and whatever future that held.

Life had never been easy for Hoss. Born in 1941 in Paragould, Arkansas, population nine thousand, he was christened Lois Weldon Bowlin. He figured out quickly that life would be easier if his pals didn't know his name was Lois. (His mom was going to name the baby Lois if it was a girl, but when it came out a boy, she named him Lois anyway.) He'd also shed his middle name of Weldon, preferring to go by Hoss, the name his father gave him for always trying to outrun the family's team of workhorses.

Hoss grew up on a tenant cotton farm in Pumpkin Center, ten miles outside Paragould in the northeastern corner of Arkansas. His dad was a hard-as-nails sharecropper, his mom "a good Christian woman." With his sister and four brothers, he had to help his dad on the farm from an early age, milking cows, gathering eggs, picking cotton. It was a hardscrabble existence: no running water, no indoor plumbing, no television, and lots of home remedies—kerosene and sugar to cure the croup or slippery elm for cuts and diarrhea. When his shoes got holes in the soles, his mother lined them with cardboard. For bathing, Hoss's mom would give him and his brothers a bar of lye soap and send them down to Sugar Creek, where his dad had piled sandbags to create a little pond. A water moccasin often lay curled on a nearby rock. Hoss named it Oscar, but then one day Hoss's dad showed up with a shotgun, and that was the end of Oscar.

Hoss not only didn't have a bedroom of his own, he had to share a bed. For Christmas one year, he got an orange. Another year he asked for a new baseball glove but got homemade peppermint candy instead. In the second grade, he learned how to handle a rifle, hiking out with the family's coonhound to shoot squirrels and other critters for dinner. It was his job to kill the rabbits he'd find in the traps his father set. He didn't like that job, but saying no to his father wasn't an option. He watched his brother get knocked right off his chair as payment for sassing back at the dinner table. Hoss wouldn't make that mistake.

With no Little League or organized competition, he and his brothers invented their own games behind the barn. Using a rake handle, he'd try to hit the corncobs or bottle caps his brothers pitched. And if his brothers weren't around, he'd pick up rocks from the road and toss them in the air and then swing away, pretending he was Marty Marion, the player he idolized on his favorite team, the St. Louis Cardinals. When he ran out of rocks, he persuaded his father to drive the old pickup into Paragould and pick up a load of gravel. To perfect his swing, Hoss didn't just throw the rocks up and flail away. He tossed them high and tight, low and away. It was even better when his dad crafted a bat for him from a weeping willow. He also honed his hand-eye coordination swinging a hoe when he was working in the cotton field. When he was tired of swinging, he'd lie down in the tall grass and stare up at the sky, watching planes passing overhead and dreaming about the day he'd be riding one of those planes all the way to the big leagues.

By the time he reached eighth grade, he'd already been asked to play on the local semi-pro team. There were no blacks on the team, nor any in the school. In fact, there weren't any in the whole county except the help at the big house up the hill where his future wife, Madelyn, lived with her parents and three sisters. The N word flowed among locals like mud washing off the foothills of the Ozarks after a big rain. Once, Hoss went into town with his father and they met a black salesman who was traveling with his young son. The two fathers decided it would be a good idea for their sons to have a "rasslin'" match. Hoss easily pinned the other boy. To celebrate the victory, his father treated him to a Coca-Cola.

If they were choosing players for Birmingham's first-ever integrated team based on experience with racial diversity, Hoss's name wouldn't have been among the first drawn. He'd grown up in a Jim Crow–ruled Arkansas, where its governor, Orval Faubus, had defiantly blocked the integration of Little Rock's Central High, forcing President Eisenhower to call out the federal troops in one of the nation's first confrontations over the *Brown vs. Board of Educa-*

tion ruling. But in his first five years in pro ball, he'd played with a handful of blacks, and had no problems.

Every Little Ache

Waiting to use one of the pay phones in the rec room at Diamond City, the A's minor-league complex in Daytona Beach, Hoss felt a dull ache in his groin... and an immediate sense of panic. He hoped it was just one of the effects of the rigors of spring training, but after his ordeal with cancer, he worried. Like most young men, he'd always taken his body and his health for granted. Now he was on hyper-alert, with every little ache, every little twitch a cause for concern. His doctor's warning that the cancer could return rattled regularly through his brain.

He was waiting to call Madelyn back home, eager to hear her voice. They'd been married four years already—she was eighteen and he was nineteen when they tied the knot. Their plan was for her to join him in Birmingham—or wherever he got assigned—when her classes got out in June. She was living at her parents' big house in Paragould while she attended school. The previous three years she had joined him in Billings, Montana; Portsmouth, Virginia; and Lewiston, Idaho. In each city, his teammates always asked him the same question: "How'd a hillbilly like you get such a smart and pretty wife?"

As he continued to wait for the phone, the ache in his groin disappeared as mysteriously as it had appeared. He breathed easier.

When it was finally his turn to use the phone, he noticed one of the other players, Charlie Shoemaker, a pretty-boy second baseman from California, glaring at him. When the glaring continued, he paused his conversation with Madelyn. "What's your problem?" he asked.

"You, you stupid bumpkin," retorted Shoemaker.

Hoss ignored him, figuring that Shoemaker was resentful of the way the coaches, who all knew of Hoss's condition, bent over backward to go easy on him. Or maybe he was just jealous of all the praise that Hoss and a flashy young shortstop named Bert Campaneris had been getting for the way they turned double plays together in practice.

Finally, after saying his good-bye and I-love-you to Madelyn, he turned, ready to return to the barracks that housed the players. Shoemaker was blocking his way.

"You're a pussy," said Shoemaker.

Again, Hoss ignored him. As much as he wanted to rearrange Shoemaker's pretty face, the prospect of getting a knee to his surviving testicle didn't seem like a risk worth taking.

Living the Dream

Hoss sat in the clubhouse, swapping stories with Paul Lindblad. In a minor-league spring training camp, where stories of luck and disaster flowed like cheap beer, few players had a narrative more down-home than Hoss's tale of getting started in pro ball.

For most young players, failing to advance past A ball after half a decade would induce a fatalistic gloom—a sense that failure was inevitable, and that they were just waiting on their walking papers. But Hoss was only in his second year in the A's organization after spending four wheel-spinning years with the Cardinals. Getting picked up by the A's, he believed, had rejuvenated his career. The belief that he still actually had a shot at the big leagues helped fuel his decision not to quit after his surgery.

In high school, he'd played shortstop, but the scouts hadn't beaten down his tenant farmhouse door to sign him. In his senior year he traveled to a regional pro tryout, and although he was the fastest player there, scouts from the Yankees and Redlegs thought he was too small. Finally, a scout from the Cardinals decided to take a chance, asking Hoss's father if he would accept a $2,000 bonus and a first-year salary of $250 a month.

"Hell yes," replied Mr. Bowlin, who had never had more than two hundred dollars to his name. "It'll be one less mouth for me to feed."

The icing was that it was the Cardinals. There'd been many nights when the only sound in the house was the radio play-by-play of Harry Caray. In the month it took for the bonus check to arrive, Hoss practically wore a path to the mailbox, and when it finally did show up, the mailman drove all the way up to the house to personally deliver it, his horn blaring. Two days later, Hoss bought himself his first car, a '56 Chevy with mud flaps and a brodie knob. When he departed for spring training two months later, he left the car with his brother Jimmy. (It was the car Jimmy would drive through the snow to rescue Hoss from the hospital.)

Hoss rode a train to get to his first spring training in Brunswick, Georgia, in 1958. His mother packed a couple of chicken sandwiches for him and admonished the conductor to make sure he got off at the right stop. When he arrived in Brunswick, he got lost and spent the night sleeping on a bench at the Y. The next day he found his rooming house, where he would be the only ballplayer. He unpacked his two pairs of pants, two shirts, and worn-out pair of spikes, and spent the next six weeks eating his meals with railroad workers, who tried unsuccessfully to get him to have a beer with them. He'd never touched alcohol. That was one of the things that had attracted Madelyn. In the 1950s, when all the guys were smoking and drinking and doing all the things to make them

James Dean–cool, Hoss kept it clean. Madelyn liked his values and that he came from a big, close-knit family.

At his first day of spring training that first year—1958—he was surprised to discover there were over three hundred players in camp. When the coaches asked the players to line up by position, forty-three hustled to shortstop, but only eighteen to second. That's when Hoss decided he was a second baseman.

Like all the other players in Brunswick, he wore an itchy generic wool uniform that was too big and too hot. Excess belt hung down to his knees. His number—209—was safety-pinned to the back of his uniform. He was nonetheless a pro ballplayer, living his dream.

He spent the next four years bouncing around the low minors in the Cardinals organization, including Hobbs, New Mexico; Dothan, Alabama; and Lancaster, Pennsylvania. He first tasted the demon rum in Hobbs. He was playing pool in a local tavern with two of his older teammates when they decided he needed to get drunk. Going behind the bar, they poured whatever they could get their hands on into a big tumbler, and after handing it to Hoss and goading him into chugging it down, they put him on a bar stool and started him spinning. He woke up in his bathtub. He'd only sipped a few beers since then. And in an era when most players smoked cigarettes and chewed tobacco, he was a gum chewer and a milk drinker.

Common Language

The first game of spring training was an intra-squad contest between the Kansas City A's top two farm clubs—AAA Dallas and AA Birmingham. With his Rawlings glove hiding his face, Hoss opened his mouth wide, the signal to shortstop Bert Campaneris that he'd cover second if the runner on first, pretty boy Charlie Shoemaker, tried to steal. In the arcane world of baseball signs, the shortstop and second baseman didn't have to speak the same language to know what to do. Good thing. The slender, Cuban-born Campaneris, aka Campy, spoke very little English. His favorite American words so far were used primarily in restaurants—"hamburgee" and "cheekin." According to teammates, there was no real language barrier, since Hoss didn't speak English, either.

On the mound for the Barons, Paul Lindblad checked Shoemaker, the Dallas runner, on first and then delivered. The batter, Santiago Rosario of Puerto Rico, hit a sharp grounder up the middle that looked like a sure base hit. But ranging far to his left, Campy lunged for the ball and snared it. From his knees, he backhanded it to Hoss, who stepped on second, and then leaped over the spikes of the hard-sliding Shoemaker and fired to first for the double play.

In the dugout, Manager Haywood Sullivan applauded. In his years as a player in the bigs, mostly with Boston, he'd seen many great double-play combinations—Aparicio to Fox, Kubek to Richardson—but the double play he'd just witnessed was as good as anything he'd seen, raising hope that the Barons could be solid defensively up the middle.

As the dust settled at second, Hoss and Shoemaker stood jaw-to-jaw, Hoss taking exception to Shoemaker's spikes-up slide. "Let's go," growled Shoemaker.

This time Hoss stood his ground, ready to rumble, never mind the potential consequences. But before any blows were thrown, Campy grabbed Hoss from behind, lifting him off the ground and spinning him around like a rag doll, and then pointing Shoemaker back toward the dugout.

With peace temporarily restored, Campy and Hoss trotted side by side off the field. Hoss couldn't help but marvel at the ease with which the skinny little shortstop had lifted him off the ground and prevented a fight. But what amazed him even more was the incredible play Campy had just made, including the perfect backhand toss from his knees.

Screw Charlie Shoemaker, he thought. *And Charlie Finley, too.*

CHAPTER 7

Paul Lindblad

Bladder Control

Paul—or "Bladder" as his teammates sometimes called him—checked the runner on second. Campaneris was sneaking in behind him. In practice the day before, pitchers and shortstops had spent half an hour working on the "daylight" pickoff play. (Pitchers had also worked an hour on the covering-first-base drill for the sixth day in a row.)

Spotting daylight between Campy and the runner, Bladder whirled and fired to the bag.

"Out!" shouted the ump.

Lindblad turned and hustled to the dugout, his three-inning stint on the mound over—no runs, one hit, one walk, four strikeouts, and one incredible Campy to Hoss to first double play. At the top step, Sullivan greeted him with a pat on the back.

Lindblad knew that one sure way to make a good impression on any manager was to properly execute the fundamentals, such as the pickoff play they'd just practiced. He smiled, happy that his arm had felt great—not even a twinge of elbow pain. He wouldn't have to pack up the wife and kids and go back to Kansas and that miserable job he'd had in the meatpacking plant last winter... at least not for the time being.

He took a seat on the bench, draping his windbreaker over his left arm. Prior to the inflammation in his elbow, he'd been sailing through the Class A Midwest League, winning ten and losing only two, with an eye-popping 1.58 ERA, giving up only sixty-nine hits and twenty-three walks in ninety-seven innings.

His excellent numbers had surprised the Kansas City brass. When he signed for a modest $2,000 bonus before the 1963 season, scouts had rated his control and breaking ball as above average, but weren't dazzled by his velocity. The big bonuses—those over $10,000—went to pitchers who blew it by the hitters.

But what Paul had shown in Burlington was that he "knew how to pitch." He threw strikes, got ahead of the hitters, and worked the ball in and out, and up and down in the strike zone. He was a left-hander with control, a great combination for moving up in any organization. Plus, his fastball had movement. There'd also been some concern that he was "too nice a guy," and would be afraid to come inside or knock down hitters. He'd dispelled that notion.

Lindblad had his heart set on going to Birmingham. That would not only be the next logical step in his career; it would give him a chance to earn the $1,000 "progressive bonus" if he stayed ninety days in Double A. And God knew he and Kathy needed the money. They'd had to take out a $500 loan from a bank in Chanute, as well as an additional loan from her mother, just to get through spring training. He was vaguely aware of the civil rights unrest in Birmingham, and he'd overheard black players in camp talk about not wanting to get assigned there, but for him, Birmingham simply meant progress in his career.

Gathering up his glove, he jogged out to the right-field foul pole. He hadn't told anybody in the front office, but he'd worried all winter that his left elbow was messed up. Since leaving Mayo, there'd been no medication, no special therapy, no guarantee it would get better. He'd run wind sprints and done his calisthenics prior to heading to Florida, but not much else. Players who spent the off-season in the warmer climates like California often threw a lot before spring training, arriving in camp in better baseball condition. (Of the 640 players on Major League Baseball rosters in spring training in 1964, 92 were from California. Pennsylvania was second with 47; Cuba produced 22.) But in wintry Kansas, Paul had spent the winter months working in that meat processing plant for $1.55 an hour while Kathy, pregnant, stayed home and took care of their toddler.

Not the Stuff of Poems

Finishing their wind sprints across the outfield grass, the pitchers bent at the waist and gasped for air. Except for Paul. He kept going, foul pole to foul pole.

"Hey, Bladder, you can't run the ball across the plate," yelled Hoss.

Paul smiled, and then held up two fingers. "Just two more," he promised.

He'd always had good stamina, whether it was baling hay during the summers in Kansas, boxing with his brothers, or running up and down the court in basketball. He wasn't running extra wind sprints to wow Sullivan or to show up the others—he just liked to run. He felt especially pumped up because his three-inning stint had gone so well.

For many players, spring training was pure torture—too much running, too many calisthenics, too much sweating under the blistering Florida sun, too much being cooped up with too many guys.

For fans, however, the very notion of spring training summoned poetic reveries—the verdant outfield grass, the magical sound of balls and bats colliding, the untrammeled hope for a better season. Ignored were the sunburned necks, or the painful blisters from new spikes, or the tedium of the endless outfield relay drills that measured players' days.

For the minor leaguers nervously waiting to see if they were about to get pink-slipped and sent home to start looking for a "real job," spring training was often an unpoetic ending rather than a beginning. They'd leave Daytona Beach with a tattered suitcase filled with broken dreams and no money in their pocket.

Spring training meant living on a shoestring. Paul's $2,000 bonus was long gone, a big chunk of it having been spent on a down payment for a '63 Chevy Impala—the Red River Rock was no longer practical. He and Kathy had already talked about getting a station wagon, maybe even one with air-conditioning. To get to spring training, they'd crammed everything they owned into the Impala for the drive from Kansas to Daytona Beach, the car packed so tightly that Kathy had to ride with towels and pots and pans at her feet.

Unlike most players in camp, Paul at least got to go home at the end of each spring training day to his family and the luxury, such as it was, of their efficiency apartment. The other players slept in barracks, on bunks with mattresses as thin as second base, eating bland cafeteria food, and hanging out with the same sun-parched faces day after day. These players didn't have enough money to go out bar-hopping and chasing girls every night, which limited their chance to be, as one sage put it, "boys in the thoughtless pursuit of being themselves."

For minor-league players in the Kansas City organization in 1964, spring training in Daytona was a little cushier than the experience other organizations provided. The Diamond City Complex included multiple fields and a perfectly manicured main diamond with a covered grandstand. Other teams' minor-league facilities looked as if they'd been dredged out of alligator swamps, their infields pocked with more craters than a country road. Still, Diamond City wasn't exactly Club Med. Players were discouraged from having cars in camp, and a cab ride to the beach was too expensive for all but a few of the bonus babies. And sleeping in the barracks was like a Boy Scout campout, with water balloon fights, snoring, and general mayhem to disturb the nights.

At Finley's urging, Kansas City's management had selected Daytona Beach for the team's minor-league spring training site in part because it believed black and Latino players would be treated better there. Even though white Florida participated in Dixie's staunch resistance against integration, Daytona Beach was viewed as being slightly more progressive. It went back to Jackie Robinson and 1946, the year before he became the first black player in the major leagues (but eighteen years before Birmingham would field an integrated team). Robinson came to spring training in Florida with the Montreal Royals' AAA team…and encountered hostility everywhere he went. An exhibition game scheduled between the Royals and the Dodgers in Jacksonville was canceled when city officials padlocked the stadium. The game was then offered to the city of Sanford, but it, too, declined, the chief of police proclaiming he would "arrest any Negro trying to enter the ballpark, including ballplayers." Eventually, Daytona Beach stepped forward and hosted the game, which was played without incident. Slowly, the city's Jim Crow laws began to at least show cracks, if not crumble. The next year, the city's auditorium was desegregated, followed by its buses, parks, restaurants, and beaches. One East Coast reporter called the city "an island of enlightenment in a sea of bigotry."

Paul's Secret

Paul waited in front of the ballpark for Kathy to pick him up, anxious to tell her how well he'd done and that his arm didn't hurt. He paced. In Burlington his first season, she had come to most of the games, bringing the baby with her, but in Daytona, the games were in the day, right in the middle of the girls' naptime.

Finally, she pulled up to the curb and slid over to the passenger side. "So?" she immediately asked. "How'd you do? How was your arm?"

"Couldn't have gone better," he said.

"Are you going to call your dad and tell him the good news?" she asked.

"No," he replied, the smile disappearing from his face.

CHAPTER 8

Blue Moon Odom

Waiting for the Bell

Blue Moon sat in fourth-period wood shop, glancing at the clock, wishing the bell would hurry up and ring. Seemed like he was always watching the clock. It wasn't just senioritis—although in truth he was ready to be done with high school. His impatience had more to do with his rush to sign a contract and start playing pro ball.

On this day, his girlfriend, Perrie, would be walking home with him for lunch. She'd forgiven him for choosing to go fishing with his friends over the chance to go out with her in her daddy's car. How could she not have forgiven him? As disappointed as she'd been, she appreciated his sense of right and wrong, an attribute she knew he'd learned, along with a solid work ethic, from his mother. Blue Moon was always telling her how he needed to hurry to practice or to get to work. She just wished that sometimes he would show that same commitment to her. She was dreading the day Blue Moon would leave Macon to take off in pursuit of his dream, not to mention her worries about all those other girls he would surely meet. His mother, Florine, believed he learned his values from going to the Methodist church with her every Sunday, but Blue Moon wasn't buying that theory. He didn't like going to church and sitting still for an hour. The sermons flew by him.

With one eye still on the wood shop clock, Blue Moon continued to apply the lacquer to his latest project, a shoeshine kit. He was pretty sure he was getting an A on this project, as well as in the class. In his math, social studies, and English classes, however, he was just limping along with C's, finding it hard to get motivated to do his homework and study like his mother kept harping on him to do. Why should he? He knew that the baseball scouts coming to see him pitch didn't give a rip whether he got a C or a D in algebra.

College was still an option—he'd gotten a football scholarship offer from

41

Southern University—but with a couple of months left in the school year, he was 99 percent sure he would sign a baseball contract the day he graduated. He didn't know how much of a bonus he'd get, but scouts from the Giants and Red Sox were hinting he could get as much as $20,000. That would be enough, he reasoned, to buy his mom a new house and allow her to quit that job cleaning those white people's house. And he had visions of that new car.

Teams were prohibited from making him a formal offer until after he graduated, but there were rumors that at least a dozen teams would have a scout at the ceremony, ready to get his John Hancock before he even got out of his cap and gown. He didn't have an agent. Nobody did in 1964—not Mickey Mantle, Willie Mays, Sandy Koufax, or his hero, Bob Gibson. Robert Slocum, his high school coach and as close as he had to a father figure, had promised to help advise him and his mother with the negotiations, knowing that a naive eighteen-year-old teenager who'd never had more than a couple of nickels to rub together would certainly be no match in financial negotiations with a slick and seasoned representative of a major-league franchise. The two things Blue Moon would have going for him in these negotiations, however, were a cannon for an arm and the fact that a lot of teams wanted his services. A bidding war could erupt.

The bell finally rang, and he hustled out of class. As usual, Perrie was waiting dutifully by his locker, ready to follow.

Baseball in Macon

It was a chilly spring day as Blue Moon and Perrie walked the five blocks from Ballard-Hudson to his home. As he did most days, he was spending his lunchtime with her. He had friends at school, but no best friend. He considered himself a loner.

The street near his house wasn't paved, so he picked up a few rocks off the gravel road and halfheartedly gave them a toss. Growing up, he'd spent many hours on that road, picking up rocks and throwing them at the nearby trees. He might pretend to be Bob Gibson, or Don Newcombe, or even Satchel Paige, the legendary star of the old Negro League. Macon never had a team in the Negro League, but occasionally teams would come to town on barnstorming tours. Blue Moon never went to any of those games. Attendance was a financial luxury his mother couldn't afford.

With the exception of a couple of years, Macon had fielded a team in the South Atlantic (SALLY) League, a Class A league. But now Macon was moving up to AA for the 1964 season—the Southern League—joining franchises in Birmingham, Columbus, Knoxville, Lynchburg, Chattanooga, Asheville, and Charlotte…with integrated teams, as well as integrated grandstands in each city.

Unlike Birmingham, Macon had fielded integrated teams over the past decade. That's not to say that Macon fans at Luther Williams Field greeted black players on opposing teams with open arms. (The stands were segregated, with black fans required to sit in bleachers down the left-field line.) Many nights, white fans brought megaphones to the ballpark, and any time a black stepped to the plate, they started chanting: "Hit the nigger in the head." If he got on base, they started a new chant: "Watch out. That nigger's gonna steal."

In a couple of months, these fans would overflow Luther Williams Field for Blue Moon's debut.

Called to the Principal's Office

Sitting in the back of his senior comp class, Blue Moon eyed the principal's secretary entering the room and whispering something to the teacher, who turned and motioned for Blue Moon to come to the front of the class. The principal wanted to see him in his office, on the double.

He had no idea why he'd been summoned. He wasn't a troublemaker, he didn't sass his teachers, he didn't bully, and he never skipped classes. About the only bad thing he'd done was smoke a few cigarettes, but not on campus.

Nearing the office, he passed a framed photo of John F. Kennedy. When Kennedy was assassinated five months earlier, Blue Moon heard the news at football practice. Play-off games across the state the next day were postponed, and on Monday kids were still crying in the hallway, especially the girls.

Entering the office, he was greeted by the principal, as well as Coach Slocum. They were both smiling.

"There's somebody on the phone who wants to talk with you," said Coach Slocum, handing him the receiver.

On the other end was Charlie Finley, the owner of the Kansas City A's. Blue Moon knew who he was, but just barely. Team owners weren't on his radar.

He listened to Finley for a moment, then put his hand over the receiver and whispered to the two men: "He wants to fly to Macon next week and talk to me about signing with the A's."

CHAPTER 9

Haywood Sullivan

A Comeback?

Barons' first-year manager Haywood Sullivan picked up a thirty-five-inch Louisville Slugger and stepped into the batting cage. He signaled to pitcher Ken Sanders, a scrappy right-hander, that he wanted to take a few cuts. At thirty-three, Sullivan, who had a six-foot-four, 215-pound frame, was still in good shape.

Sullivan seemed like a questionable choice to be the manager of Birmingham's first-ever integrated team, a baseball experiment that had already generated angry opposition from the city's staunch segregationists, including the Ku Klux Klan. These hard-liners didn't want blacks playing in their city, even if Babe Ruth managed them. The opposition to Sullivan as manager came mostly from Birmingham's black community. They wondered if his Southern roots would cloud his judgment of black players.

Their anxiety was based on valid reasoning. After all, as a native of Alabama, Sullivan had grown up in Dothan in the full flower of Jim Crow. He attended an all-white high school and competed only against all-white teams. After high school, he attended the University of Florida, a school with no blacks, whose teams played in the SEC, a conference with no blacks. As a big leaguer, he'd played in Boston, a city with a long and troubled history of racism. During his first three years with the Red Sox, the last team in the major leagues to integrate, he had no black teammates. Tom Yawkey, the team's owner, lived part of the year on an old plantation in South Carolina ("I have lots of Negro help") and was regularly criticized about the absence of black players on the team. Sullivan's manager with the Red Sox, Pinky Higgins, was an unrepentant racist. "As long as I'm the manager of this team," he once said, "there'll be no niggers."

Sullivan's credentials for running an integrated team were thus suspect. But as he dug in to the batter's box for his first swings of the spring, the issue at hand was whether he could still swing the bat. Back injuries had constantly dogged him during his career.

Sanders fired the first pitch, a fastball that tailed in on Sullivan's hands. The ex-catcher swung, and the ball jammed him, sending a million bees swarming through his hands. The ball dribbled back to Sanders.

"Hey, just groove it," hollered Sullivan. "This isn't the World Series."

Sanders delivered his next pitch, this one a sinking fastball, low and away. Feebly, Sullivan swung and missed. Stepping out of the box, he glared at Sanders, not sure whether to cuss him out or compliment him on his good stuff.

"I repeat... just groove it," he said, holding his hand out about pecker-high to show him where he wanted it.

He was, after all, the manager, just up there to take a few easy swings.

This time Sanders piped one down the middle, and Sullivan took a smooth cut, the ball rocketing off his bat, a line drive to left field.

Sanders offered up another cream puff, and again Sullivan drove it hard to left.

A handful of players still running sprints in the outfield noticed, and applauded.

Sullivan had been hired to manage the Barons, but in the back of his mind he hadn't ruled out the possibility of playing, too. With a limit of only twenty-two players on a minor-league roster, he figured that, at the very least, he needed to be ready to step up in case of an injury. Despite his commitment and enthusiasm for his new career as a manager, part of him still believed he belonged in the big leagues.

"One more swing," he said, digging in.

Sanders was being converted to relief after spending his first four years in pro ball as a starter, and the bulldog in him wanted to show his new skipper that he deserved consideration for the starting rotation. Instead, he served up a grapefruit down the middle. Sullivan unloaded, and all heads turned to watch the ball disappear over the left-field fence.

Baseball Résumé

Leaving practice, Sullivan stopped at a pay phone and plugged in two quarters to call his wife, Pat, back at their home in Lake Worth, Florida, 150 miles to the south. She hadn't joined him for spring training this year, deciding that it would be easier on her and their three young kids not to have to uproot and move again, especially with their older son now in school. They'd been college sweethearts, and Haywood and Pat had been married for eleven years, having wed in San Francisco when he played in the Pacific Coast League. By his calculations they had moved thirty-three times in those eleven years, putting on many miles with kids in diapers. During the off-season, he'd done PR for a Buick dealership. This would be the first spring training Pat hadn't joined him.

Sullivan's blast over the fence in batting practice was a far cry from how his playing days had ended the previous year, hitting .213 at Portland in AAA— an ignoble end to a career that had started with such clear promise back when he was a star athlete at Dothan High. Not only was he an outstanding baseball player, he'd also excelled in basketball and football, earning a total of nine varsity letters. In the summer prior to his senior year, 1949, he grew four inches, put on twenty pounds of lean muscle, and led his football team to an undefeated season, earning all-state honors. After a game in which he ran the opening kickoff back for a touchdown, the opposing coach called him "a man among boys." Heavily recruited, he turned down offers from the football coaches at Alabama and Auburn, as well as Bear Bryant at Kentucky, and he chose the University of Florida.

While attending Florida on a football scholarship, he would hitchhike the two hundred miles between Dothan and Gainesville on holiday breaks. During his sophomore and junior seasons, he set twelve passing records (that stood until broken by Heisman winner Steve Spurrier in 1966) and was named to the all-SEC team twice. He also starred as the catcher on the Gator baseball team. In the spring of 1952, a steady stream of major-league scouts beat a path to his dorm room, dangling bonus money and trying to convince him to drop out of college and go pro. When the Red Sox offered him the princely sum of $45,000, he couldn't pass it up, starting his climb to the big leagues in Albany, Georgia, the Red Sox team in the Class D Florida State League.

But as the Korean War crept on, a military draft had been instituted, requiring all men between eighteen and a half and thirty years of age to sign up. Sullivan enlisted in the army and was assigned to artillery, learning how to shoot bazookas, howitzers, and machine guns. But instead of seeing active duty as did his future teammate Ted Williams, he was assigned to play on the Fort Jackson (South Carolina) baseball team and to coach its football team, a talented squad of mostly ex–college players. This was his first taste of coaching, and his players loved him. Whenever the baseball team had a game, the whole football team showed up to cheer for him.

He resumed his baseball career in 1955, spending the next three years in AAA, including 1956 with the San Francisco Seals in the Pacific Coast League (where he hit .296 with eleven homers). Each of those three years, the Red Sox called him up for the last month of the season, although he mostly warmed up pitchers in the bullpen. He got to bat a total of only six times in those three years, failing to get a hit.

Just as military duty had slowed his progress, so did a serious back injury. Surgery forced him to miss the entire 1958 season. After another year in AAA, he finally got promoted to the Red Sox, spending the entire 1960 season in the big leagues, appearing in fifty-two games. He called the pitch when Mickey Mantle hit the longest home run of his career. Sullivan hit a pitiful .162 for the season. He did, however, have his first black teammates, second baseman Pumpsie Green and pitcher Earl Wilson.

Despite the fact that Red Sox owner Tom Yawkey liked him personally, Sullivan was traded, ending up with the perennial doormat of the American League, the Kansas City A's. With the A's, he got to see much more playing time, appearing in 252 games over the next three years and hitting .239. But in 1963, he fell into a horrific slump, going 2 for 50 in the month of June, including 0 for 14 in what would be his last four games. But like Tom Yawkey, A's owner Charlie Finley was drawn to Sullivan's personal charisma and thought he had a future in the game as a manager.

Sullivan's understanding of the game impressed Finley. As a catcher, Sullivan saw everything unfolding in front of him, and he'd studied how players in each position responded in different situations. Like a coach on the field, he positioned players and kept teammates alert. With pitchers, he had a reputation for his defensive skills—blocking balls in the dirt, throwing out base stealers— but he was even more highly regarded for calling a game. He had an innate sense of each pitcher's strength, whether the guy could throw a breaking ball behind in the count or had the confidence to come inside with heat and knock a long-ball hitter back from the plate. He also instinctively knew how to keep his pitcher calm in tight situations, a leadership skill he attributed to his experience as a quarterback in football and a platoon leader in the army. He was well liked by all of his teammates... not an easy accomplishment in baseball. He just couldn't hit.

In an era when the majority of ballplayers signed straight out of high school, his three years of college provided a scholarly tint to his image. In locker rooms, while teammates read the St. Louis Sporting News, he was reading newsmagazines and the front page. He also liked biographies of men of accomplishment, such as Lincoln and Teddy Roosevelt.

There was a commanding presence about him. He carried himself tall and erect, and although in the homophobic world of professional sports his teammates would never tell him so, he eased along like Gary Cooper, movie-star handsome, with crystal blue eyes, chiseled jaw, perfect teeth, and tall, lean frame. Whether it was his time spent in New England or just something in his genetics, he had about him a sense of patrician dignity and strength, yet at the same time, he was approachable and friendly. His voice also added to his presence. With a Southern drawl, it was soothing yet deep and senatorial.

None of those qualities, however, qualified him to manage Alabama's first-ever integrated team in any sport.

Alabama Black and White

Barons pitcher Stanley Jones had just retired the side in order, and as he headed to the dugout Sullivan met him halfway. "You okay to go one more inning?" he asked.

Jones hesitated. This was his first outing of the spring, and in truth, after two innings of a scheduled three-inning stint, he felt tightness in his shoulder. But he was reluctant to confess it to Sullivan. He knew that the stereotype of black players was that they sometimes "jaked it," the players' term for either not hustling or taking yourself out of the lineup with nothing more than a hangnail.

More than any player in camp, Jones wanted to make the Barons. Birmingham was his hometown, and the chance to be one of the black players on its first integrated team was important to him. So far in spring training, he hadn't been able to gauge Sullivan's racial temperament.

Sullivan noticed the hesitation, and managers tend not to like hesitation in their pitchers. "Let's let Sanders close the game," he said. "Go get your running in."

Trotting toward the outfield, Jones felt an odd ambivalence. On the one hand, he'd pitched two scoreless innings, striking out three. He felt good about that. But he'd also come out of the game after only two innings. Born and raised in Bessemer, ten miles west of Birmingham, he'd tasted the bitterness of Jim Crow his whole life—segregated schools, segregated neighborhoods, segregated lunch counters, segregated everything. Located in the midst of the iron ore, coal, and limestone district of Alabama, Bessemer was a major steel-manufacturing town. Stanley's father worked in one of the city's mills, earning half what his white co-workers made, always struggling to put food on the table for Stanley and his six brothers and sisters.

In some ways, Stanley's career path in baseball had been as torturous as his dad's struggles in the mill had been. Signed out of high school in 1958 by the Birmingham Black Barons in the dying gasp of the Negro League, he achieved local notoriety when he pitched a no-hitter against the barnstorming Kansas City Monarchs. Signed the next year for $1,000 by the Cincinnati Reds, he didn't possess a blazing fastball, relying instead, much as Paul Lindblad did, on control, ball movement, and a good curve. At twenty-four, he was one of the oldest players in camp. A married father of three, he was starting his seventh year in pro ball, and like Hoss Bowlin he had never progressed above Class A. To some, it was a mystery why. Was it because of race? In his first year at

Geneva in the New York/Penn League, he was 19–4 with a 2.55 ERA, the best record of any pitcher in the Cincinnati chain that year. Over the next four years, he never had a losing record. Yet even with a strikeout-to-walk ratio of four to one, he watched white teammates with inferior records advance ahead of him.

During the off-season, he'd been purchased by the A's from the Reds organization. He hoped the change would give a rebirth to his stalled career. No player on the Barons' roster better understood the importance of baseball's return to Birmingham after a two-year absence—the two most violent years in the city's history. He was home in Bessemer in September when the KKK blew up the 16th Street Baptist Church, where his mother had once worshipped. He remembered trying to tell his oldest daughter why those four little girls died, and then trying again to explain two months later why the president was shot in Dallas. He remembered going to Baron games at Rickwood Field when he was a boy, and being told he had to sit on the other side of a chicken-wire fence, apart from the white folks. Now he hoped to return to Rickwood and have his kinfolks come out and cheer for him and sit anywhere they wanted. He wasn't interested in being a foot soldier in the war against bigotry...he just wanted Sullivan to give him a fair chance to make the team.

But he had to wonder. On the surface, Sullivan seemed nice enough, but Jones knew he was from Dothan, down in the southern part of the state, an area not known for racial tolerance. How could anybody who'd grown up in a town full of segregationists, as Sullivan had, not have at least some of it seep into his blood?

When Sullivan was ten years old, the big news in town was the lynching of Claude Neal, a black accused of killing a white girl in nearby Marianna, Florida. The *Dothan Eagle* urged citizens to attend the lynching, its headline proclaiming: NEGRO TO BE MUTILATED, SET AFIRE IN EXTRA LEGAL VENGEANCE FOR DEED. Never mind that there had been no trial. More than a thousand people, including women and children, turned out for the event. The following day, the *Eagle* reported it this way: "After slicing and shooting his body to mincemeat, citizens drug his naked body to the county courthouse where they strung him from a tree for all to see. Children stuck sharp sticks into him." (Neal proclaimed his innocence all the way to the end, and years later evidence was uncovered to support his claim.)

Stanley Jones didn't like his odds with Haywood Sullivan.

CHAPTER 10

Tommie Reynolds

Waiting for the Turk

Reynolds sat in front of his locker in the clubhouse of the Kansas City A's training camp in Bradenton. He eyed Manager Ed Lopat walking slowly in his direction. Today was the day the team would be cutting five or six players and sending them to the minor-league camp at Daytona for reassignment.

The players called it a "visit from the Turk." It was a bus ticket to Palookaville, a knife to the heart of a big-league dream. The words were usually the same: "We like your talent, kid, but we want you to get some more experience in the minors. Keep your head up...and remember, you're only a phone call away." In many cases, the phone call never came.

Reynolds felt like hiding. But of course the Turk always found his victim.

So far, Reynolds had played well, getting six hits in nineteen at-bats, including a home run. He'd struck out five times and misplayed one ball in the outfield, but he was happy overall with his performance. His chances of breaking camp with the big club, he knew, most likely depended on whether the team's best hitter and outfielder, Rocky Colavito, ended his holdout. If he did, Reynolds had done the math—there were six outfielders left in camp, not counting Colavito, and the team would probably carry only five. He had the least experience.

"Tommie, I want to see you in my office," said Lopat.

He could feel the Turk's breath. But going to the minor-league camp at Daytona, he rationalized, had a couple of things going for it. In Bradenton, he'd been staying in a boardinghouse across a bridge in Palmetto on the edge of its "shotgun shack" section, a cluster of run-down, narrow, rectangular houses in a black neighborhood. In Daytona, he'd be housed in the barracks with all the other players, black and white.

But the even bigger upside was his girlfriend, Penny—she lived in Daytona.

They'd talked on the phone about her coming over to Bradenton to visit again, but they were holding off to see if he survived the Turk.

One thing was for sure—he didn't want to get assigned to Birmingham. He'd listened to other blacks on the team talk about playing in the South, and they didn't have good things to say. Third baseman Ed Charles, who spent nine seasons in the minors before finally making it to the big leagues in 1961, recalled road trips in the SALLY League where blacks not only couldn't go into restaurants, but also weren't allowed to use the restrooms and would have to relieve themselves in the bushes. In cities like Knoxville and Macon they had to stay in flophouses with no air-conditioning, while the white players stayed in nice hotels and came to the park fresh and rested. Charles also talked about how management expected all black players to project their best image in public. If a player spoke out on issues, he'd be labeled a "troublemaker," the word would get around to other teams, and pretty soon the "troublemaker" was out of baseball.

But Tommie Reynolds was no troublemaker. Following Lopat into his office, he hoped for the best.

"Tommie, I like the way you've swung the bat this spring," said Lopat. "We're going to take you north with us."

Reynolds could barely believe his good fortune. After only one season in the minors, he was going to The Show. There was a caveat, however. For the first three weeks of the season, big-league teams could carry twenty-eight players, but then they had to cut down to twenty-five. The Turk would still be lurking.

Not the Normal Route

In high school, Reynolds had dreamed of following in the footsteps of other San Diegans—Ted Williams, Don Larsen, and Bob Skinner—but in talent-rich Southern California, the scouts didn't take much notice. He had decent size—six feet tall, 170 pounds—decent speed (4.2 seconds to first), and a good but not great throwing arm. He was a line-drive hitter. But the scouts weren't impressed enough to offer him a contract, so he enrolled in San Diego Junior College. His heart, however, wasn't in school, so after one semester he and two of his buddies drove down to the army recruiting station in downtown San Diego and signed up. At the time, young men between the ages of eighteen and twenty-three and not in school were required to serve in the military.

Joining the army offered him the chance to get out of San Diego. He'd spent all but the first year of his life in Southern California, and he was anxious to see other parts of the country and meet new people . . . and he didn't have a girlfriend to cloud the issue.

In January 1960, the threat of the Cold War hung heavily, especially after the Russians launched Sputnik and beat America into outer space. But to Tommie, the odds of actually seeing combat seemed remote. In the army, he figured, he'd learn skills that could help him later in life. In addition to his college prep classes at Lincoln High, he'd taken all the shop classes—wood, metal, drafting, auto—but after the army, he'd be eligible for the GI Bill and could get his college paid for.

Despite logic indicating otherwise, he thought the army was his best path to a pro contract. He'd be more mature, physically and mentally, and he would get to play on an army base team against good competition and catch the eye of scouts. Never mind that he would be twenty-two when he got out—relatively old to start a pro career—and that scouts rarely traveled to army bases in search of prospects.

After basic training at Fort Ord in California, he was stationed at Fort Leonard Wood in Missouri, where he encountered a different kind of racism than what he'd grown up with in California. On and off the base, black soldiers were routinely assaulted and subjected to taunts and racial epithets. Reynolds went out of his way to avoid trouble. He followed the advice to walk only in pairs.

After a posting to Germany, he got the chance to play on a base team, and although there were no scouts, a teammate was impressed and contacted a relative back in California, who got in touch with Art Lilly, the A's scout in Southern California. Lilly promised he'd be willing to talk with Tommie in a year, after he was out of the service.

It was not an easy year. Reynolds regularly confronted racism. On the marching grounds, fights between blacks and whites were common. And in a bar in Munich, a drunken brawl broke out between white and black troops. Several soldiers were arrested and faced court-martial. Although Reynolds was involved in the fight, he avoided arrest because his commanding officer learned he had rescued a white soldier who was being pummeled by a black.

Nearing the end of his tour in October 1962, the Cuban Missile Crisis pushed the world toward the brink of nuclear annihilation. When President Kennedy demanded that Khrushchev turn Soviet ships around, American troops were ordered on high alert, including Reynolds's unit of the 24th Infantry Division. He packed his combat gear, signed his last will and testament, and watched atomic warheads being loaded onto trucks. Even though he had only three months left on his tour, if war erupted, he'd be on the front line. Like everyone else in the world, he was scared.

Fortunately, the United States and Russia stepped back from war, and he was soon discharged, returning to San Diego. During his two years, he had indeed matured mentally and physically, gaining twenty-five pounds and more upper-body strength. Like so many of the men he'd served with, however, he'd picked up a nicotine habit and now smoked Pall Malls.

He enrolled in junior college again, but before the semester began Art Lilly showed up as promised. Going solely on the report of the friend, he signed Reynolds to a contract in January 1963—a $500 bonus, a new glove, and a $400-a-month salary.

Now, just fifteen months later, he was going north with the A's. He'd be making the major-league minimum of $7,500 for the year. Maybe he would use it to pay off his Malibu Super Sport, or at the very least get the front bumper fixed from the damage it had suffered when he had fallen asleep at the wheel on his way to spring training.

Or maybe he'd use it to buy Penny an engagement ring.

Penny

Tommie parked his Super Sport in front of the Bradenton Greyhound station and hustled inside. He didn't want to be late to pick up Penny, who was coming in from Daytona.

Although they were in love, he could count the times they'd been together on his fingers. There'd been the letters and phone calls when he was playing in Burlington, and the few days they'd spent together when she took a bus to Bradenton last fall to see him during Instructional League. That visit came the week before Kennedy's assassination—Tommie heard the news just before the start of a ball game in Tampa; Penny found out walking to campus at Bethune-Cookman. Sharing their grief helped.

Tommie had fallen in love almost from that very first meeting when she tried to sell him a ticket to a play. He learned later that it wasn't even a school play. It was a community play that had been written by the wealthy woman Penny was working for—scrubbing her floors, getting her five-year-old daughter ready for school, fixing lunch for her elderly mother, selling tickets to her play. Strapped for money, Penny had dropped out of college for a semester to work full-time to earn money to pay for next year's tuition. She'd learned this work ethic from her mother while she was growing up in Chattahoochee, Florida, right next to the Georgia state line. Her mother worked eighteen hours a day on three jobs—an aide in a mental hospital, a cook in a restaurant, and the cleaning lady for her church—so that she could pay for at least some of Penny's college education. Penny's father had suffered a stroke when she was ten and was disabled. Growing up, Penny had taken care of the house and her younger siblings.

There was plenty that Tommie liked about Penny besides her good looks and work ethic. Like him, she was quiet, serious, and independent. He was learning from her what it was like to have grown up in the South. From her perspective, racism permeated everything, and bigoted people were all cut from the same cloth, whether they lived in Birmingham or Daytona. She didn't buy the proposition that Daytona was more "enlightened."

"With racism, there's no in between," she maintained.

As a student at Bethune-Cookman, she had taken part in a boycott of a local cafeteria, but didn't consider herself on the cutting edge of the movement—her focus was doing what she had to in order to get through school. She wanted to be a teacher, no matter how long it took, or how many floors she had to scrub. To Tommie, she had a no-nonsense determination that he hadn't seen in the girls he knew in California.

He wanted to marry her.

She wasn't quite as eager. He had all the right stuff—he was attractive, mature, and gentlemanly—but she worried that his career and its travel would get in the way. She wasn't a baseball fan, and had no illusions that he was rich. When she'd approached him about buying a ticket to the play, he had admitted that he couldn't afford it. She knew he was telling the truth—he was, after all, frequenting an all-you-can-eat cafeteria during its early-bird special, not exactly haute cuisine.

Right on time, the bus rolled into the station. Watching Penny walking toward him, looking beautiful in her new sundress, he was ready to propose right there on the spot.

Haywood Sullivan

Conferring with the Boss

Seated behind home plate at Diamond City, Haywood Sullivan and A's owner Charlie Finley watched the Barons take batting practice. For a major-league owner to drive all the way across the state to observe his minor-league charges was unusual. Then again, Finley was all about the unusual—fancy new uniforms, a mascot mule named Charlie O, orange baseballs, pretty ball-girls, strange trades, firing managers, cussing out the league president.

Stepping into the batting cage, shortstop Bert Campaneris, the slender twenty-year-old who'd fled Fidel Castro's Cuba, lined the first two pitches to left, and then on his third swing crushed a towering drive over the left-center-field fence, the ball clearing the 370 mark by a mile.

"Who is this little guy?" asked Finley.

Sullivan explained that not only did Campaneris have great power for such a skinny kid, but he also had a rifle for an arm and was the fastest guy in the camp.

"The only thing that could hold him back is his temper," said Sullivan. "It got him suspended last year in A ball."

"You're the perfect guy to calm him down," said Finley.

Finley had a special interest in the Barons. He'd grown up in Birmingham and still had lots of friends in the area. The violence that had rocked his hometown over the past couple of years, and its long history of racism, and all of the ugly national media coverage it generated, embarrassed him. When the Barons' local owner, Albert Belcher, approached him at the winter meetings to discuss the idea of bringing professional baseball back to Birmingham, Finley, who'd made his fortune in insurance, jumped at the chance. One of his first moves was to hire Sullivan as the Barons' manager.

Minor-league managers, like players, usually start their careers in A ball, and then work their way up through the organization—AA, AAA, and then, if they're lucky, The Show. That's why eyebrows were raised when Finley hired Sullivan and then promptly leapfrogged him over several more experienced managers into the AA job at Birmingham.

It was no secret that Sullivan was a favorite son with Finley (although with seven children of his own, Finley didn't really need a son). "The first time I addressed the team in Kansas City, Haywood stood out," he told reporters. "He understands the game."

The pundits speculated that Birmingham would be only a stepping-stone for Sullivan, and that Finley was grooming him to take the reins of the big-league team. It was also no secret that the A's current manager, Ed Lopat, the ex–Yankee pitcher, was on borrowed time after the team's last-place finish in 1963. Patience wasn't Finley's strong suit. In his four years of owning the A's, he'd already fired three managers—Bob Elliott, Hank Bauer, and Joe Gordon.

Because of his connection to Birmingham, Finley had promised to do whatever he could to make the Barons a winning team. He believed it would help rebuild the city's tarnished image and provide a diversion for the summer of '64, which had the potential to be a powder keg again. A backlash was brewing among white Alabamians angry over a court order to begin desegregating schools, and fearful of the passage of a civil rights bill in Congress.

"Sully, what can I do to help you?" Finley asked.

His apparent willingness to supply Birmingham with a winning team was unusual in a minor-league/big-league relationship. The primary purpose of any minor-league team is to develop players for potential ascension to the majors. Winning a Southern League title, as nice as it would be, was supposed to take a backseat to nurturing talent.

An obvious answer for Sullivan would be for Finley not to raid his team and call up players. Nothing can kill a minor-league team's pennant hopes faster than losing a couple of its best players in the heat of a title chase. But of course, Sullivan wasn't going to tell his boss how to run his organization.

After three weeks of spring training, Sullivan believed Baron pitching would be strong, but he worried about the team's offense, especially its lack of a long-ball threat.

Finley mentioned Tommie Reynolds, explaining that Lopat was taking him north for the start of the season, but as soon as Colavito ended his holdout, Reynolds was the likely choice to be sent down.

"If he is," said Finley, "I'll make sure he's sent to Birmingham rather than Dallas. He's exactly the kind of Negro that would be good for this team. Very mature, very serious."

Finley then rattled off the names of four amateur players the A's had their eyes on—Rick Reichardt, an outfielder from the University of Wisconsin; Willie Crawford, a high school outfielder from Los Angeles; Jim "Catfish" Hunter, a high school pitcher from North Carolina; and John Blue Moon Odom of Georgia.

"According to our scouts, all of them are certain big leaguers," said Finley. "I won't hesitate to send any of them to you. Wouldn't it be great to have a Catfish and a Blue Moon pitching in Birmingham?"

The Beautiful Family

With his squealing six-year-old son, Marc, riding atop his broad shoulders, Sullivan trotted out onto the ball field before any of the players or other coaches had arrived. It was a Saturday morning, and his wife, Pat, had driven up from Lake Worth with their three kids to spend the weekend. She was back at the motel with their two-year-old twins, Kyle and Sharon.

In many ways, Haywood and Pat Sullivan were polar opposites. Growing up in Dothan, he never had much. His mom and dad, Ralph and Ruby Lee Sullivan, had lived hardscrabble lives in Donalsville, Georgia, trying to scratch out a living as peanut farmers before moving to Dothan with Haywood and his younger brother and sister during the Depression. Ralph and Ruby Lee found work at Blumberg's department store, Ruby Lee as a seamstress and clerk, Ralph as a maintenance man. They lived in a simple two-bedroom home. What it lacked in comforts was offset by a family togetherness—eating supper, reading at night, church on Sundays. There was also plenty of discipline. When Haywood misbehaved, which wasn't often, he'd have to go out to the willow tree in the backyard and retrieve a switch to get smacked with. The first thing he did after signing his $45,000 bonus contract with the Red Sox was to buy his parents a new house in a nicer neighborhood.

Pat, on the other hand, grew up in a wealthy family and was part of the Palm Beach socialite crowd—debutante parties, big house, fancy cars. She was beautiful and fun to be around. Like Haywood, she attended the University of Florida, and when they started dating, they were the glamour couple on campus—the beautiful coed and the handsome quarterback. Unlike Haywood, however, she wasn't diligent with her studies and failed to keep up her grades. She moved back to her parents' big house in Lake Worth. That's when Haywood declared he wanted to marry her, but not until he finished college.

And they did get married. Dutifully, she followed him to all his many baseball stops along the way—Louisville, Minneapolis, Miami, San Francisco, Boston, Kansas City, Portland—and at the end of each season, or sometimes before, she'd pack up the kitchenware and the diapers and off they'd go. Now her plan was to stay in Lake Worth until school was out in June, and then come to Birmingham with the kids for the rest of the summer.

Managerial Style

Sullivan flashed the steal sign to Campaneris on first, with Hoss at the plate. In the first three weeks of exhibition games, Sullivan loved the way that the two worked together, defensively and offensively, even though they didn't speak the same language.

As Campy took off running with the pitch, Hoss saw out the corner of his eye that he'd slipped and gotten a terrible jump and would be thrown out by an Arkansas mile. Instinctively, he flicked his bat at the outside pitch and fouled it off, preventing Campy from getting thrown out.

Sullivan flashed the steal sign again.

With Campy taking a big lead, the pitcher whirled and threw to first, Campy diving back to the bag.

"Out!" shouted the umpire.

Furious, Campy dusted himself off, and then as he marched back to the dugout, he threw his helmet in disgust, low-bridging Lindblad seated on the top dugout step.

Sullivan's eyes followed Campy into the dugout. He was keenly aware of Campy's temper. In Campy's first season as a player for Daytona Beach in the Florida State League, he'd been repeatedly warned—by umpires, team-mates, opponents, and his manager, Bill Robertson—about throwing helmets and bats. After one particularly egregious bat-throwing incident, he was sus-pended for a game and came close to getting released. Sullivan contemplated his response.

Since being hired to lead the Barons, Sullivan had thought about the style of manager he wanted to be. One option was to be a "players' manager." But what the hell did that mean? Was he supposed to be buddy-buddy with his players? No, that was a recipe for disaster.

Or would he be a manager who treated his players like men? Yes, of course...what kind of manager would treat his players as if they were in junior high? But he knew he needed to establish that he was the boss, with a firm and clear set of rules. Discipline was critical. Players needed to know his limits and what he expected. But he didn't want to be a manager who preached or gave long pep talks and lectures. His response to Campy could go a long way in setting the parameters, not only to Campy but to the whole team, black and white. If he let him get away with throwing a helmet, it could set a tone; he could be perceived as weak, afraid to stand up to a star player.

As Sullivan headed back to the dugout, he veered his course to intercept Campy heading out to his shortstop position. The situation, he knew, was loaded with problems.

One was language. Would Campy even understand what he was trying to say?

Another was culture. Would Campy think he was being picked on because of the stereotype in baseball that Latin players were hotheaded?

A third possible problem was the embarrassment factor. No player wanted to be dressed down in front of his teammates or the crowd, especially not one as competitive and fiercely proud as Campy.

And finally, there was the consideration that how Sullivan handled this situation would send a big message to the other players. If he did nothing, he'd lose respect, especially with the white players. If he came on too strong and got in Campy's face, he'd be viewed as too hard-ass.

Stopping Campy next to the baseline, he motioned for first baseman Santiago Rosario, a Puerto Rican, to join them. Rosario spoke English, and often served as a translator for Campy in the clubhouse.

Sullivan towered over Campy. Maintaining a respectful distance, he spoke, his voice calm but firm, and with no wild hand gestures.

"If you throw helmets and bats," he said, "you won't be playing for me."

Rosario relayed the message.

"Comprende?" asked Sullivan.

Campy nodded. In the Barons' dugout, the players took notice.

CHAPTER 12

Paul Lindblad

What's My Role?

The question was not whether Paul would make the Barons but whether he'd be in the starting rotation or the bullpen. At Burlington in his first year, he was a starter. That's what he'd always been. Then again, so had every pitcher in camp when he was in high school and college. In 1964, nobody signed as a reliever. The age of specialists—long reliever, middle reliever, setup man, closer—was still years in the future. In the minor leagues, the prospects were the starters. Pitchers assigned to the bullpen were long shots to ever make the big leagues. Most had no chance.

With only a week to go in spring training, the pitching staff for the Barons was almost set. In Paul's last outing, he had pitched six innings and given up only one run on four hits. His elbow, the one that had sent him to the Mayo Clinic last season, had given him no trouble.

By Paul's calculations, there were six pitchers who had a legitimate chance to get the coveted opening-night assignment—Paul Seitz, Joe Grzenda, Ron Tompkins, Stanley Jones, Nicky Don Curtis, and himself. Sullivan had given no indication of who it would be. Seitz and Tompkins had been in the big-league camp, so maybe they had the inside track. They both threw harder than he did.

He wondered if Sullivan would be a manager who explained to players what their roles were. Most managers didn't feel obligated to explain their decisions. Lindblad hoped Sullivan wasn't one of those.

Doing the Right Thing

Of the many things Kathy loved about her husband, near the top of the list was his strong code of right and wrong. She first detected it during his senior year at Chanute High. One night he and a friend were driving past Anderson's Gas Station where Paul worked, and they spotted a shadowy figure running out of the office. Paul had locked up the station many nights, and he knew something was wrong. The office door was wide open

"Stop!" yelled Paul.

The man didn't stop, so Paul jumped out of Red River Rock and took off in pursuit. He'd never been the fastest guy on any team. but he'd always prided himself at having good wind and being the hardest worker on the team.

Paul had also never thought of himself as particularly brave or tough or morally virtuous—he'd never been a regular churchgoer. He wasn't a fighter, although when he was growing up his father had made him and his brothers put on the boxing gloves when there was a dispute.

He quickly overtook the thief, tackling him from behind, landing on top of him. As the man struggled to get free, Paul threw a punch. A block away, Paul's friend heard the guy's jaw break.

Two days later, Paul's picture appeared on the front page of the *Chanute Tribune*. The headline read: LOCAL ATHLETE THWARTS ROBBERY.

The second time that Kathy witnessed his sense of right and wrong was a month after he'd left home to attend college at the University of Kansas in Lawrence, a hundred miles to the north. She called and said they needed to talk...in person. It was urgent.

An hour later, he was driving past the farms that dotted the countryside along Route 59 to Chanute. He'd made the trip home every weekend since he'd started school, and Kathy had come up once to visit him, and every time they parted, she cried. They'd talked about marriage; he'd even gone so far as to order an engagement ring out of a catalog. But she was only nineteen and he was twenty. He worried that starting a family at this age would derail his dreams of playing for KU and becoming a pro ballplayer.

When he finally arrived at her house, she broke the news. She was pregnant.

He didn't hesitate. The next day they drove to Miami, Oklahoma—a state with no waiting period—and got married at the county courthouse. After the ceremony, Paul borrowed $10 from the justice of the peace so he could take Kathy out to dinner. The next day, he dropped out of college, and a month later he signed a contract with Kansas City, repaying the justice of the peace out of his $2,000 bonus.

Bad Dad/Good Dad

Another thing Kathy loved about Paul was that he was such a good father to their two daughters. Maybe he wasn't as demonstrative toward her as she'd like, but when it came to the girls, he was always there—changing diapers, feeding them in the middle of the night, reading bedtimes stories, giving horsey-back rides.

One of the reasons Paul was trying so hard to be a good father, Kathy reasoned, was because his relationship with his own father was so strained. Paul hated the way his dad, Paul Sr., regularly abused Paul's mother, physically and verbally. Mrs. Lindblad and Paul and his four brothers all liked it when Paul Sr. spent the week in Kansas City on his job with the railroad. But domestic abuse wasn't talked about back then, especially not in small-town America. It was the Lindblad family secret. To outsiders, Paul seemed like a handsome, well-mannered, and athletic young man. They didn't know his secret. Or Kathy's, either.

In the four years that Kathy had known him, she had rarely heard Paul talk about his father. One of the few times she'd seen him show any emotion about his dad was after a game he'd pitched in the Ban Johnson League, a summer semi-pro league for college-age players in the Kansas City area. Kathy never missed a game, and this was the first time she'd seen Paul Sr. at a game. Every time Paul (or "Junior," as everyone in his family called him) struck out a batter, his father would remind everyone that Paul was his son.

Paul pitched a no-hitter that evening. As his teammates mobbed him, Kathy stood at the edge of the well-wishers, waiting to add her congratulations, proudly watching Paul soak it up in his usual modest way. She spotted Paul Sr. approaching. But instead of congratulating his son, he reached out and shook the hand of the shortstop, who had gotten two hits and made a leaping catch of a line drive in the seventh inning to preserve the no-hitter. Without saying anything to Paul, he turned and walked to his car. Paul watched the taillights disappear into the night.

The Answer to His Question

After seven weeks in Florida, the players were eager to head north. There was an apprehension, especially with the players of color, about the reception that awaited them in Birmingham.

After finishing his running, Lindblad wiped the sweat from his face. It had been a good spring for him, if for no other reason than his arm felt great. He'd pitched well, giving up only four runs in twenty innings. By his estimation, he'd earned a spot in the starting rotation.

"Paul, can I talk to you for a minute?" said Sullivan.

"Sure, what's up?"

"You've really thrown well this spring..." Sullivan began.

Lindblad sensed there was a *but* about to follow.

"But I'm going to have you start the season in the bullpen."

Sullivan explained that he was going to open with Paul Seitz, Stanley Jones, Ron Tompkins, Gary Sanossian, and Nicky Don Curtis in the starting rotation. "I want a left-hander to be able to come in and shut it down."

But none of those other guys was a left-hander, Lindblad thought. Wouldn't it have made sense to also have a left-handed starter?

"I know you want to start," said Sullivan, "but I think you can help us the most this way."

Lindblad nodded, but Sullivan sensed the disappointment.

"This is just to start the season, Paul," he said. "I may need you as a starter sooner rather than later."

As he usually did, Paul tried to look on the positive side—his manager had just told him what his role would be, and although he didn't like what he'd heard, he appreciated that Sullivan had taken the time to inform him.

"I'll just go out and prove I should be starting," Paul later told Kathy.

Segregation will keep our nation from becoming another Brazil,
where the intermingling of the races, I am told, has produced a
hapless, helpless nation.

—Bull Connor, Birmingham commissioner of public safety

PART II

WELCOME TO BOMBINGHAM

CHAPTER 13

Birmingham

Hoss stared out the window of the Barons' bus as it chugged through the streets of downtown Birmingham. Night had fallen, and after a ten-hour ride from Daytona Beach, he was ready to check into the hotel. His cancer had shown no sign of returning during spring training, but the grind had exhausted him. He was running a fever of one hundred degrees.

The bus pulled to a stop in front of the Gaston, a single-story motel in a black part of downtown. "Is this where we're staying?" Hoss asked, slightly incredulous.

From his front seat, Sullivan stood and directed the black players to grab their bags and go check in.

"Welcome to Birmingham," said pitcher Stanley Jones, the native of nearby Bessemer.

The Gaston Motel would be the black players' temporary housing until they could get settled in boardinghouses closer to the ballpark. Located only a few blocks from the 16th Street Baptist Church, the Gaston (owned by A. G. Gaston, a wealthy black businessman involved in the civil rights struggle) had often served as temporary headquarters for Martin Luther King Jr. and other civil rights leaders when they visited Birmingham. During one stay by King the previous year, the motel had been bombed. Nobody was injured, and nobody was arrested. Gaston's house was also bombed a few months later after he attended a state dinner with President Kennedy. But again, no arrests had been made.

After dropping off the team's five players of color—Stanley Jones, Bert Campaneris (Cuba), Santiago Rosario (Puerto Rico), Woody Huyke (Puerto Rico), and Freddie Velázquez (Venezuela)—the bus continued to the Tutwiler Hotel, where Sullivan and the white players checked in.

At the Tutwiler's front desk were copies of the *Birmingham News*. The front-page headline proclaimed: WOMEN WEEP, MEN STRUGGLE TO TOUCH TRIUMPHANT WALLACE.

The Alabama governor, whose inaugural address included the infamous "segregation now, segregation tomorrow, segregation forever" line, had just returned to the state after his surprising second-place finish (with 35 percent of the vote) in Wisconsin's Democratic presidential primary.

> Women with small babies in their arms wept out of sheer joy at seeing their governor back home.
> Men, less emotional, but charmed by the Wallace magnetism, pushed each other around to get close to the governor.

In another front-page story, Birmingham mayor Albert Boutwell declared the last twelve months in the city "a year of spectacular and tremendous progress." He added that despite "all the difficulties imposed by civil disorders and the sniping of malcontents," the atmosphere in the city was "very nearly a miracle."

Magic City

Sitting atop Red Mountain near downtown, the Vulcan, a fifty-six-foot-high statue and the city's most famous landmark, symbolized Birmingham's prominent position in the iron and steel industry. Established six years after the Civil War by speculators and industrialists, Birmingham did not have the antebellum traditions or studied gentility of older, more pretentious Southern cities. It quickly grew to be the third most populated city in the New South, behind Atlanta and New Orleans. Essentially an overgrown mining town, it owed its existence to one industry—steel—and although it was often referred to as the "Pittsburgh of the South," its citizens preferred its other nickname—"Magic City." In its early years, the majority of its people were working-class, uneducated, poor, and racially divided.

During the late 1920s and '30s, the Depression hit Birmingham especially hard. Unions fought to protect the rights of miners and steelworkers, and the Communist Party sought to gain influence and protect the rights of black laborers. It was from this effort that the early seeds of the civil rights movement were sown.

Of Birmingham's population of 350,000 in 1964, 36 percent was black, but the inequality between the two races was staggering. Racial segregation of public and commercial facilities was still *legally required and rigidly enforced.* Only 10 percent of the city's black population was registered to vote; the average income for blacks was less than half that of whites. Steel mills routinely paid black workers half of what they paid whites . . . if they hired black workers at all. There were no black police officers, firefighters, salesclerks, bus drivers, bank tellers, or store cashiers. The unemployment rate for blacks was two and a half times higher than that for whites.

It was this discrimination that had made Birmingham a crucible of the civil rights movement and an inviting target for Dr. King's strategy of non-violent, direct action. Confrontations between black protesters and white civic authorities had focused the national spotlight on the city's discriminatory laws and practices. The confrontation had landed Dr. King in jail, but it also energized a stalled movement.

History of Violence

Despite an upturn in the city's economic growth following World War II, the pattern of violence toward blacks established in the first half of the century remained part of life in Birmingham, with lynchings, beatings, and even castrations. Blacks had no recourse against endemic police brutality. A city-zoning ordinance mandated that blacks and whites live in separate neighborhoods.

In 1947, a black church was bombed, the first strike in a terror campaign by the Ku Klux Klan, which reportedly had twenty thousand Alabama members. No arrests were made. More unsolved bombings followed, but still no arrests. This violence was widely viewed as the KKK's response to the emerging civil rights movement, echoing the violence that had erased the experiment with racial equality during Reconstruction. Jim Crow grew ever more solidly entrenched as a way of life, with segregated parks, restaurants, restrooms, drinking fountains, schools, and just about everything else, including baseball.

With a ledger of forty-five unsolved bombings of black churches and houses from the previous twenty years, the city earned the nickname of "Bombingham."

Christmas Night Bombing

Of the many acts of violence that would cast Birmingham in a negative national spotlight, one of the first occurred on Christmas night 1956. After dinner with his family, the Reverend Fred Shuttlesworth, pastor of Bethel Baptist Church in north Birmingham (also known as Dynamite Hill), sat in his underwear on the edge of his bed in his home next to the church. He was working on plans for a protest the next day against Birmingham's segregated buses. In the next room, his ten-year-old son was wearing his Christmas present, an Alabama Crimson Tide football jersey; his daughter was playing with a new doll. Suddenly, a loud thump sounded on the front porch.

It was well known that the thirty-four-year-old Shuttlesworth was a potential target of the KKK. He was a leader of a new coterie of black preachers, social activists who believed in working to improve living conditions in the present rather than trying to save souls for the hereafter. The city's commissioner of public safety, Eugene "Bull" Connor, labeled him a "hothead." Over the previous two years, Shuttlesworth had campaigned hard and very vocally to improve conditions in his community, seeking paved streets and better police protection. His efforts had been met with stiff opposition: Connor rejected his proposal to hire black policemen to patrol black neighborhoods; the state's attorney general brought an injunction against the Alabama chapter of the NAACP (of which Shuttlesworth was president), effectively putting it out of business for many years; and Birmingham Fire Department trucks, under Connor's orders, regularly showed up at his Sunday-morning sermons, leaving their sirens wailing so that the congregation couldn't hear his words, and if that didn't work, the firemen would enter and evacuate the church. But Shuttlesworth remained undaunted, becoming the founding president of the Alabama Christian Movement for Human Rights (ACMHR), which in the absence of the NAACP quickly became the leading organization for civil rights in Alabama. He was also present at the founding of Martin Luther King's organization, the Southern Christian Leadership Conference (SCLC). His aggressive leadership not only put him in the crosshairs of the KKK but also ruffled the feathers of some of the more conservative black leadership in Birmingham, people who feared reprisals and worried that bolder efforts to end segregation would doom any hope for change. There was little doubt what that thump on the porch portended.

The dynamite blast shattered the walls of Shuttlesworth's wood-frame house, blowing off the roof and caving in the floor beneath his bed. It blew out windows a mile away. Somehow in all the rubble, the lights of the Christmas tree still shone. More amazingly, neither Shuttlesworth nor any of his family members were seriously injured.

A crowd of black neighbors quickly gathered, some armed with pistols and sawed-off shotguns. "God saved me to lead the fight," Shuttlesworth declared.

One of Connor's first police officers to reach the scene advised him that it would be in his best interests to leave town as quickly as possible. Shuttlesworth declined the advice.

The FBI quickly identified Bull Connor's good friend "Dynamite" Robert Chambliss as its main suspect, but no arrest was made.

Nat King Cole Attack

Not long after the Shuttlesworth bombing, on April 10, 1956, Nat King Cole was performing at Municipal Auditorium before a whites-only audience when four men charged the stage, yelling, "Let's get that coon." Earlier in the day they had accused Cole of playing "jungle music." Jumping on stage, they knocked Cole to the floor, and before order was restored, Cole was taken to a nearby hospital and the concert was canceled. The attackers were members of the Northern Alabama White Citizens Council, a KKK- affiliated group with ties to Connor. The mastermind of the attack, Asa Carter, was never arrested. Later, he would become a speechwriter for Governor George Wallace, and is credited with being the author of Wallace's inaugural "segregation now, segregation tomorrow, segregation forever" speech. (Carter would also go on to write novels under the assumed name of Forrest Carter, including *The Outlaw Josey Wales*—made into a movie with Clint Eastwood—and the faux–Native American "autobiography," *The Education of Little Tree*, a *New York Times* number one bestseller and an Oprah pick.) Nat King Cole never played in Birmingham again.

Castration

Another incident under Connor's rule served to highlight the threat of violence faced by blacks in Birmingham. It was in response to the Supreme Court's unanimous decision in 1954 in *Brown vs. Board of Education*. Perhaps more than any issue, the mandate to integrate schools raised the hackles of segregationists.

On September 6, 1957, the day before school was to start in Birmingham, thirty-four-year-old Edward "Judge" Aaron, a slightly built black United States military veteran, walked with his girlfriend alongside Tarrant Huffman Road on the north side of town. Aaron was a painter's assistant who lived with his mother. Behind him, he heard a car approaching. Inside rode six Ku Klux Klanners.

Over the summer, segregationists had made the blockage of school integration their top priority and were prepared to use whatever means necessary. Civil rights activists, on the other hand, were just as committed to implementing the *Brown vs. Board of Education* decision. The Reverend Fred Shuttlesworth had gone so far as to announce publicly that he personally was going to escort several black teenagers to previously all-white Phillips High on the first day of school, further infuriating segregationists.

Determined to send a message, the six men in the car, including Jesse Mabry, a lieutenant in Asa Carter's paramilitary Ku Klux Klan of the Confederacy and a participant in the attack on Nat King Cole, had stopped at a drugstore earlier in the evening to purchase razor blades and a bottle of turpentine. On this night, they were dead-set on going further than the customary tactic of putting on hoods and "scaring a nigger."

Pulling next to the couple, three men jumped out and grabbed Aaron, manhandling him into the backseat. The driver quickly sped away as one of the men sat on Aaron and pistol-whipped him. Within minutes, they pulled up in front of their lair, nicknamed "the slaughter house," a cinder-block cube with a dirt floor and windows draped with black curtains. As the others watched, one of the men grabbed Aaron by the nape of the neck and forced him to crawl like a dog into the lair. They didn't know his name or anything about him...just that he was black.

Inside the lair, they all donned their hoods and began kicking him and firing questions. Did he think he was better than a white man? Did he think black kids should go to school with whites? Did he think he should be allowed to eat or go to the toilet where whites did? Did he know Fred Shuttlesworth? He didn't.

They told him to tell Shuttlesworth that if didn't quit trying to send "nigger kids" to school with whites, they would do the same thing to him that they were "fixin' to do to you."

They then took off his pants and forced him to spread-eagle on the floor. One of the men dropped to his knees over the half-naked Aaron and, using one of the newly purchased razors, cut off his scrotum and penis, plopping them into a paper cup as a souvenir. He then poured turpentine onto the open and bleeding wound.

As Aaron screamed in pain, the men dragged him back to the car and stuffed him into the trunk. Then they drove back to the highway and dumped him. A passing motorist spotted him and called the police, who rushed him to the hospital.

Aaron would survive the attack (partially because the turpentine helped to sterilize the wound). As word of this violence spread, moderate segregationists denounced it, but the message had been delivered, sending chills down the spines of Birmingham activists. (Perpetrators of the crime were convicted and sentenced to twenty years in prison, but shortly after George Wallace took office as governor, he appointed new members to the prison parole board, and the men were released.)

Two days after the castration of Aaron, the Reverend Shuttlesworth was beaten by an angry white mob when he tried to enroll his children in the previously all-white Phillips High. No arrests were made.

The Birmingham Campaign

In 1961, Freedom Riders arrived at the Greyhound bus terminal in Birmingham, greeted by a mob of men armed with clubs and chains. Bull Connor had been alerted of the potential for trouble but purposefully delayed the arrival of his police officers by fifteen minutes, thus allowing the savage beating of the Freedom Riders. Again, nobody was arrested.

In a 1962 *New York Times* article detailing the darkness that hung over Birmingham, reporter Harrison Salisbury wrote:

Every reasoned approach, every inch of middle ground has been
fragmented by the emotional dynamite of racism, reinforced by the
whip, the razor, the gun, the bomb, the torch, the club, the mob, the
police and many branches of the state's apparatus.

In 1963, the civil rights movement was stalled. Dr. King had led a march in
Albany, Georgia, that one critic claimed "was successful only if the goal was
to get arrested and thrown in jail." Leaders of the movement realized that they
desperately needed a significant national victory.

And out of that realization, the Birmingham Campaign was devised.

The real architect and force behind the daring strategy was Fred Shuttlesworth, while Dr. King advocated a more cautious approach. It was Shuttlesworth's idea to stage mass demonstrations, fill the jails, and force the opposition
to enact change. It was James Bevel—a civil rights leader—who came up with
the idea of using children to march. Adults had shown a reluctance to demonstrate, but on May 2, 1963, a thousand black students boycotted schools and
assembled at the 16th Street Baptist Church before marching toward downtown. They were quickly confronted by the police, ushered into buses, and
taken to jail, among them Dr. King and Shuttlesworth.

Thousands more showed up the next day, and this time they were met with
Bull Connor's flesh-tearing police dogs and high-pressure fire hoses strong
enough to blast the shirt off a person's back. The national media were there to
record it, sending out news footage and photos that captured the viciousness
of the opponents of civil rights. The dramatic photos of firemen blasting demonstrators were front-page news around the world. The *New York Times* ran
a startling photo on page one of a dog biting a demonstrator. And positioned
defiantly in the middle of it all, standing next to his personal white tank and
praising his officers, was Bull Connor.

The architects of change had achieved their significant victory. The civil
rights movement was now stronger than ever. And in Bull Connor, they had an
identifiable villain.

Four Innocent Girls Murdered

It had been a peaceful Sunday morning, September 15, 1963, as worshippers
filled the 16th Street Baptist Church, among them dozens of children. The
morning calm was shattered when a powerful dynamite bomb blast knocked a

walrus-size hole in the steel-reinforced east wall of the church restroom, sending chunks of concrete and brick flying in every direction. The blast blew out stained-glass windows, driving shards of sacred scenes into oblivion. In the basement, massive pieces of concrete tore into the four girls gathered in front of mirrors to primp before going upstairs to take part in the church services for "Youth Day." They were all wearing their best white dresses. The blast was so powerful that it blew the clothes off all four girls and scattered their bodies under an avalanche of concrete and beams and glass. All four were killed instantly. One was decapitated.

Everyone suspected the Ku Klux Klan, just as it had been suspected of being behind all the other bombings around town. But those bombings had all been at night...this one had come not just in the morning but on a Sunday morning, violating the holy space of a sanctuary in a city that prided itself in its churches.

In the hours immediately after the bombing, tension and anger raced through the city. Two more blacks were killed: A ten-year-old black boy riding on the handlebars of his brother's bike was shot and killed by a white teenager, and a sixteen-year-old black boy was shot by police after he allegedly threw rocks at passing cars and refused to stop for police officers. Only a week earlier, Governor George Wallace had told the *New York Times* that to stop integration, Alabama needed a "few first-class funerals."

The bombing and shootings evoked an outpouring of sympathy for the victims and a surprising spell of guilt throughout Birmingham and Alabama. The city offered a $52,000 reward. Governor Wallace, implicitly acknowledging that his sanctimonious segregationist attitude might have contributed to the terror, put up an additional $5,000. But the money did little to soothe the national outrage. Dr. King wired Wallace that "the blood of four little children...is on your hands. Your irresponsible and misguided actions have created in Birmingham and Alabama the atmosphere that has induced continued violence and now murder."

Within days, Robert Chambliss, aka Dynamite Bob, an admitted member of the Ku Klux Klan, Connor's friend, and a suspect in several other bombings, was arrested and charged with murder and with possessing a box of 122 sticks of dynamite without a permit. With his arrest, there was renewed hope that a measure of justice would be achieved. That hope was quickly squashed. Despite considerable evidence, including a witness identifying Chambliss as the man who had placed the bomb under the church steps, an all-white jury found him not guilty of murder, slapping him on the wrist with a $100 fine for illegally possessing dynamite.

This was the Birmingham into which the young athletes of the Barons were about to step.

CHAPTER 14

Bull Connor

The Checkers Rule

Until 1964, integrated baseball in Birmingham had been illegal. City ordinance #597 declared:

It shall be unlawful for a Negro and a white person to play together or in company with each other in any game of cards, dice, dominoes, baseball, softball, football, basketball or similar games.

Nobody took the enforcement of this ordinance (called the Checkers Rule because it also prohibited people of different races from playing checkers) more seriously than Bull Connor. He was the primary force in enforcing the Checkers Rule, not only in professional baseball, but among kids, too. Birmingham police officers regularly drove by parks and sandlots, and if they spotted black and white kids playing games of pickup baseball, they screeched to a halt and chased after these kids, threatening them with going to jail if they didn't break it up. One of these kids was future Hall of Famer Willie Mays, a Birmingham native. The kids would scatter, wait for the cops to leave, and then resume their games.

In November 1961, Major League Baseball mandated that all minor leagues had to integrate, including the Southern Association, the league Birmingham had belonged to for over sixty years. Connor and other hard-core segregationists pressured the owner of the Barons, Albert Belcher, to fold the team rather than allow blacks to play in Birmingham.

"We cannot allow the mongrelization of our great national pastime," said Connor.

Rather than defy Connor and the Checkers Rule, Belcher yielded to the pressure and folded the team. With Birmingham out of the league, the

Southern Association collapsed. The official explanation for the decision was declining attendance, but everyone knew the real reason: race. Or more specifically, the racism of Bull Connor.

Voice of the Barons

In mid-century Birmingham, nobody wielded more power than Eugene Bull Connor. As the commissioner of public safety, he ruled the police department with dictatorial force. It was Connor who'd ordered the cops to aim the fire hoses and unleash the police dogs on non-violent demonstrators, many of them children, in Kelly Ingram Park the previous spring. Along with George Wallace, he had become the face of racism in America. Connor's vicious tactics elicited widespread sympathy for their victims. President Kennedy asserted: "Bull Connor has accomplished more for integration in this country than Abraham Lincoln."

Ironically for the 1964 Barons, it was baseball that had offered Connor a path to power.

In the 1920s, Connor, a high school dropout, was working as a young telegrapher for the railroad. Although he was never much of an athlete—he had a high-waisted, chicken-chested body and he'd been shot in the eye with a pellet gun as a kid—he was an avid fan of the Barons. The '20s were a golden time for minor-league baseball in America. With no TV to bring major-league games into America's living rooms, baseball fans across the country packed the ballparks of their local teams. In Birmingham, the Barons regularly drew capacity crowds. As fate would have it, the team's radio announcer called in sick when the team was on the road, and Connor volunteered to take his place for the day for $5.

Soon, his booming voice and his ability to take the skeletal account of the play-by-play coming in on the wire and then fill the airwaves with homespun baseball chatter and contrived re-creations of the action (this was the origin of his nickname, Bull) made him an immediate hit. (Ronald Reagan's career, too, was launched by his winning radio personality when he re-created Cubs games for an Iowa station.) Connor quickly became a permanent hire, his devoted listeners using his baseball narrative as a diversion from the drudgery of the mines, mills, and industrial slog of blue-collar Birmingham. Soon he was an Alabama celebrity, his fans jamming into the billiard parlor below the radio station where he manned his telegraph machine just to watch him call the game. His friendly, country cornball idioms, filled with bad grammar, became part of the Birmingham vernacular of the day. The St. Louis Sporting News called him "Dixie's most popular announcer."

From the Barons to Politics

After a few years in the baseball spotlight, Connor was encouraged by his influential fans to run for public office. In 1934, with no training or background in politics, he ran for the Alabama House of Representatives and was elected. In 1937, Birmingham's "Big Mules" (an unofficial amalgam of business and financial leaders who controlled the city's public policy) were anxious to rid the city of its "New Dealers," so they convinced Connor to run for the city commission. He ran as "the people's candidate," and the voters, almost exclusively white, elected him. (At the time, Birmingham city government had a mayor and three commissioners.)

"My door will always be open," he vowed. To prove his point, he took the office door off its hinges. He also promised not to improve his grammar, to end dissension on the all-white police force, and to bring honesty to city government. When he took office, he inherited a police department in which many patrolmen and detectives couldn't write their own names. Seventy-five percent of the force was alleged to either be members of the Ku Klux Klan or have connections to it. Everyone knew that Connor also had multiple connections to the Klan, if he wasn't a member himself.

Reelected to office three times, he was popular with the rank and file on the police force. But a handful of officers believed he played favorites, and he did little to disavow it. He called those in his good stead "my nigguhs." He was also accused of being susceptible to the influence of the "Big Mules." If they needed the police to turn a blind eye, he willingly obliged.

Like so many white Southern politicians, he wore his racism on his sleeve. At the 1948 Democratic Convention in Philadelphia, Connor helped lead a delegation of Alabamians, including George Wallace, as it walked out of the convention in protest of a proposed civil rights plank in the party's national platform. A few days later, he welcomed a crowd of over six thousand states' righters and segregationists to Birmingham, who had gathered to form the "Dixiecrat" party and nominate South Carolina governor Strom Thurmond as its avowedly segregationist candidate for president. The extent of their delusion could be measured by the Dixiecrats' confident claim that Thurmond would "ignominiously" defeat President Harry Truman in the general election.

When a series of bombings rocked black churches and homes in the Dynamite Hill neighborhood, leaders in the black community accused Connor of stonewalling the investigations. The longer he was in office, the more entrenched he became in opposing integration. "Negroes and whites will not segregate together in Birmingham as long as I'm commissioner," he declared with malapropic verve.

With the season opener and professional baseball's return to Birmingham now only a couple of days away, he was the unofficial leader of the segregationists determined to prevent it... and the most dangerous.

Caught in the Act

Technically, the 1964 opening night for the Barons would not be the first integrated game in Birmingham. That happened in 1954, but only because Bull Connor was caught with his pants down.

At the time, a city ordinance called the Hotel Rule prohibited unmarried couples from occupying the same hotel room. Connor had vigorously enforced the rule to help cut down on prostitution, but following a Christmas Eve party in 1952, he escorted his secretary to room 703 of the Tutwiler Hotel (where Sullivan and the white players had checked in upon arriving in Birmingham). When a disgruntled detective on Connor's police force found out that Connor was at the Tutwiler, he showed up with a reporter and a photographer and started pounding on the door. Eventually, Connor opened it and denied anything inappropriate was going on, but it was obvious that he had been caught in flagrante delicto and was forced to resign.

In Bull's absence, a more moderate commission overturned the Checkers Rule, opening up the possibility of bringing lucrative major-league exhibition games with integrated teams to Birmingham. On April 2, 1954, fewer than three months after the repeal of the Checkers Rule, baseball fans streamed into Rickwood Field for an exhibition game between Jackie Robinson's Brooklyn Dodgers and the Milwaukee Braves, the first game ever in Birmingham involving white and black players. Nobody knew what to expect. The new police commissioner ordered extra security.

Black professional baseball players, including greats like Satchel Paige, Josh Gibson, Buck O'Neil, and Artie Wilson, had previously played in Birmingham, but as part of the Negro League. There were the white Barons and the black Barons... and the two teams never competed against each other. White fans rarely attended games of the Negro League.

Anxious to see black Dodger players like Robinson, Roy Campanella, Don Newcombe, and Joe Black, over five thousand black fans showed up for the 1954 exhibition game, overflowing the small segregated section of bleacher seats in right field and spilling onto the grass around the outfield fence and down each foul line. At the same time, fewer than two thousand white fans showed up, leaving most of the 9,612 seats reserved for whites empty. Playing for the Braves was a twenty-year-old rookie, Hank Aaron.

In the game, Aaron had a double and scored a run for the Braves, while

Duke Snider and Carl Furillo each homered for the Dodgers. But the most memorable moment occurred when Robinson stepped to the plate for the first time. The five thousand black fans stood as one, giving him an ovation that lasted over a minute. Poetically, in a reply to their ecstasy, he slammed a double. Years later, Aaron would recall: "The crowd had been roaring as soon as Jackie left the dugout, and when he stepped to the plate, it was hard for me to hold back tears."

The next night, the two teams played again, and this time, perhaps emboldened by the fact that the previous night's game hadn't caused a riot, white fans showed up in record numbers, packing Rickwood Field, giving supporters of integrated baseball in Birmingham and the Southern Association cause for optimism.

Segregationists, however, were appalled at how quickly an exhibition game had been scheduled in Connor's absence. But he wasn't about to roll over and go harmlessly into the hooded night. In 1954, with the support of one of Birmingham's most powerful Big Mules, Sid Smyer, he helped form the American States Rights Association, a group focused on stopping integration. Its first campaign was sending canvassers door-to-door collecting signatures demanding a voter referendum to reinstate the Checkers Rule. Their slogan was: "Keep Baseball White."

It took only three days to collect the necessary signatures, and on June 1, 1954, two months after the Dodgers-Braves exhibition game, the voters of Birmingham went to the polls and, by a margin of three to one, reinstated the Checkers Rule. The white voters had spoken—no integrated baseball.

Two years later they spoke again, voting Connor back into office. "I will never support the ruination of our national pastime," he proclaimed.

And in 1961, he backed up those words, bullying the Barons owner into killing the game.

CHAPTER 15

Albert Belcher

Somebody's Gonna Die

Lighting another Pall Mall, sixty-two-year-old Albert Belcher, a Birmingham millionaire and the owner of the Barons, fidgeted at his desk in his office at Belcher Lumber. Five months earlier, he'd been sitting at the same desk when he got word that President Kennedy had been shot in Dallas. At the time, he assumed that the assassin was from the Ku Klux Klan, angry at Kennedy's efforts to cram civil rights down the throats of Southerners. Like most white people in Birmingham, Belcher wasn't a big Kennedy fan.

In a few minutes, he'd be leaving his office and heading over to Rickwood Field, the venerable home of the Barons. It had been standing empty for the last two years. But now, thanks to him, baseball was flickering back to life. He was boldly committed to bringing Birmingham into the Southern League, a radical 180-degree turn from two years earlier when he had pulled the plug on the team rather than challenge Bull Connor and the Checkers Rule.

A lot of people around town weren't happy with him.

Putting out his cigarette, he grabbed his coat and hat and headed for the door. His phone rang.

"This is Albert Belcher."

He listened to the person on the other end for a few seconds, and then hung up. The caller's message was the same one he'd heard—by his count—a dozen times: "If the niggers play, somebody's gonna die."

The Chicken-Wire Fence

Arriving at Rickwood, Belcher parked his Cadillac Coupe deVille near the main gate and hurried inside. In the two years since professional baseball had deserted Birmingham, Rickwood had fallen into disrepair. But thanks to

Belcher, it was now almost ready for opening night. On this day, he intended to take care of the one task more than any other that he hoped would symbolize a new era in Birmingham.

Exiting a tunnel on the first-base side, Belcher stepped into the sunlight and squinted, surveying the box seats in front of him. Painters were slapping on the last touches of green and gold paint, the colors of the Barons' parent club, the Kansas City A's. Charlie Finley had made the color combo part of the working agreement between the Barons and the A's. The money to refurbish the ballpark—already in excess of $100,000—was coming out of Belcher's own pocket. This was his baby. Neither the city nor any other person or organization, including Finley, was making a contribution—he was shouldering the risk alone.

Belcher could afford it. In a city where the majority of the wealth came from one industry—steel—he had made millions in lumber, buying up vast tracts of Alabama timberland and converting them to lumber. Married and the father of three children in their twenties, all of them shareholders in Belcher Lumber, he had survived a conviction for income tax evasion in the 1950s. He didn't serve any jail time over that dispute, although some in town suspected he bribed the judge. For years he'd been a member of the elite and powerful Big Mules. He wasn't a member of the KKK—at least not that anyone knew— but he counted many of its members as friends or acquaintances.

He liked playing golf, but baseball had been his true passion since childhood. He attended the University of Alabama on a baseball scholarship, but eventually gave up his dream of pro ball to go into the lumber business. In 1949, he became a part owner of the Barons, and then in 1958 he bought out the other owners and became the sole owner and president. When he pulled the plug following the 1961 season, he said it was the hardest thing he'd ever done. To resurrect the team for 1963, he bought the Nashville franchise of the going-out-of-business SALLY League. He wanted a pennant winner with the new Barons badly enough that he promised the A's general manager, Hank Peters, an all-expense-paid vacation to Hawaii if he sent the Barons the talent to win the championship.

Dressed in a suit and tie, he climbed the stairs to the top of the bleachers down the right-field line. Using a claw hammer, he began ripping down the chicken-wire fence that divided the stands. For sixty years, blacks had been required to sit on the far side of the fence, farther away from home plate and the action. Whites called it the "coal bin." (For Black Baron games, the few white fans who attended also had to sit on the other side of the fence.) In two days, not only would the teams on the field be integrated, so would the fans.

"This worries me more than what will happen on the field," he confided to a reporter after hauling the fence away. "With all the hatred around here, who knows what's gonna happen. But the chicken wire has to come down."

Behind the Decision to Bring Back the Barons

After removing the chicken-wire fence, Belcher sat down in a box seat behind first base and lit another Pall Mall. His decision to bring back baseball hadn't come out of a sudden conversion to the tenets of the civil rights movement or out of admiration for Martin Luther King Jr. He loved baseball and believed it should be part of the fabric of Birmingham. As a fan, he missed going to games. As a businessman, he believed he could make money at it. And as a realist, he believed that integration was inevitable—whether he favored it or not—and the Barons could offer a healthy alternative to the violence that had rocked the city and stained its image.

But there was another, perhaps bigger, reason for his decision to fund the return of the Barons. Bull Connor was no longer in office. Voters had passed a measure that changed the city's form of government, switching to a mayor and city council from the three-commissioner system that had given Connor so much power. Despite threats of lawsuits, Connor was ousted from office and the Checkers Rule was repealed.

But as it had been a decade earlier when Connor had been forced to resign, nobody assumed Bull would move to Florida and spend his days lawn bowling with other seniors, talking about the good old days when nobody, other than a few blacks, paid much attention to bombings. Privately, he told friends he wasn't about to "let the niggers take over baseball."

With the Checkers Rule gone, and only after careful consideration, Belcher had given the Barons the green light...or rather the green-and-gold light. He hadn't gotten to be a multimillionaire by dumb luck—he studied the market—and he'd also studied Bull Connor. More than any politician in Birmingham, it was Connor who was responsible for the absence of the Barons the previous two years. And he could, despite no longer being in office, still bring his power to bear and ruin the team's return.

Many in town thought Belcher was taking too big a risk in bringing back the Barons. But Bill Lumpkin, the sports editor of the *Birmingham Post-Herald*, thought it was a noble cause. He wrote:

From a city which has gotten little but bad press for many, many a moon, a Baron comeback would be one hopeful sign the place was stirring again in the right direction. Baseball didn't make Birmingham one of the country's great cities, but it gave it one of its most favorable images. It could do it again, too, Baron baseball could.

Who the Hell Is Knocking at My Door at This Hour?

Belcher looked out his front window and noticed the headlights of an older-model Ford pickup slow down as it passed. He got up to look, but as he peered out the window, the pickup disappeared around the corner.

It was fewer than forty-eight hours until the much-anticipated season opener, and Belcher was cautiously optimistic. The publicity had been good, and ticket sales were going reasonably well considering that a lot of people in town still didn't like the idea of integrated baseball in the Magic City.

Belcher loved his hometown. He'd supported Connor's and Wallace's campaigns for office, and loved sitting next to Alabama's revered football coach Bear Bryant, a regular at Barons games before the team folded. He took pride in the fact that Birmingham, unlike cities such as Memphis, Mobile, and Charleston, wasn't tied to the myth of *Gone with the Wind* and an agrarian South. It was a post–Civil War industrial city, an engine pulling the New South forward. Echoing the Old South nonetheless, Belcher also took pride in the fact that Birmingham was "churchgoing, flag-waving, slow-moving, and conservative to the point of being paranoid about people and ideas that deviate from the status quo."

Returning to his chair, he lit a cigarette and smiled at his wife, Nell, sitting across the room. Suddenly, a knock at the front door startled him. He checked his watch. It was 10 p.m., awfully late for anyone to come calling.

"Who could that be?" asked Nell.

"No idea," he replied, glancing out the window, noticing that the pickup he'd just seen was now parked across the street.

Maybe it was Bull coming to get him to change his mind, but that seemed unlikely.

The knocking continued.

"Who's there?" he called out.

"Fletcher Hickman," a voice replied.

Belcher knew Hickman. He was Imperial Wizard of the local Ku Klux Klan, and a friend of several nefarious characters, including Asa Carter, the man behind the Nat King Cole beating, and Robert "Dynamite Bob" Chambliss. Belcher cracked the door and peeked out.

"What brings you here at this hour, Fletch?" he asked.

"I want to talk about the Barons," replied Hickman.

"What about them?" said Belcher, stepping onto the porch, figuring the guy wasn't there to find out who was pitching opening night or to give his opinion on the Barons' new kelly-green and Fort Knox–gold uniforms. He could smell alcohol.

Hickman was alone. In the dark shadows of the front porch, his shoulders looked as wide as his Coupe deVille.

"Albert, you and I have known each other for a long time, so I think I can be honest with you," Hickman said.

"Fire away."

"It's no secret that a lot of other folks ain't happy with y'all planning to go ahead and let the niggers play ball here."

"If we want baseball here in Birmingham, we got no choice."

"I don't care if it's the Southern League or the American League. It's against the city ordinance."

"Not anymore," said Belcher. "Did Bull send you?"

"Nope."

Belcher didn't believe him.

"So why you doin' it?" continued Hickman. "It's not like you. Y'all not caving in to that nigger preacher Shuttlesworth and those outside agitators, are ya?"

Belcher contemplated his response. "Fletch," he finally said, "sometimes a man has to pick his battles. And it just seems to me, baseball ain't it. This city needs something to cheer about."

"Depends on how you look at it," replied Hickman. Then he took a long pause. "Well, I sure as hell don't much agree with what you're doing, but I'm gonna make you a promise."

"What's that?"

"The Ku Klux Klan is picking its battles, too, and we won't stand in your way," he said, extending a handshake.

"Well, I thank you for that," said Belcher, not sure whether to believe him.

"You got my word on it," replied Hickman, turning to leave.

Belcher nodded, keeping in mind the fact that this guy was the Imperial Wizard and the Klan's history was thick with deceit.

As Hickman walked toward his pickup, Belcher yelled after him. "Hope to see you out at Rickwood for the opener."

"Ain't no way I'm coming out to watch no niggers less'n you promise one of 'em gets hit in the head."

CHAPTER 16

Charlie Finley

Rickwood Field

The Barons were holding a final tune-up at Rickwood Field on the eve of the season opener. Standing in front of the dugout, Finley, Belcher, and the Barons' general manager, Glynn West, watched Haywood Sullivan step into the batter's box.

"I got a feeling Sully's gonna help this team with his bat before the season is over," offered Finley.

On the second batting-practice pitch, Sullivan crushed it over the scoreboard, a towering drive that brought gasps from the crowd and a smile to Finley, Belcher, and West.

"Like I said..." added Finley.

It was more than just Sullivan's tape-measure drive that had the three men in suits smiling. Over the past couple of days, everything was falling into place for the opener. Season ticket sales and fence advertising were up from 1961, and the advance sales for the opener had Belcher predicting a crowd in excess of five thousand. No game in '62 had drawn that many. And on this night, an estimated twelve hundred fans had shown up just to watch the players take batting practice.

Birmingham fans had always been proud of Rickwood. Built in 1902, it was the oldest baseball park in America, older even than Boston's Fenway Park or Chicago's Wrigley Field. Over the years, it had hosted most of the great players, either in exhibition games, Southern Association games, or Negro League frays—Ted Williams, Joe DiMaggio, Babe Ruth, Ty Cobb, Satchel Paige, Josh Gibson, Willie Mays, Mickey Mantle. It was a place where families walked through darkened tunnels into bright sunlight and a welcoming vista of perfectly mowed green grass, Georgia red clay, white chalk lines, and outfield fences brightened with billboards of the leading local merchants. It was where

Charlie Finley worked as a batboy when he was twelve. It was impossible to think of baseball in Birmingham without thinking of Rickwood.

Publicity Whore

Over the past week, nobody had garnered more ink in the Birmingham papers than Charlie Finley. Before coming to Birmingham for the opener, he had defiantly vowed to move in the outfield fences at Municipal Stadium in Kansas City so that it had the same dimensions as Yankee Stadium, whose inviting measurements, Finley claimed, gave the Yankees an unfair advantage. He was calling his promised new right-field fence his "pennant porch." The commissioner's office had promised to stop him…which was just the publicity he was seeking. He had challenged Belcher to move in the fences at Rickwood, but so far Belcher had resisted.

"Charlie does things his way, I do things my way," stated Belcher. "I'm not moving any fences until I see what kind of power hitters we have."

As a concession to Finley, however, he agreed to paint a white line on Rickwood's outfield fences and keep track of balls landing above the line (which would supposedly be homers if the fences were moved in).

In the days leading up to the opener, the Birmingham media had fallen all over themselves in praise of Finley. One column advocated ousting Ford Frick as commissioner of baseball and replacing him with Finley. Another labeled him "free-wheeling and free-thinking," with "piercing blue eyes" and the "persuasiveness of a million-dollar salesman." A speech to the Rotary Club was "marked with evangelistic fervor." After the speech, he received a "rousing ovation."

Seemingly, he was everywhere in Birmingham strumming up publicity for the season opener. A promotional visit to a minor-league town was unheard of in the world of big-league owners. But Birmingham was his hometown, and he'd personally set up this whirlwind tour. He talked to the media, Rotary clubs, even the student body of the high school in Ensley, the blue-collar community where he lived as a youngster. At every stop, he reminded listeners that he'd been a batboy for the Barons, and would be again at the opener. Whether it was a lunch in Hueytown or a meeting with downtown bankers, he wore a green, satiny A's jacket and boasted how the Barons would be wearing the same colors adorning the splashy, sleeveless uniforms worn by his big-league players.

With impassioned fervor, he talked about the importance of the Barons and baseball to Birmingham, and how he hoped the team would provide a healthy diversion to help keep the lid on a potentially incendiary summer.

"Here's my guarantee," he said. "I will do everything in my power to give the Barons the best available talent it needs to be a winner. Birmingham deserves it."

Self-Made Millionaire

Finley came from a poor, working-class Southern Baptist family, his grandfather and father working backbreaking jobs in the steel mills of Birmingham. He mowed lawns and sold eggs to help pay family expenses. When he was thirteen, his dad lost his job in the Depression, and the family moved to Gary, Indiana, where his dad found work in a steel mill.

After graduating from high school in 1936, Finley went to work in the mill as well. He also worked in a butcher shop, took classes at a Gary junior college, got married, and indulged his passion for baseball by playing first base for mill teams. When World War II broke out, he tried to enlist in the marines but was rejected because of an ulcer. During the war he worked in an ordnance plant, but his new father-in-law encouraged him to moonlight selling life insurance.

Finley quickly discovered he was a natural salesman. In 1946, however, he contracted tuberculosis and had to spend a year in a sanatorium, struggling to breathe and needing assistance just to get out of bed. He lost a hundred pounds. But as fate would have it, while he was in the sanatorium he hatched an idea to sell disability insurance to doctors. Within two years of his release, he'd sold policies to 92 percent of the doctors in the Chicago area. He soon expanded nationally, and within a few years he was a multimillionaire, with a twenty-one-room farmhouse on 260 acres near La Porte, Indiana. Married with seven children, he was rarely home.

In the late 1950s, he became obsessed with buying a major-league team, making unsuccessful bids for the Philadelphia A's, Detroit Tigers, Chicago White Sox, and the rights to a new team that would become the Los Angeles Angels. Finally, in 1960, he purchased the dreadfully inept Kansas City A's for $1.975 million. Initially, he charmed the Kansas City media and fans with his folksy demeanor, guaranteeing to keep the team in Kansas City and promising to build a winner. He anointed himself the "savior of Kansas City baseball." The honeymoon was short-lived, however, as he began threatening to move the team to Dallas. People began to doubt his word; he promised to end the A's history of trading its top players to the Yankees, and then six days later he traded his best pitcher, Bud Daley... to the Yankees.

Finley developed a reputation as a maverick with offbeat promotions, such as using players to ride the mascot, Charlie O. He lobbied to use orange baseballs; he installed a pop-up mechanical rabbit behind home plate to deliver balls to the umpire; he personally interviewed the good-looking ball-girls. He also developed a reputation as hot-tempered, penurious, confrontational, over-bearing, loud, and obnoxious...but charming when he needed to be. It didn't take him long to alienate the other American League owners, as well as the commissioner's office.

Many worried that his roots in Birmingham had made him a racist. But those who worked for him claimed otherwise. For the most part, his players liked him. "He's equally rude to whites, blacks, Puerto Ricans, everybody," said outfielder Jimmy Piersall.

Pep Talk and a Challenge

Following the workout, the Baron players sat in front of their lockers, admiring the brand-new wedding-white uniforms hanging in front of them. "Pretty nice, huh?" extolled Finley, sitting in a corner next to Belcher.

Sullivan signaled for the players' attention, and then after announcing the starting lineup reviewed the signals, all eyes on him. In the ranking of baseball no-nos, missing a signal was near the top, proof that a player's head was in the clouds.

"Right hand to the face will be the indicator," said Sullivan. "Everybody got that?"

Lindblad leaned close to Hoss. "Need me to show you which is the right hand?" he whispered.

After repeating the signals, Sullivan turned to Finley. "Gentlemen, Mr. Finley would like to talk to you for a moment," he said.

Finley stepped into center stage, his piercing blue eyes scanning the players. They fell silent, realizing that an address from a major-league owner to a minor-league team wasn't normal.

"I'll keep this brief," he started. "My goal is to turn the Kansas City Athletic organization into the best in baseball. I want us to be World Series winners. I want our players to be homegrown, raised in the Athletics way of playing ball. We're going to do everything possible to make this team a pennant winner. In a couple of weeks, the big-league team will have to trim three players off its roster...and some of them might be coming here.

"This city has been through a lot in the last year and deserves a winner. Some of you may know that I grew up around here. Used to be the Barons' bat-boy, as a matter of fact. So this team and this city mean a lot to me. I want you to go out there and play like hell...and it's not impossible that I'll see some of you in a big-league uniform before the season is over."

As he spoke that last sentence, he looked straight at Campy, who smiled but had no clue what Finley had just said.

"Anything you want to add, Mr. Belcher?" he asked.

Belcher stood, remembering his promise of a free trip to Hawaii to Hank Peters. He looked directly at Finley. "I agree with you how important it is that this team wins," he said, "so I've got a challenge for you. If the Barons win the Southern League championship, you and I will go together and treat all these guys and their wives to a week in Hawaii. Whattya say?"

The players all looked at each other, mouths open, shocked by the proposal. For most of them, scraping together enough money just to get home was a challenge, let alone accumulating the stash needed for a week in Hawaii.

Finley stared at Belcher, the challenge totally catching him by surprise. Prior to the start of the big-league season, he'd told his A's that if they just finished in the first division, he'd give them $100,000 to divvy up among them, an offer that seemed super-safe considering that the moribund Washington Senators were the only team the A's even remotely had a chance of finishing higher than.

"Come on, we can afford it," added Belcher.

"Well, I'm pretty sure my wife would like to go to Hawaii...so I say, Damn right, let's do it. But we better ask the players and make sure it's all right with them."

A roar as loud as Alabama thunder shook the clubhouse.

As the exuberant players started to retreat to their lockers, Finley called out the names of Stanley Jones, Bert Campaneris, Santiago Rosario, Luis Rodriguez, and Freddie Velázquez.

"I'd like a minute with you guys," he said, leading them off to a corner.

Separated from their white teammates, the five drew around Finley, who nodded toward Rosario. "You can translate for Campy," he said.

Speaking in a hushed tone, Finley's face drew serious: "I don't know what you guys have heard about the way they treat colored people around here," he said. "But a lot of it's true. You guys are going to hear a lot of shit this season. Lots of ugly names. I'm sure you've all heard them before. You might get thrown at. You might get spit on. But I want you to stay cool. I know it'll be hard, but you can't yell back at these people. Not in Birmingham, not on the road. Some of these people are nuts. And if you get in a situation where you feel threatened or in danger, you can't fight. You need to walk away. The last thing we need is for there to be stories about you guys getting in fights. There's a lot at stake. So it's important that you behave in a good way.

"You need to be like Jackie Robinson. When he broke in, the abuse was horrible. But he handled it beautifully. He changed baseball. You can do the same here in Birmingham."

He hesitated, eyeing each of the five men. "A lot of people will be watching," he said. "I'm counting on you."

That's baseball, and it's my game. Y'know, you take your worries to the game, and you leave 'em there. You yell like crazy for your guys. It's good for the lungs, gives you a lift, and nobody calls the cops. Pretty girls, lots of 'em.

—Humphrey Bogart

PART III

THE SEASON

April

CHAPTER 17

Albert Belcher

The Odd Couple

Albert Belcher was not a man to wear his emotions on his sleeve. He was easy to smile, but like so many men who'd survived the Depression, he wasn't given to tirades or jumping up and down with joy. It didn't matter whether he'd just closed a deal on another trainload of lumber, or watched a ninth-inning rally by the Barons, or attended one of his children's weddings...he was steady-Eddie, low-key, unflappable, reliable, and usually close-to-the-vest. That's why it surprised his wife, Nell, and their friends to learn he'd coaxed Finley into agreeing to take the Barons to Hawaii if they won the championship. Some suspected he did it to one-up the ostentatious Finley. Although they were both rich and shared a love of baseball and Birmingham, their personalities were on opposite sides of the moon. Finley wasn't afraid to wear a houndstooth hat and a green satin warm-up jacket; Belcher always looked as if he were on his way to a CPA convention. He would no more set up his own promotional tour than bark at the pitcher's mound.

He did, however, appreciate Finley's stepping up to offer the A's as the Barons' parent club. Given Birmingham's troubles over the past year, as well as the uncertainty of how the city would respond to an integrated team, it was a ballsy move. When Belcher had approached other big-league franchises, they expressed concern. Finley jumped at the chance.

As much as anything else, Belcher worried that Finley's considerable ego and penchant for hogging the news could lead to the two of them bumping heads down the road. They were both strong-willed, and each owned his own business, employed lots of people, and was used to doing things his own way.

Pre-Game Publicity

On the morning of the opener, Belcher sat at his desk at Belcher Lumber, reading the news accounts of the big event. Although the game was given front-page coverage, as well as space in the sports section, the local writers tiptoed around the historical importance of the game, perhaps fearful of reminding readers of recent events, even though anybody in Birmingham who wasn't aware of what was happening would had to have been vacationing on Neptune. The *Birmingham News* sports editor Benny Marshall cautiously put it this way:

It's integrated baseball, the only kind of professional sport there is anywhere, anymore. Thus, this season opener is given a touch of history.

Only sportswriter Alf Van Hoose, the Barons' beat writer for the *Birmingham News*, dared to contemplate the game's importance:

Owner W. Albert Belcher has bet strongly that his town is ready again for the nation's great summertime game, and he's playing his hand with confidence.

Five of the 22 Barons are Negroes—and this will make history all the world will carefully watch.

It's more than an ordinary occasion, and to label it a historic Birmingham sports day might not be too extravagant. Baseball, as you know, returns to Rickwood tonight, and for reasons not to dust off and re-run, the occasion will be noticed and checked from afar.

Outside the South, one could guess, more people will be interested in how things come out at Rickwood than any Legion Field football game in years.

To ensure the peace, Belcher had requested extra police protection, and as many as twenty additional officers were expected to be on hand for the opener. When Belcher was reminded that these policemen were from the same Birmingham police force that a year earlier, under the guidance of Bull Connor, had beaten black demonstrators and had deep connections with the Klan, he could only shrug.

Armed and Dangerous

Belcher and the Barons' thirty-year-old general manager, Glynn West, sat in box seats behind the Baron dugout, anxiously eyeing the crowd making its way into Rickwood. It was a slow-arriving bunch, and both men looked concerned, despite advance sales.

Black fans entering the park hesitated when they came out of the tunnels and reached the concourse, not sure which way to go. In the sixty years of white Baron baseball, the chicken wire had always mandated where they should sit. But now the screen was gone, the bleachers stretching in uninterrupted rows across the tiered stands.

Out of habit, or maybe fear, many of the Barons' black fans retreated to the right-field bleachers, where they'd always sat. Others, however, headed toward seats previously forbidden. Although perhaps not as bold as moving to the front of the buses in Montgomery a decade earlier, it was nonetheless an empowering moment.

All of the fans, black and white, were entering the park with a pack of Schick razor blades. It was an opening day promotion created by West, an idea he'd gotten attending a baseball convention over the winter.

"Is this a good idea?" asked Belcher.

"Whattya mean?"

"You've armed the crowd," replied Belcher.

Bomb Threat

Sitting next to his wife, Nell, Belcher scanned the stands, taking note of the fifteen Birmingham police officers spread around the ballpark. He took comfort in their presence, although he still didn't know what to make of Fletcher Hickman's late-night visit and his promise that the KKK wouldn't cause any problems. An usher approached.

"Mr. Belcher, you've got a phone call in the office. They said it's urgent."

Belcher entered the Barons' front office and picked up the phone, listening to the muffled sound on the other end: "Y'all making a big mistake playing them niggers," the voice said. "Don't be surprised if something bad happens."

And then the caller hung up.

Belcher stood frozen, staring at the wall, trying to figure his next move. Was this guy serious? It wasn't the first phone threat he'd had in the months since announcing integrated baseball was coming to Birmingham. But it was the first one with people pouring into the ballpark.

The Barons' president considered his options. He could go up to the press box and make an announcement to the crowd that there'd been a bomb threat and everybody needed to evacuate the ballpark as quickly as possible. That was the safe and prudent thing to do. He'd lived in Birmingham his whole life and knew what the KKK was capable of doing.

Or maybe he should go tell Finley and see what he said.

But then the business side of his brain kicked in. It would take at least a couple of hours for the police to search for a bomb, and by then most of the very large crowd of fans who had now settled into their seats would be long gone. He'd have to refund their money, and in the minor leagues, large crowds were rare gold.

He also knew that if he evacuated the park, it would be all over the news, and not just in Birmingham. Definitely not what the city needed. On the other hand, if there was a bomb and it went off, lives could be lost. And so could the season. Birmingham might not ever recover.

Slowly, he exited the office, pausing as he neared one of the policemen. He looked back over his shoulder and eyed a line of people a block long still queuing up to the ticket booth. Automobiles were searching for parking.

Taking a deep breath, he quickly returned to his box seat. "Who called you?" asked Nell.

"I don't know," he answered. "They hung up before I got there."

CHAPTER 18

Haywood Sullivan

Opening Night Jitters

Standing in front of the dugout, Sullivan glanced up into the box seats behind first base, hoping to catch a glimpse of his parents and wife. He'd left them tickets at will-call, but with the opening night festivities about to start, they still hadn't arrived.

He was surprised at how jittery he was, and not because his family wasn't there yet, but rather because his managerial debut was about to commence, ushering in a whole new chapter in his life. Every spring and summer since he was a kid, his life had been consumed with being a baseball player—catching, throwing, hitting. He'd put on his spikes, jock, and uniform at least two thousand times. He looked like a baseball player. He talked like a baseball player. He thought like a baseball player. His tax returns said he was a baseball player. But on this night, April 17, 1964, for the first time in his life, he was no longer a baseball player. He was a manager.

He no longer had to worry only about his own performance. Now he was responsible for every player on the team, every hiccup, every pulled muscle, every thrown bat, every passed ball, every loss. He couldn't wait to get started.

"How do you feel?" asked Finley, on the field for his duties as batboy.

"I wouldn't mind having a couple more power hitters," replied Sullivan. "But I'm excited."

Finley turned to the real batboy and asked him how much he got paid per game. "Fifty cents," the boy replied.

"All I got were broken bats and scuffed-up balls," said Finley.

Sullivan glanced toward the stands again. Still no sign of his family. His parents, Ralph and Ruby Lee, were driving up from Dothan to see their son's managerial debut. So were several carloads of Haywood's old high school friends. Since signing his big bonus contract and starting his playing career,

97

he and Pat had made their off-season residence in her home state of Florida, but he had always managed to return to Dothan at least once a year to visit his parents, show off his kids, and reconnect with old buddies. For opening night, Pat had left the three kids with her parents in Lake Worth and flown to Birmingham.

As he looked out over the field and its lush green grass and pristine chalk lines, there was a sense of calm and confidence in Sullivan's posture, as if all roads he'd taken in his life had ordained his arrival at this moment. He'd been the captain of the football, basketball, and baseball teams in high school; at the University of Florida, he was elected captain of the football team as a junior. As a major leaguer, despite never having achieved stardom, he had always been a student of the game. Sitting in the dugout or in bullpens across America, he didn't waste his time spitting, scratching, or checking out the girls in the stands; he did what managers constantly harped on their players to do: "Keep your head in the game." He always paid attention to detail.

As the Jones Valley High School marching band took the field in preparation for playing the national anthem, he turned once more to the stands. Finally, he spotted Pat and his folks. They waved. He nodded.

For the Sullivan family, the baseball axiom "You can't see the whole game unless you see the first pitch" had now been honored.

The Coveted Starting Pitching Assignment

In the bullpen, starting pitcher Paul Seitz, a six-foot-three, twenty-three-year-old right-hander from Columbus, Ohio, took off his green jacket and slowly started warming up. Sullivan had tapped him for the prestigious opening night pitching assignment after a commanding seven innings of two-hit ball in his last start in spring training. Not only was he getting to pitch the first-ever integrated game in Birmingham, he would be getting to do it with Charlie Finley watching—a good night to shine. He was the hardest thrower on the staff.

For Sullivan, choosing the starting pitcher for opening night had been the hardest decision in his new career so far. With an abundance of good arms to choose from, he fretted over the potential damage to the fragile psyches on his staff that his decision might have. He had to think both in the short and the long term.

As Seitz started to throw a little harder in his warm-ups, he felt tightness in his shoulder. Nothing serious, he figured, probably due to the change from the heat of Florida to the cool night air of April in Birmingham. And as far as it being cool, it wasn't nearly as cold as the game he pitched his sophomore year at Ohio State against Xavier. It was snowing at the start of that game … and he pitched a no-hitter.

Prior to spring training, *Baseball Digest* had listed him as a "can't miss" prospect in its summary of top young players. For the third year in a row he was on the A's forty-man roster and spent the first month in Florida with the big-league team. And for the third year in a row, he didn't get in an exhibition game. Not a B-squad game, not even a "scare" (the players' term for getting the call to warm up in the bullpen but not getting in the game). No records were kept on such things, but Seitz was pretty sure it was a major-league record for futility.

Getting ignored at big-league camp three years in a row had not been good for his ego, but his spirits were buoyed on his first day at Diamond City in Daytona. Coming out of the locker room, he was greeted by Sullivan with a big smile. "Welcome," Sullivan said. "Really glad to have you with us." For Seitz, it was the first time in his five years of pro ball that he felt valued by a manager, although he hadn't even thrown a pitch. Other than that, he knew little about Sullivan.

As for the historic significance of the game he was about to pitch, it was something he was only vaguely aware of. He'd seen news footage of the church bombing, and he'd witnessed the South's Jim Crow way of life during his initial year of pro ball in 1960, first with the Selma Cloverleafs in the Class D Alabama-Florida League, and then with the Burlington Indians of the Class B Carolina League. By and large, however, current events and civil rights were outside his purview. At Ohio State, he was a PE major.

Pre-Game Distractions

There had been no rah-rah pre-game pep talk from Sullivan. That wasn't his style. Besides, he figured Belcher and Finley's promise to take the team to Hawaii if they won the pennant was better than anything he could say to fire them up. He assumed they'd all watched the news or read the paper and knew what was at stake.

In the bullpen, Seitz paused his warm-ups. The stiffness he'd initially felt was still there, but he figured it would go away once the game started. He was more concerned with all the opening night hoopla that was throwing him off his normal pre-game routine. He stepped off the mound to watch.

On the field, the Jones Valley High School marching band played what seemed like the tenth straight football fight song, and when that mercifully ended, Birmingham mayor Albert Boutwell summoned Finley to home plate and presented him with a key to the city. Surprisingly, Finley kept his remarks short.

"I just want everybody here tonight to know how much I love this city," he said. "I'll do everything I can to make the Barons a winner, even if it means I gotta take 'em to Hawaii. I'm glad to see such a nice turnout tonight. I hope you'll continue to support us during the year."

In the bullpen, Seitz resumed his throwing as the Barons and visiting Asheville Tourists were introduced, players trotting out to line up along the first- and third-base lines. The second loudest cheer was for Sullivan, a lot of it generated by his buddies from Dothan. The loudest cheer went to "Shaky Joe" Grzenda, the ace of the 1958 pennant-winning Barons and arguably the most popular Baron ever. (Teammates nicknamed him Shaky Joe because he drank two pots of coffee and smoked three packs of Lucky Strikes every day, sometimes working so fast on the mound that he would light a cigarette on the bench, leave it burning as he went out and retired the side, then come back and finish it off with a final quick puff or two.)

Following the introductions, Seitz concluded his warm-ups, draped his jacket over his right shoulder, and then stood at attention as the Jones Valley High School marching band played the national anthem.

After the last note, he plopped a fresh wad of Red Man tobacco into his cheek and headed for the dugout as Sullivan and Asheville manager Ray Hathaway met at home plate with the umpires.

"How do you feel, Droopsy?" asked Lindblad as Seitz sat down next to him on the bench.

"Guess I'm about to find out," replied Seitz.

Droopsy

Nicknamed Droopsy because of his laid-back, laconic personality and the slope-shouldered way he ambled on and off the field (*Baseball Digest* called it a "farmer's walk"), Seitz had deadpan facial expressions that sometimes made it hard for coaches to get a read on whether he was fully engaged in the game. It wasn't that he didn't care . . . he was just a taciturn young man, courteous and polite, but a guy who could yawn in a house fire.

Birmingham would be Droopsy's eighth team in five years in the game, and it had not always been a smooth journey. Like every player in pro ball, he'd been a star in high school, pitching a no-hitter and earning a scholarship to pay for the $75-per-semester tuition at Ohio State. He lived at home with his parents in the working-class Linden McKinley neighborhood and drove a Cushman to school. After pitching the no-hitter against Xavier in his second start his sophomore year, he heard the dreaded four words from his girlfriend: "I think I'm pregnant." Turned out she wasn't, but he didn't win another game the rest of the year. His junior year, however, he set the Buckeyes' single-season strikeout record. In June, he signed a $15,000 bonus (spread out over three years) with his favorite team, the Cleveland Indians.

After going 13–12 in his first two years in the Cleveland organization, two important things happened to him over the winter of 1961: The A's purchased his contract and he got married in a big church wedding in Wooster, Ohio, not to the girl who'd thought she was pregnant but to Carol Gordon, a tall, brown-eyed black-haired beauty who taught baton twirling for the Columbus Parks and Rec.

He spent the next two seasons putting a lot of miles on his Oldsmobile Delta 88 hardtop, bouncing from Albuquerque, New Mexico, to Binghamton, New York, to Portland, Oregon, to Lewiston, Idaho, and then back to Columbus in the off-seasons, where he tried to sell insurance, although no matter how many pep talks he got from the sales manager, he couldn't peddle the policies.

But all that was behind him. Heading to the mound at Rickwood to start the 1964 season—with the Jones Valley High School marching band playing another football fight song in the background—he had high hopes. Carol, pregnant with their second child, was back in Columbus with their young son and the Olds 88.

A First Inning from Hell

After a pat on the butt from Sullivan, Seitz took his "farmer's walk" to the mound. Completing his eight warm-up pitches, he could still feel the twinge in his shoulder. Of course now wasn't the time to complain. It would work itself out, he hoped.

He wasn't going to complain about the mound, either, but it was way too flat for his liking. Like all pitchers, he preferred a mound that made him feel as if he were standing on Mount Everest, throwing downhill at the cowering Sherpas. This mound made him feel as if he were in a foxhole, throwing uphill.

After the throw down to second, he took the ball from twenty-eight-year-old third baseman Tony Frulio, the oldest player on the team and Sullivan's pick to be team captain.

Finally, after months of anticipation, tension, and an unreported bomb threat, professional baseball was back in Birmingham. The Checkers Rule was dead, and now a raucous crowd of 6,592, with blacks and whites sitting shoulder-to-shoulder, heard the umpire's cry:

"Play ball!"

Seitz peered in for the signal from catcher Velazquez. One finger. Fastball. Seitz fired a room-service fastball right down Broadway. Asheville's leadoff hitter, center fielder Don Bosch, swung, sending a screaming line drive into the gap in left center, the ball rolling all the way to the wall for a stand-up double.

Seitz walked the next batter on four pitches.

Stepping off the mound, he stretched his right arm over his head, the knot still there.

He walked the next hitter, too, loading the bases with no outs.

Sullivan hustled to the mound to settle him down. "Paul, you're steering the ball," he said. "Is your arm okay?"

"Just a little tight, but I'm fine," Seitz answered.

On Sullivan's way back to the dugout, he motioned toward the bullpen for Rich Allen, a lefty, to start warming up...and in a hurry.

When Seitz fell behind in the count to the cleanup batter, the crowd stirred, hesitant to start booing their starting pitcher in the first inning of the first game. Kneeling next to the Barons' dugout, Finley shouted encouragement. Next to him, Sullivan motioned for first baseman Rosario to go talk to Seitz to buy time for Allen to get loose.

With the count 2–2, Seitz uncorked a wild pitch, allowing the runner on third to waltz home as the other runners advanced to second and third.

"Come on, Paul," encouraged Sullivan, fighting to stay calm.

The next pitch was ball four, loading the bases again. Even though he'd faced only four batters, Sullivan had seen enough, signaling to the bullpen for Allen.

Waiting for Sullivan to come and give him the hook, Seitz's shoulders sagged. He wanted to cry; he wanted to hide.

In front of the biggest Baron crowd in a decade, and with Charlie Finley taking it all in, he had just laid the biggest turd ever. He hadn't retired a single hitter; he'd walked three and thrown a pitch so wild that a dump truck couldn't have blocked it. His ERA was infinity. And worst of all, he'd let down his manager—the man who'd picked him above all the others to open the season.

Leaving the field, his eyes stayed fixed to the ground. He could only be thankful that Carol, who wasn't enamored with the baseball life, was in Ohio and had missed this catastrophe.

"Hang in there," offered Sullivan.

His words did little to soothe the pain. Seitz wondered if was time to resurrect that career, such as it was, in insurance.

Post-Game Promise

After the game, Sullivan was joined in his office by Finley and Belcher. If anybody could find sunshine in an opening game loss, it was Belcher. He'd orchestrated the first integrated game in Birmingham Baron history, and the largest Rickwood crowd in years had shown up to witness it. There'd been no fights, no ugly racial slurs at the players, no attacks with razor blades, and best of all the bomb threat before the game turned out to be a hoax...at least on this night. Belcher still hadn't told anybody about it.

"Not the way I wanted to start," said Sullivan. "I think we're going to have trouble scoring runs."

"I'm gonna get you some help," promised Finley.

Sullivan hoped that meant Tommie Reynolds would be coming soon.

CHAPTER 19

Haywood Sullivan

Taking His Temperature

Arriving at the park the next day, Sullivan was upbeat, smiling. Some players had worried, especially Seitz, that because it had been his managerial debut and so much had been made of Birmingham's first integrated baseball game, he'd be grumpy, pissed off that the team had stunk it up in front of Finley, the big crowd, his parents, his wife, and all his pals from Dothan.

If the players were looking for clues to their new manager's temperament—and they were—his relaxed manner was a good sign. They'd all been around the game long enough to know that an antsy manager equaled uptight players.

Sullivan and Hoss

Over the next two days, the players got more clues on Sullivan's managerial temperament by watching the way he handled several potentially ticklish situations. The first was with Hoss Bowlin.

Hitting fungoes before the second game, Sullivan noticed that Hoss, who had even quicker hands than Campaneris, was turning double plays like he was standing in molasses. As they walked off the field, Sullivan eased up next to him.

"You okay?"

"Sure," he replied.

But judging from the sallow gaze in his eyes, Hoss didn't look okay. He'd gone 0 for 4, and had taken some feeble swings on opening night. His temperature was 102.

"Don't bullshit me," said Sullivan. "I want a straight answer. You don't look good."

"I think I'm just a little tired from spring training and I haven't slept well since we got here, and..."

Sullivan stopped him mid-sentence. He knew about Hoss's surgery for testicular cancer in the off-season. As much as he wanted him in the lineup, he was starting to question Hoss's health.

"I'm okay to play tonight, really," Hoss claimed.

"Where you staying?" asked Sullivan.

"I'm still at the Tutwiler. Why?"

Sullivan called the office and lined up a ride to take Hoss to the hotel. "We'll make you a doctor's appointment for tomorrow," he said. "And don't let me catch you at the ballpark tomorrow, either."

The next day the doctor determined that Hoss was suffering from exhaustion and needed at least three or four days' rest. Familiar with the uncertain calculus of baseball's deliberations, Hoss knew that a couple of days off for an injury could mean an eternity on the sidelines...just ask Wally Pipp, the guy Lou Gehrig filled in for. As Hoss recuperated at the Tutwiler during the last two games of the opening series, his replacement, Dan Greenfield, went 0 for 7, struck out three times with runners in scoring position, and made an error. Sullivan called Hoss at the hotel.

"Take as long as you need to get healthy," he said. "Your job will be here when you get back."

Sullivan and Droopsy

The next clue to Sullivan's style was seeing how he dealt with Paul Seitz. The day after his first-game disaster, Seitz sat in front of his locker, slowly putting on his uniform, every fiber soaked with the weight of his failure. His arm ached.

Sullivan summoned him to his office.

He'd only been on the job a short time, but he'd already figured out that the hardest part wouldn't be knowing when to bunt or steal—most of the knuckleheads in the stands knew that stuff—the hardest part would be learning how to handle the diversity of personalities and temperaments on the team. He'd have to be hard-nosed with some, and then go easier on others. He didn't want a one-size-fits-all approach, even if it meant getting accused of not being evenhanded.

For Seitz, the humiliation of not retiring a single hitter had swirled through his brain all day, and to make it worse, when he rolled out of bed, he felt the throbbing in his arm. He could barely lift his spoon to eat his Cheerios.

Heading toward Sullivan's office, he weighed the possibilities of what he was about to hear. Was he getting sent down to A ball in Lewiston? If that was true, he was sure his wife, Carol, wouldn't be happy about going there again. She'd probably choose to stay in Ohio the whole season...and that wouldn't be good for a marriage that was already on rocky ground.

Or maybe Sullivan was demoting him to the bullpen. That would be a new experience—he'd been a starter his whole life.

Or maybe Sullivan was going to give him his pink slip. One bad game and poof, he's gone. He'd seen it happen to other players. Half the guys he played with his first year in Selma were history. Some cried when they got the news. Others cussed and threw their uniforms into a heap, and then just disappeared off the baseball map. If this was what Sullivan was about to tell him, then what? He'd never really liked being a student at Ohio State, and now with a family, the idea of resuming undergraduate life didn't appeal at all.

Nervously, he entered Sullivan's office. "What's up, Skip?" he asked.

Sullivan looked him in the eye. Seitz thought Sullivan seemed like a straightforward guy. He knew Finley liked him—everybody could see that—and maybe when Sullivan and Finley met behind closed doors after the first game, Finley had told him to get that pitcher the hell out of Birmingham.

"Paul, I don't want you to bullshit me," said Sullivan, echoing his earlier comment to Hoss. "Is your arm okay? It didn't look like it."

Seitz had been in the game long enough to know that management, to say nothing of the other players, expected guys to be tough and to be able to play through the pain, or as the baseball cliché went, "rub a little dirt on it." Being labeled a "pussy" was to sink to the lowest phylum among baseball species. On the other hand, it was impossible to pitch through a sore arm.

"I noticed a twinge warming up," confessed Seitz.

"Why didn't you say anything?"

"I figured it'd go away."

"How's it feel today?"

"Okay, I guess," he lied.

Sullivan wasn't buying it. "I'm putting you on the disabled list," he said. "You've got a future in this game. We don't want to jeopardize it."

Returning to his locker, Seitz felt an ambivalence, disappointed to be out of action, but happy to hear that Sullivan still thought he had a future in the game. He was surprised at how quickly Sullivan had made the decision to put him on the disabled list, but then again, maybe Sullivan had seen him struggling just to lift his arm to put on his jersey.

Sullivan and Stanley Jones

Another hint as to Sullivan's managerial style was his decision to start Bessemer native Stanley Jones in the second game. It surprised other pitchers on the staff. In spring training, Jones had pitched well and earned his spot on the team. But at least three others had pitched better—Paul Lindblad, Ron

Tompkins, and Nicky Don Curtis—and were naturally more gifted. Was this the first sign of an early-day affirmative-action assignment, a harbinger of Sullivan bending to the pressure, spoken or unspoken, from integrationists? Was he protecting himself against being accused of being a racist? Or did he really believe Jones deserved to start game two?

Before a crowd of 2,493, the Barons won that second game against Asheville 7–6, coming back from a four-run deficit after Jones had gotten drilled for seven hits and five runs in four innings. Not the hometown debut he'd hoped for.

Unofficially, twice as many blacks turned out to watch Jones's debut as had attended opening night, lending credence to the argument that black players would attract black fans, an axiom posited first when Jackie Robinson's exhibition appearance in 1954 drew more black fans than white. Jones knew he'd pitched like crap and possibly disappointed all the family and friends who'd shown up to watch him pitch. Maybe Sullivan wouldn't give him another start.

In the locker room after the game, Sullivan approached, patting him on the back. "Hang in there," he encouraged. "Get 'em next start."

Sullivan and Campy

In the Barons' clubhouse after losing the series finale to Asheville, Campy sat in front of his locker, his dark eyes cast to the floor. If a human could have steam coming out of his ears, Campy would've had enough to power a rail yard full of locomotives. For the series, he'd gone 1 for 13, struck out four times and made two errors, both on balls hit directly at him.

Sullivan eyed him cautiously, trying to design his approach. He knew the slender shortstop would be okay in the long run—he was probably the best prospect on the team. Campy was pressing too hard, eager for a good start but going to the plate looking as tense as a fiddle string. How could he get him to relax?

Campy was the team's biggest enigma, and Sullivan's biggest challenge. A lot of it had to do with language. Even though this was his third year in pro ball, Campy still spoke very limited English, and so far he'd shown little interest in learning. Other Spanish-speaking players who'd been in America the same amount of time had developed much better language skills. Sullivan communicated with him mainly by gesturing and pointing. And sometimes he got Rosario or one of the other Latin players to translate for him.

Until he'd gone 1 for 13, Campy seemed upbeat, smiling and looking as if he enjoyed being a Baron. But he was shy. Since coming to America, he'd kept mostly to himself. He didn't have a girlfriend. Sullivan worried he was, even after three years, still experiencing culture shock. He'd grown up impoverished in Cuba during Castro's rise to dictatorial power, living in a house with no electricity or running water. He'd spent long hours wielding a machete in the sugarcane fields. At a tournament in Costa Rica, a Caribbean scout for the A's told Campy that if he could get to Miami, he would get him a place to stay and a $500 bonus. It would take years for Campy to earn that kind of money in the cane fields, so with only the clothes on his back, he smuggled himself onto a fishing boat and set sail for America. When the scout came through for him and paid the bonus, Campy mailed most of the money back to his parents in Cuba. Knowing that he risked being imprisoned if he set foot back on the island, he hadn't been home since, communicating with his parents only through censored letters.

Sullivan eased next to him and reached out to put his hand on his shoulder, but quickly pulled it away, uncertain whether touching him on the shoulder would be violating a cultural taboo. Instead he smiled and spoke.

"No problemo," he said, imitating Campy's swing with an imaginary bat. "Mañana. Base hits mañana."

"Gracias," replied Campy with a hint of a smile.

Sullivan and Bladder

In the sixth inning of the last game against Asheville, Paul Lindblad sat in the bullpen, wondering if he was ever going to get in a game. The Barons trailed 7–1, and just as in the first two games, Sullivan hadn't even had him warm up. He felt discouraged.

Spring training had gone well for him—no sign of the arm problem that ended his first year and no runs allowed in his final twelve innings. He appreciated that Sullivan had told him he wouldn't be in the starting rotation to start the season, and had told him to "stay ready." But it was hard to stay focused sitting in the bullpen and never getting the call.

And then the call came. He was going in the next inning. Coming in out of the bullpen was new to him. His first pitch to the first hitter was a fastball down the pipe. The hitter connected, blasting it halfway to the Smoky Mountains. One pitch, one home run, an inauspicious Southern League baptism. At least Droopsy's first pitch had stayed in the park.

But Lindblad settled down after that, pitching three innings, giving up no more runs, and striking out four. Of all the Baron pitchers to take the mound in the opening series, he was the most effective.

"You looked good," said Sullivan.

That was nice to hear, thought Lindblad. But he wanted more. He wanted to hear Sullivan tell him he'd be starting one of the games on the upcoming road trip, but there was no such promise.

And that was just another of the vagaries of Sullivan's first week on his new job.

No Wild-Eyed Zealots, No Demonstrations...

The opening series had not gone as well as Sullivan had wished—winning one and losing two—but for Albert Belcher, baseball's return to Birmingham could not have gone better. The three-day attendance was 11,459, almost 5,000 more than had shown up for the first three games of 1961. There'd been no racial incidents, on or off the field; the bomb threat was a hoax; the KKK and Bull Connor stayed away; and nobody had gotten arrested, been blasted with a fire hose, or demanded reinstallation of the chicken-wire fence.

With a day off following the opening series, Sullivan went home to Dothan. His dad was building a backyard deck, and Haywood liked building things and working with his hands. It helped him relax. So he volunteered to help. In Birmingham, the newspapers offered analysis of the first series. Sportswriter Bob Phillips of the *Post-Herald* wrote:

> Professional baseball has returned to Birmingham, and the return was successful sociologically and financially. The emphasis is to be placed on the sociological. That the racial integration of both the spectators and the participants at Rickwood was accomplished in an orderly, unobtrusive manner must be hailed as a huge step in the right direction for Birmingham.

Benny Marshall, the sports editor of the *Birmingham News*, wrote:

> You will be aware that this was an integrated gathering. Both white and Negro citizens of Birmingham were at Rickwood over the weekend, watching integrated teams play baseball...
>
> No wild-eyed zealots, no demonstrations accompanied. And it happened, my friends, in Birmingham, Alabama, U.S.A.
>
> You know, old Birmingham, Hate Capital of the World. Say fear and say Birmingham.
>
> Or isn't it a story when people of Birmingham can gather together—just like people at Yankee Stadium or Busch Stadium or Shea Stadium—and watch young men play baseball?

CHAPTER 20

Paul Lindblad

Road Trip

The bus rolled south out of Birmingham on the team's first road trip, a 130-mile journey to Columbus, Georgia. Three days later they would cross the state to Macon for three more games. On board were twenty-two players (average age of twenty-two), with no college grads, eleven married men (eight with children), and fifteen smokers, with Marlboros and Winstons being the cigarettes of choice.

"Hey, Bussie," hollered Hoss, "could you pull over?"

"A piss stop already?" asked Lindblad.

"No, I want to see if I can find that home run you gave up. Oh, wait. Bussie, keep going. It's at least another ten miles."

In the minor leagues, bus trips are as much a part of the players' experience as foul balls. The team is both isolated and confined, a rolling band of brothers, sleeping, snacking, cussing, lying, spitting, farting, playing cards, and one-upping each other. There are no outside distractions. Being away from wives, kids, and trips to Piggly Wiggly to pick up some TV dinners translates into talking about cars, girls, and sliders on the corner. Bus trips can make or break a team. It's where team chemistry is built... or destroyed.

The Barons' bus passed through a corridor of tall pines in the gently rolling countryside. Using his own money, Belcher had bought the bus—a converted Greyhound, nicknamed "Iron Lung" by the players. Its air conditioner was broken, windows wouldn't open, and the smell of diesel fuel permeated the inside. In April, this was not a problem. In July and August—watch out.

Lindblad handed the sports page to Hoss and then pulled it back. "Oh, I forgot," he said. "They don't teach reading down there in Arkansas. And what about math? Do they teach you how to do averages? If not, I can help. You've got zero hits for the season. That means you're batting zero."

"Keep going, Bussie," said Hoss, "that ball should be up here somewhere."

110

Meanwhile, in Other Civil Rights News

Despite the "sociological success" of the opening of the baseball season in Birmingham, other parts of Alabama continued with segregation as usual. In Notasulga, a hundred miles southeast of Birmingham and not far from Auburn University, Ku Klux Klan arsonists set fire to a high school scheduled to enroll six black students in the fall, forcing its closure. No arrests were made.

In Montgomery, Governor George Wallace's strong showing in Midwest primaries had given his presidential campaign a new concern—his personal safety. At campaign events away from Alabama, he had sometimes encountered hostile crowds, despite being surrounded by three or four armed guards. With primaries coming up in Maryland and Indiana, his advisers requested more security. (This concern foreshadowed by eight years the assassination attempt in 1972 that would leave him paralyzed.)

Bolstered by Wallace's success, Bull Connor began to stir again politically, resurfacing as a spokesman for White Citizens' Councils, traveling around the state to raise funds to fight the civil rights movement.

"Segregationists might be on the one-yard line with our backs to the wall," he said. "But we will fight back. I guarantee it."

In Birmingham, Belcher was keeping himself informed about Connor's actions . . . just in case. And along with everyone else in the city, he was following the FBI's attempt to bring justice in the bombing of the 16th Street Baptist Church. Despite the most extensive investigation in the Bureau's history, as well as eyewitness testimony, no arrests had been made.

An editorial in the *Post-Herald* argued that the civil rights bill being debated in Congress was a "threat to traditional liberties of American people." If passed, the editorial concluded, "it would give the government too much power over the daily lives of citizens."

Columbus

As had been the case in Birmingham, Columbus's game with the Barons would be its first-ever integrated game. Although Columbus (a Yankee farm team) had a long minor-league history, it had been five years since its last professional game. Local ownership there had also shut down the team there rather than integrate.

With a population of 150,000, Columbus advertised its white colonial houses with well-tended gardens, lush lawns, forests of azaleas, and elaborate wrought-iron verandas. The city was home to RC Cola and Tom's Roasted Peanuts. Locals liked to call it "simply one of the best places on Earth." But in the early 1960s, urban blight and white flight had taken their toll on its once bustling core.

The city had a troubled history of racial violence. Assaults on black people were frequent and often brutal. In 1954, Dr. Thomas Brewer, a black physician who helped create the Columbus chapter of the NAACP and orchestrated voter registration drives, was shot by a white police officer seven times in front of his own office. Despite several witnesses to the shooting, no arrest was ever made.

In recent months, racial tension in the city had ratcheted up, due in part to the increased number of black soldiers arriving for basic infantry training at nearby Fort Benning. Many of these soldiers would be leaving soon for the escalating war in Vietnam. They not only faced hostility from white soldiers on the base, but when they ventured into Columbus they were banned from whites-only restaurants, bars, restrooms, and public parks. That they were soldiers prepared to give their lives for their country seemed not to matter.

As the bus stopped in front of the historic Parsons Hotel downtown, the players disembarked, grabbed their bags from the bus, and headed inside to receive their room keys—two men to a room. Or at least the white players did. As the bus pulled away from the curb, with the black players still on board, Lindblad watched it disappear around the corner.

"Where do those guys stay?" he asked.

Nobody knew.

For Lindblad, this was a new experience. During his first season with Burlington in the Midwest League, the blacks stayed in the same hotels. On one road trip, he and Tommie Reynolds had roomed together.

On the Cheap

After checking into the Parsons Hotel, Lindblad headed out on foot in search of lunch. Other than the home run on his first pitch, his initial appearance had been satisfying, even though Sullivan hadn't given him any indication if he'd get a starting assignment on this trip.

Wandering into Woolworth's in Columbus Square, he sat down at the lunch counter (where there'd been a series of sit-ins the previous year). Surveying the menu, he debated between a BLT for fifty cents, or a ham salad sandwich for thirty cents. What he really craved was a chili cone from Barker's Dairy back home in Chanute, or even a burger, but Woolworth's didn't serve burgers, not in Columbus, not anywhere.

He ordered the cheaper ham salad sandwich, mindful of the tight budget he and Kathy were on. Financially, his big hope was that he would stick with the Barons for ninety days and earn his $1,000 "progressive bonus."

He inquired as to the cost of a slice of apple pie and a large Coke. "Pie is a quarter, Coke is a dime... just like it says on the menu," answered the waitress.

He did a little quick math. The sandwich, pie, and Coke would come to sixty-five cents. Add a dime for a tip—no, she had an attitude—and he'd still have $2.35 of his per-diem meal money left. He couldn't even fathom getting the $18-per-day meal money the big leaguers got, but if he continued to watch his pennies on the road, he could return home with four or five extra dollars. He and Kathy could buy diapers for a month with that, or apply it to the $70-a-month rent on their apartment.

After inhaling his ham salad sandwich, he walked back to the Parsons. He thought about calling Kathy, but held off, deciding to wait until later when the rates were cheaper.

Never a Good Time

Kathy answered the phone in their two-bedroom Birmingham apartment, excited as always to get a call from Paul. She was also apprehensive.

For as long as she'd known him, she'd thought about telling him her big secret—that her stepfather had sexually abused her starting when she was in junior high. She had never told anyone, not her sisters, not her mother. She didn't know if her stepfather had also abused her sisters, or if her mom knew about it. In the era of Ozzie and Harriet, sexual abuse somehow seemed improbable in a small, wholesome Midwestern town. She'd never even heard anyone talk about it.

As often as she'd thought about telling her husband, she couldn't get past a feeling of shame, as if it were somehow her fault. What if she told him and he couldn't handle it? Paul was the nicest person she'd ever met, the perfect husband for her... but the fear of risking what she had with him was inhibiting. But if not now, when?

Hearing his voice on the phone, as always, made her feel better. There was just something so comforting and calm about him, a feeling that he would always take care of her and the girls. After asking her how her day had gone, he told her that he'd just pitched four scoreless innings in relief against Columbus.

"Maybe Sully will give me a start in Macon," he said.

She knew that now was definitely not the time to tell him.

"And guess what?" he added. "I'll have a little present for you when I get off this trip."

CHAPTER 21

Haywood Sullivan

What's in That Briefcase?

Boarding the bus in front of the Parsons, Lindblad and Hoss eyed Sullivan settling into his front-row seat and setting down a brown leather briefcase next to him. They had seen him carrying it several times when he left the ballpark in spring training.

"Whattya think he's got in there?" asked Hoss.

Lindblad contemplated his response. In the baseball world, there was always a fine line between wit and insult. Lindblad decided that Hoss could handle it.

"He's got your release papers in there," he said.

In the three games in Columbus, Hoss and Campy had both gone 1 for 12, including 0 for 8 the last two games. They were both hitting below .100 after the first week of the season.

Sullivan's briefcase actually contained the blank player-evaluation forms he was required to submit to the Kansas City front office after every game. It also held a copy of the *Columbus Ledger* and *Profiles in Courage* by JFK.

Sullivan wasn't about to release Hoss. He was, however, trying to figure out how to get him and Campy jump-started. He was also considering giving Lindblad a shot at starting.

"I'll bet he's also got some travel brochures for Hawaii in there," added Lindblad. "I'll send you a postcard when we get there."

"Shit. You get a couple guys out and all of a sudden you're Dizzy Fuckin' Dean."

Sullivan and Santiago Rosario

For Sullivan, one of the best surprises so far had been Rosario. He was hitting .529, easily the best on the team.

Sullivan had known that Rosario would be an asset defensively. Not only was he flashy around the first-base bag, doing the splits and sweeping his glove with flair after routine catches—which elicited calls of "*perro caliente*" (hot dog) from the opposing dugout—but he routinely dug balls out of the dirt. This was his fifth year in pro ball, the first four spent in the Cardinals' organization. In those four years, he had a combined batting average over .300, as good as anybody in the organization, but the Cardinals thought he had an "attitude problem" and left him unprotected in the draft. Kansas City decided to take a chance and purchased his contract. Sullivan had read the reports of the "attitude problem," but knew from experience that players sometimes get on the bad side of a manager, for either real or perceived issues, and get written off. (This was especially true with black and Latin players.) Sullivan was determined not to pre-judge Rosario. So far, he had seen no signs of the "attitude problem," and as long as Rosario was making all the plays at first and ripping the cover off the ball, he'd let him be as flashy as he wanted. He also seemed to have a steadying influence on Campy.

In the first week, Sullivan had Rosario hitting eighth, but he was going to juggle the lineup and move him up to fifth. With the sometimes fragile psyches of players, most of whom had batted cleanup in high school, Sullivan knew this could create ripples. But he'd told himself that he couldn't get bogged down worrying about players' feelings every time he made a move... otherwise he'd go nuts. He was a manager, not a shrink.

Statistically, the logical choice would be to move Campy and Hoss down to seventh and eighth in the order, or even sit them on the bench. But playing a hunch, Sullivan elected to leave his keystone combination in the one and two slots.

In the first game against Macon, they got five hits between them: three for Campy, two for Hoss.

The Good People of Macon

A few days prior to the Barons' arrival in Macon, seventeen black college students decided to stage a sit-in at the lunch counter of Liggett's Drug Store in nearby Warner Robins. In the past, blacks had been allowed to buy merchandise at the store, but not to eat there. "You niggers need to leave," the manager told them as they sat down at the lunch counter. "This place will never integrate." The police quickly arrived, arrested the students, and hauled them off to jail, where they sat for two days with nothing to eat but cold beans. Shortly after that, blacks demanded access to the swimming pool at Macon's Baconsfield Park, but rather than integrate, city officials closed the pool.

Before the first game, Sullivan warned the black players that Macon fans had a reputation for hurling racial insults.

"Just ignore them," he advised.

Sullivan's warning proved accurate. A fan behind third kept up a steady bar-rage aimed at Campy. "Hey, Banana Boy," he yelled. "Go back to Africa."

Sullivan's first reaction was to question the guy's grasp of geography. Then he realized that Campy didn't understand a word the dimwit was yelling, so the dimwit was wasting his breath.

Keeping His Cool in the Face of a Bonehead Play

Sailing along with a five-hitter going into the bottom of the ninth—the Barons leading 2–1—Stanley Jones was in control, justifying Sullivan's faith in giving him a second start after a bad first outing. The decision had been based not on the color of Jones's skin or the fact that he was from Birmingham, but on his confidence in Jones, who'd pitched well in spring training, and the fact that he'd had a 2.47 ERA the previous year, the second best in the Carolina League, with 121 strikeouts and only 34 walks.

But when Jones walked the first two hitters in the ninth, including the Peaches' cleanup hitter, Lee May, Sullivan waved in twenty-two-year-old right-hander Ken Knight from the bullpen. In his fourth year of pro ball, Knight had compiled an impressive 21–7 record, mostly in relief.

With two outs and runners on second and third, Sullivan signaled Knight to intentionally walk the next hitter, Len Boehmer, who was hitting over .400 in the young season.

Catcher Woody Huyke gave Knight a target a foot outside. Knight lobbed the pitch, but instead of hitting Huyke's target, the ball floated like a beach ball over the outside part of the plate. Boehmer swung, lining a shot to right for a base hit, scoring the runners from second and third, losing the game for the Barons and sending Jones to his second loss.

In the Barons' clubhouse, the players waited to see if Sullivan would upbraid Knight. It's frustrating enough to get beaten in the ninth inning, and to have a starting pitcher lose after pitching so well. But to lose it on a careless mistake was an invitation for a manager to throw chairs.

Knight sat in front of his locker, head down, looking for a rock to crawl under. Sullivan approached, putting a hand on his shoulder.

"Don't do that again," he said calmly.

Scouting Blue Moon

Sullivan waited in front of the Dempsey Hotel, where Blue Moon Odom washed dishes on weekends. Accompanied by Bill Posedel, the minor-league

Four innocent girls were murdered in the dynamiting of the 16th Street Baptist Church. *Courtesy of Birmingham Public Library*

The nation was shocked by the vicious attacks on protestors. *Courtesy of Charles Moore*

The threat of violence hung over the Barons season. *Courtesy of Birmingham Public Library*

"Bull Connor has done more for integration in America than Abraham Lincoln."—President John F. Kennedy *Courtesy of Birmingham Public Library*

Albert Belcher, owner of the Barons: the man who made it happen. *Courtesy of Friends of Rickwood—Clarence Watkins*

Charlie Finley, owner of the Kansas City A's: "I'll do whatever is necessary to bring a championship to Birmingham." *Courtesy of Friends of Rickwood*

Charlie Finley and legendary Alabama football coach Bear Bryant watching Blue Moon Odom pitch. *Courtesy of Friends of Rickwood*

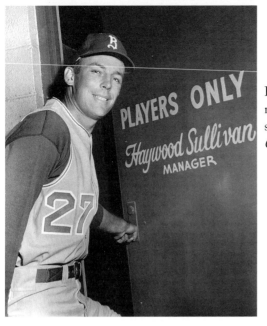

First-year manager and Alabama native Haywood Sullivan was no stranger to the ways of Jim Crow. *Courtesy of Friends of Rickwood*

Haywood Sullivan was a record-setting All-SEC quarterback at the University of Florida. *Courtesy of University of Florida Athletic Department*

Haywood Sullivan signed with the Red Sox for $45,000 in 1952, one of the largest bonuses ever given at the time. *Courtesy of Boston Red Sox*

Over 16,000 turned out to Rickwood Field to see the Barons play the A's. *Courtesy of Friends of Rickwood—Clarence Watkins*

Blue Moon Odom was the richest player on the team. *Courtesy of Friends of Rickwood— Clarence Watkins*

Bert Campaneris escaped from Castro's Cuba to lead the Barons in hitting. *Courtesy of Friends of Rickwood—Clarence Watkins*

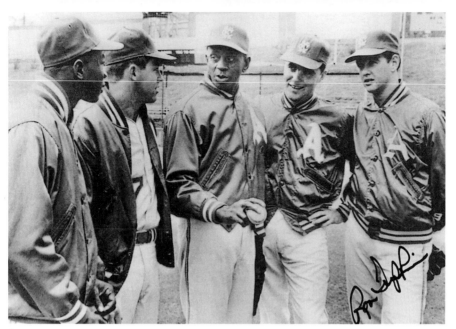

Satchel Paige shows Blue Moon, Catfish Hunter, Dick Joyce, and Ron Tompkins the tricks of the trade. *Courtesy of Ron Tompkins*

For Hoss Bowlin, fighting a slump wasn't as hard as battling testicular cancer. *Courtesy of Weldon "Hoss" Bowlin*

Teammates always asked Hoss, "How'd you get such a pretty wife?" *Courtesy of Madelyn Mack*

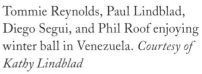

Tommie Reynolds, Paul Lindblad, Diego Segui, and Phil Roof enjoying winter ball in Venezuela. *Courtesy of Kathy Lindblad*

Kathy and Paul Lindblad at the prom in Chanute, Kansas. *Courtesy of Kathy Lindblad*

Joe DiMaggio taking it easy with Lindblad. *Courtesy of Kathy Lindblad*

Lindblad finished second in the national junior college javelin competition. *Courtesy of Kathy Lindblad*

Maybe the most popular player in Barons history, "Shaky Joe" usually downed six cups of coffee and smoked a pack before noon. *Courtesy of Friends of Rickwood—Clarence Watkins*

JOE GRZENDA

Set club record for most strikeouts by fanning 190 men in 1958. The previous record was set by Phil Morrison in 1922 at 170 strikeouts. Burleigh Grimes struck out 158 in 1915 for the next best record by a Baron.

Army vet Tommie Reynolds was packed to go to war during the Cuban missile crisis. *Courtesy of Friends of Rickwood—Clarence Watkins*

Tommie knew he wanted to marry Penny almost from the day they met. *Courtesy of Tommie and Penny Reynolds*

The 1964 Birmingham Barons. Front row: Richard Allen, Tony Frulio, John Stutz, John Stahl, business manager Glynn West, manager Haywood Sullivan, president W. A. Belcher, Santiago Rosario, Woody Huyke, Nicky Curtis, Weldon Bowlin, Johnny Odom. Back row: trainer Fred Posey, Stan Jones, Stan Wojcik, Tom Reynolds, Lou Hemauer, Bill Meyer, Ron Tompkins, Ken Knight, Paul Seitz, Joe Grzenda, Wayne Norton, Paul Lindblad, Ossie Chavarria. *Courtesy of Jim Goodwin Studios*

pitching instructor for the A's, Sullivan was waiting for a ride to go scout the high school pitching phenom. Minor-league managers and pitching instructors didn't usually scout amateur players, but Blue Moon was an exception. Sullivan had received a call from Charlie Finley asking him to check out Odom when the Barons were in Macon. Was he as good as advertised? The only two games he'd ever lost had both come on passed balls by the catcher.

Kansas City scout Jack Sanford picked up Sullivan and Posedel and drove them to Ballard-Hudson High, home of the Maroon Tigers, the defending state champions in Georgia's Negro Class AA Conference. Sullivan had talked on the phone to Finley, who'd personally flown to Macon to try to persuade Blue Moon to sign with Kansas City. Finley had eaten dinner with Blue Moon and his mother at their duplex, and listened to Blue Moon's high school coach say that Blue Moon wouldn't be making his decision until after he graduated in five weeks. Finley promised he would top any offer Blue Moon received.

Arriving at the field, Sullivan and the other two men took a seat in the rickety bleachers behind home plate. They weren't alone—eight other scouts were also on hand. In the top of the first, Blue Moon struck out the side, nobody even getting a foul tip off him. "That last pitch must've sunk a foot," Sullivan enthused. "You can't teach that."

In the bottom of the first, Blue Moon drilled a savage double to left, driving in a runner from first.

"He's a great all-around athlete," added Sanford.

In the second inning, he struck out the side again.

In the seventh and final inning, he still had a no-hitter. With two outs and the count 1–2 on the hitter, Blue Moon tugged at his hat, and then fired a fastball. The batter swung, but not until the ball was in the catcher's glove.

Blue Moon nonchalantly walked off the mound, greeted by his coach and teammates. Not only had he pitched his seventh no-hitter and struck out seventeen (out of a possible twenty-one), he was also the star at the plate, getting three hits and driving in the Maroon Tigers' only two runs.

"I'd love to have him pitch for the Barons," said Sullivan.

"Finley may take him straight to the big leagues," said Posedel.

"That would be a mistake," said Sullivan.

Superstitions

Baseball players, by both custom and instinct, are wildly superstitious. Infielders won't step on the foul line coming off the field; batters won't change their underpants if they're on a hitting streak; pitchers will smoke Kools instead of Marlboros on the days they start; hitters will put on their left shoe first and drink half a Coke before a game. But of all baseball's rituals, one of the oldest and most rigidly observed is the superstition of teammates' not acknowledging that their pitcher has a no-hitter going.

Going into the bottom of the eighth of the final game of the Macon series, with the Barons leading 5–0, right-hander Nicky Don Curtis hadn't given up a hit…and in the Barons' dugout an odd silence was interrupted only by inane chatter, including banal contributions from Sullivan.

Sullivan had taken a chance in keeping Curtis on the Barons' roster. The handsome twenty-two-year-old right-hander with a thick Oklahoma drawl hadn't done well in 1963, recording an unspectacular 4–10 record and a 4.58 ERA in A ball. But in spring training, Sullivan had seen something he liked— a lively fastball and decent control—so he brought him north with the Barons. Curtis lost his first start against Columbus, but as he'd done with Jones, Sullivan gave him a second start.

With one out in the eighth inning and only five outs to a no-no, Boehmer, the guy who'd smacked the errant pitchout the night before, lined a base hit to center. Good-bye, no-hitter. Curtis shook it off and held the Peaches hitless the rest of the way for a 5–0 victory.

"The hell with superstitions," said Hoss. "Next time I'm telling him he's got a no-hitter going."

A Scouting Report on Sully

After observing the Baron pitchers for three days, Bill Posedel submitted his report to Hank Peters, the A's general manager. It included this observation:

> They've got a bunch of Major League arms here with Birmingham, and a heckuva manager to keep them developing. These boys really like Sullivan, and more importantly, they respect him and really hustle for him. I've got a feeling that this club is going to do alright in this league.

CHAPTER 22

Paul Lindblad

Surprises for the Wife

Night had fallen as Iron Lung pulled into the Rickwood parking lot after the five-hour ride from Macon. With babies in arms, wives greeted the players as they stepped off the bus. After a hug and a kiss, Lindblad handed Kathy a $5 bill.

"What's this?" she asked.

"It's the meal money I saved," he said.

She offered possible uses for the money—diapers, groceries, new shoes for the baby—and then gave him another kiss.

"I've got more good news," he said, and then explained that Sullivan had told him he'd be starting the second game of the home stand against the Knoxville Smokies.

As they headed to their Impala, Paul Seitz hailed him, asking if Paul wanted to join him for golf on their day off tomorrow. Lindblad hesitated.

"Go ahead, it'll be fun," said Kathy.

Seeing his wife with their younger daughter in her arms, he thought about the reality of the last seven days—he'd been staying in nice hotels, sleeping late, eating out, drinking beer, and shooting the bull in the bullpen; Kathy had been cooped up in their small apartment, changing diapers, cleaning baby food off the wall, and getting up in the middle of the night.

"Thanks, Droops," he replied, "but I better pass."

The Latest News in Birmingham

One of the settlements negotiated the previous spring by Martin Luther King and Fred Shuttlesworth following the demonstrations and arrests in the Birmingham Campaign was the appointment of a biracial Community Affairs

119

Committee to make recommendations for possible changes to the city's segregationist laws. In a blistering attack on Mayor Boutwell, the committee chastised him for failing to invite blacks to apply for openings on the police force, continuing a policy handed down from Connor.

Boutwell defiantly stood his ground:

> Our government does not intend to let the state of Alabama or the federal government tell us what to do. We are not going to surrender to pressure from any side. You must realize that this city government represents all the people of Birmingham. We are not dealing with one race's problems and desires. You may create a disturbance... and it doesn't have to be a thrown bomb, setting of a fire, or the inflaming of the mind.

Meanwhile, on the presidential campaign trail in Cambridge, Maryland, George Wallace was unrepentant:

> The South must let the world know that racial segregation is the only sane, sensible and non-hypocritical way in which our people can live in harmony together.

Prior to the start of the season, Albert Belcher had sent Wallace an invitation to attend a Barons' home game at Rickwood. So far, he had received no response. It was not clear whether Alabama's only pro sports team, the integrated Barons, was challenging Wallace's segregationist certainty—that the only way to preserve racial "harmony" was to keep the races apart—or if he was just too busy running the state of Alabama and campaigning for president to respond.

Despite Governor Wallace and Mayor Boutwell's resistance to integration, a front-page headline in the News pointed out that a recent Billy Graham sermon at Legion Field had drawn "the largest mixed race gathering in Alabama history." It was also noted that a group calling itself the "International Downtown Executives Association" had recently met in Birmingham, arriving in town with what it said was an attitude that "Birmingham wasn't such a good place to live, and that is putting it mildly." But after exploring the city for several days, it reported to Mayor Boutwell that it had been "tremendously impressed by the vigor of your downtown people, and the evidence on all sides of the marvelous job you are doing for Birmingham." One member of the association even marveled that Birmingham's culinary choices included "the greatest Chinese meal I have ever had in my life. There were five different entrees and they were all delicious."

The report did not mention anything about the violence that had rocked the city, or the mayor's refusal to hire a black police officer.

Seven Good Innings

In his first start, Lindblad threw well, giving up only one run on five hits and striking out ten in seven innings. The one negative was that he'd walked five and thrown a lot of pitches—143. But there'd been no pain in his left arm, no hint of the injury that had ended his first year. He just hoped that when he woke up in the morning, his arm wouldn't be so stiff and sore that he couldn't lift it to comb his hair. With the Barons leading 5–1, Sullivan brought in Rich Allen to finish off the last two innings.

The first person in the dugout to greet Lindblad was Ron Tompkins, who was still riding high from striking out a league-best thirteen hitters the night before to improve his record to 2–0. Lindblad took a seat to watch the last two innings as Allen tried to protect his first Southern League victory.

Hitters' and Pitchers' Biggest Fears

In the bottom of the seventh, the first pitch to Barons' center fielder Wayne Norton sailed just under his chin, sending him sprawling in the dirt. Earlier, he'd hit a long homer off the BELCHER LUMBER sign atop the right-field roof, earning himself $50—the bonus Belcher had promised to any Baron clearing the sign. Despite getting knocked down, he figured the pitch had just gotten away from the pitcher and was not meant to hit him.

Like all hitters, Norton's biggest fear was getting beaned—taking a ninety-five-mile-an-hour fastball to the temple. In all of major-league history, only one hitter, Ray Chapman of the Cleveland Indians, had died from being hit by a pitch. It happened in 1920 in a game against the Yankees at the Polo Grounds (before Yankee Stadium), and the sound of the ball smashing into Chapman's skull was so loud that pitcher Carl Mays thought it hit the bat, so he fielded the ball and threw to first. In those days, almost all pitchers dirtied up a new ball by smearing it with dirt, licorice, or tobacco juice, as well as sometimes deliberately scuffing it with sandpaper, spit, or an emery board. The result was a ball that was hard for hitters to see, especially in twilight. According to eyewitnesses, Chapman never moved, and after he was hit, he slowly collapsed to his knees, blood pouring from his ear. Recently married, he died later that night in a New York hospital. Forty years would pass before hitters were required to wear batting helmets.

For pitchers, the biggest fear was a wicked line drive back through the box, one that arrives so fast that there's no time to put up a glove in self-defense. To avoid the calamity of being hit, pitchers spend hours every spring on drills designed to get them to practice their follow-through so they'll be ready to field their position. But they all know that no matter how agile they are off the mound, or how fast they can throw the ball, it can come rocketing back at them even faster.

Every pitcher knew about what happened in 1957 to Herb Score, a young, hard-throwing lefty for the Cleveland Indians, a sure future Hall of Famer. Pitching against Gil McDougald of the Yankees, he threw a fastball that McDougald ripped back up the middle. The result was one of the goriest and most lasting images of the era. The ball hit Score just above the eye, and he fell in a heap to the side of the mound, his face so bloody and battered that the sight made some players retch. He missed the rest of that season and was never the same as a pitcher.

As If He'd Been Shot

In relief of Lindblad, Allen, a twenty-one-year-old bachelor from St. Paul, Minnesota, gave up two runs in the eighth inning, cutting the Barons' lead to 5–3. Rather than bring in either of his two best closers—Shaky Joe Grzenda or Ken Sanders—Sullivan sent Allen back out for the top of the ninth.

Allen retired the first hitter in the ninth, and then walked the next batter, Jess Queen, bringing the tying run to the plate. In the dugout, Lindblad paced.

With Sanders warming up in the bullpen, Sullivan stayed with Allen, a lefty, to face Bud Zipfel, a left-handed power hitter.

Pitching from the stretch, Allen's first pitch was a fastball right down the pipe. Zipfel connected, with the ball rocketing right back up the middle, head-high. Allen ducked, but not in time, the baseball hitting him squarely in the forehead, dropping him to the ground as if he'd been shot.

As the crowd gasped, the ball caromed high in the air toward short right field. Alertly, Rosario backpedaled and caught it on the fly, then hustled to first to double up Queen, who never saw the ball and was already rounding second.

The game was over—a 5–3 Baron victory—giving Lindblad his first win. But Allen lay sprawled in the dirt, motionless.

Sullivan raced out to the mound, followed closely by Lindblad and the rest of his teammates. Kneeling down, Sullivan saw Allen's eyes rolled back in his head. He turned toward the stands and yelled: "Somebody call an ambulance."

If segregation can be destroyed in Birmingham, it can be destroyed anywhere in America.

—Rev. Fred Stallingsworth

PART IV

THE SEASON

May

League Standings, May 1

	W	L	GB
Macon	11	3	
Chattanooga	8	4	2
Birmingham	9	6	2½
Charlotte	6	5	3½
Knoxville	5	7	5
Asheville	5	7	5
Columbus	4	9	6½
Lynchburg	4	9	6½

CHAPTER 23

Tommie Reynolds

On the Road to Birmingham

Just outside Memphis, Tommie Reynolds gripped the steering wheel of his '64 Malibu Super Sport, staring at the road ahead. Determined to make the 730-mile drive from Kansas City to Birmingham in one day, he rolled down the window to let a blast of air slap him in the face.

He didn't want to end up in a ditch again as he had on the way to spring training.

Getting sent down from the big leagues had him in a foul mood, especially because he'd been sent to Birmingham instead of AAA Dallas. Usually, players sent down from The Show went to AAA...but Charlie Finley had promised to send Sullivan "the best talent available," and that's what he'd done. Reynolds had heard enough about the Southern League to know that black players didn't stay in the same hotels or eat in the same restaurants as whites...as it had been in Bradenton. In the big leagues, he'd stayed with the whole team in fancy places, like the Palmer House in Chicago. No telling what kind of rat-holes he'd have to stay in now. Ed Charles, his teammate in Kansas City, had told him about one rooming house in Macon that he'd stayed in when he was in the SALLY League that reeked so badly of urine, he slept on the porch with the mosquitoes.

But Reynolds wasn't coming to Birmingham to sulk. He was determined to show Finley and Manager Eddie Lopat that they'd made a mistake. He was proud that he'd made the big leagues after only a year in pro ball, but it hadn't taken long for him to figure out that there was nothing glamorous about riding the pine. He'd rather be playing—even if it was for Birmingham—than collecting splinters.

Before leaving KC, he'd gotten a pep talk from Finley, reminding him how important it was that Birmingham have a winning team, and how he needed to comport himself like Jackie Robinson and ignore all the crap that would surely come his way. Reynolds assured him he would.

The best thing about coming to Birmingham was that he'd be closer to Daytona Beach and his girlfriend, Penny. He'd already called and told her he'd been sent down. The plan was for her to visit him when she got out of school in June. He'd spent a lot of his nights in the big leagues going to sleep thinking about how beautiful she'd looked stepping off that Greyhound in Bradenton in her new sundress, and what a great time they'd had during her visit. The word *marriage* had come up in more than one conversation. But she still had two years left before earning her degree in English from Bethune-Cookman, and she wanted to wait.

Driving through Memphis, the world headquarters for Holiday Inn, he saw several green signs beckoning motorists to spend the night. None of them had a NO NEGROES ALLOWED sign. They didn't need to...he knew he wasn't welcome.

Wide awake again, he continued to Birmingham.

Warm Welcome

He arrived in Birmingham at twilight and headed directly to Rickwood, where the Barons, now only a game out of first, were playing Macon in the second of a three-game series.

Reynolds took a seat behind first base, sitting next to Albert Belcher and Glynn West, the general manager. West had already lined up a room for him in a boardinghouse in a black neighborhood north of the ballpark.

Also arriving in Birmingham that day was another outfielder, Larry Stahl, sent to add more firepower to the lineup. Like Reynolds, Stahl had completed his military duty, serving six months in the Army National Guard during the off-season. Unlike Reynolds, he was staying temporarily at the Tutwiler downtown, a hotel that Reynolds had as much chance of staying at as he did of landing an off-season job as a Birmingham policeman.

After the game, Reynolds headed down to the Barons' locker room to meet his new teammates and manager. Looking around, he saw a couple of familiar faces from big-league spring training camp—pitchers Paul Seitz and Ron Tompkins—as well as two other pitchers he'd played with his first year in Burlington, Ken Knight and Lindblad.

He saw another familiar face from Burlington—Rich Allen. General Manager West had told him about Allen getting hit in the head with the line shot and how, miraculously, he was released from the hospital the next day after X-rays revealed he hadn't been seriously hurt.

Reynolds was introduced to Stanley Jones, who tried to assure him that Birmingham wasn't as bad as a lot of people made it out to be.

"Hope you're right," said Reynolds.

The Black Newspaper Looks at the Barons' Impact

The *Birmingham World*, the city's black newspaper, spoke to the Barons' return and its impact on the city:

Organized baseball fled this coal, steel and industrial center two years ago under the pressure of crescending [*sic*] racial conflict. The demise of the Great American game trumpeted the death knell of the Southern Association which died because of its refusal to accept Negro competitors...What a difference two years makes. Since baseball fled here, Birmingham has been heralded throughout the world as a symbol of police brutality, murder, bombings, arson, hate mobs, discrimination and prejudice...Rickwood seating is integrated. No incidents...Friendly exchange is frequent between Negro and white fans who sit side by side. Acceptance of the Negro players by the front office...has been indoctrinated into the fans, press, radio and TV, as well as the general public.

Forewarned

Ed Charles of the A's had warned Reynolds that some of the Southern cities, such as Knoxville and Macon, were particularly nasty. Players, fans, the community, and even the front offices contributed to the hostile atmosphere. But, according to Charles, Reynolds wouldn't have to deal with racism from the Birmingham front office. Baseball officials appeared to have finally figured out that black players could help win championships. Whether or not baseball executives believed in integration in their hearts was hard to determine, but supposedly blacks players weren't being held back from getting to the big leagues. (Rumors persisted, however, about quotas and black players routinely making less than whites, speculation that was hard to verify because salaries were not published, and players didn't discuss how much they made with each other. Major League Baseball's first collective bargaining agreement with the players' union wasn't signed until 1968.)

Reynolds hoped that the greeting he'd received from Albert Belcher and Haywood Sullivan was a positive sign. In his Rickwood debut the next night in a losing cause against Macon, he went 2 for 4, with a triple, double, and no racial slurs from the stands.

Rude Introduction

Taking his position in left field during batting practice prior to his first road game in Asheville, he trotted over near the foul line to toss a ball back to the infield. A middle-aged white man stood next to the fence.

"Hey, nigger, give me the ball."

Reynolds ignored him and threw the ball back to the infield.

"Hey, nigger, you don't listen so well. We don't like uppity niggers around here."

Reynolds continued to ignore him, trotting back to his position in left field.

"You're not a very friendly nigger," the man yelled. "Might wanna watch yourself tonight. We like to shoot niggers like you...right in your nigger dick."

CHAPTER 24

Hoss Bowlin

Soaking in the Culture

With a dozen other tourists, Hoss stepped off the tour bus in front of the majestic Biltmore Hotel in the mountains above Asheville. Mouth agape, he stared up at the 250-room chalet located on the eight-thousand-acre estate and gardens once owned by George Vanderbilt. He'd come up with the idea to tour the different Southern League cities he'd be playing in this season to help pass his days. In his five previous seasons, he barely went out of the team's hotel except to the ballparks, but this year he was determined to make an effort to soak up some local history and scenery, figuring that since he didn't drink and never had to worry about a hangover like some of his teammates, he'd get up early and do something other than sit in his room and watch *The Dating Game*. The idea came while he was recuperating from his cancer surgery. He'd thought about how precious life was and how lucky he was to have survived. He was determined to milk every second of every day.

He calculated that he was about a third the age of the other tourists at the Biltmore, and the only one without a Brownie camera draped around his neck. He'd already learned from the tour guide that Asheville, a city of sixty thousand, was located in the Blue Ridge Mountains in the western part of North Carolina, and during the Civil War, the area had not suffered heavy fighting. Asheville had experienced less turmoil from the civil rights movement than most Southern cities, possibly because its mountainous climate offered cooler temperatures, but more likely because tourism was a big part of its economy and local businesses, wanting to attract Northern dollars, were more receptive to negotiating with advocates for civil equality.

Disregarding the numbskull who had yelled insults at Reynolds the previous night, Hoss sensed that desegregation had, in fact, moved more quickly in Asheville, at least compared with Birmingham. Most restaurants and dime store lunch counters had opened to blacks in 1962; Jim Crow signs on drinking fountains and restrooms had been removed; the Windsor Hotel downtown, where the Barons stayed, was the only accommodation in the league where black and white players stayed together. The only significant protest in the city had occurred when the Congress of Racial Equality (CORE) demonstrated against Winn-Dixie's hiring practices. This was not to say, however, that Asheville was one big homogeneous enclave. At the city's two public pools, both supposedly integrated, whites swam in one pool, blacks in another. Same at McCormick Field—blacks on the first-base side, whites down the third. Reynolds, in left field, was in the line of verbal fire from racist white fans.

Paul Lindblad was standing in front of the hotel when the tour bus dropped off its passengers. As he spotted Hoss bidding his fellow tourists good-bye, he laughed.

"What the hell are you doing?" he inquired.

"Getting some culture."

"I didn't know they had hog-calling contests around here."

B₁₂ Shots

With the lineup card in his hand, Sullivan walked out of his office in the clubhouse at McCormick Field and eyed Hoss getting dressed. Without saying anything, Sullivan held up the card. Hoss nodded... and Sullivan penciled in his name.

This was the new ritual between them—Sullivan's unspoken way of asking Hoss if he felt okay to play today. Other than sitting out the second and third games of the opening series because of exhaustion and a temperature of 101, Hoss had not missed a game. Each day he felt a little stronger. It helped that he didn't drink, smoke, or chew. It also helped, or at least he thought it did, that he was getting a B_{12} shot in the butt every other day. In Birmingham, he had the team doctor administer it; on the road, he did it himself.

"Don't handle me with girl gloves," Hoss had told Sullivan.

Hoss wasn't sure if the shots were doing any good, but he didn't see any harm, especially since a doctor prescribed them. He figured it was probably more effective than any of the home remedies his mother might prescribe, such as milkweed extract. Someone had suggested that before games he take a "greenie," the amphetamines (aka "pep pills") that were abundant and openly dispensed like candy in most major-league locker rooms. He'd said "No thanks" to that idea. (The steroid era was still a couple of decades away.)

In the past week, both he and Campy had started to show life with the bat, nudging their averages over .200. Hoss was second on the team in RBIs, half of them coming after Campy had singled and then stolen second. Sullivan knew that defensively they were All-Stars—they'd already shown that—and if they could continue to provide a spark at the top of the order, the team's run production could start to pick up, especially with Reynolds hitting behind them.

The Lesson Learned...Don't Mess with Sully

By a quirk of the schedule, the Barons returned to Birmingham after only a two-game trip to Asheville. It was an eight-hour bus ride home, and to pass the time, Hoss joined the poker game in the back of the bus. The kingpin of team poker games was Paul Seitz, who was back off the disabled list after his abysmal opening night.

Seitz had first started gambling during the summers in Columbus when he caddied at the Scarlet and Gray golf courses at Ohio State. While he was sitting around the caddyshack waiting to get a loop, he'd play acey-deucey with the other caddies. Some days he lost more money in the caddyshack than he made on the course. But he was hooked on the rush of placing a wager. In spring training he spent a lot of evenings at the greyhound track, carefully studying the racing forms before each bet. He kept a notebook. He also read books on poker, and had studied the odds. But on the bus it wasn't as if they were playing at the high rollers' table in Vegas—it was nickel-and-dime stakes. Still, the play often got spirited and the decibel level could bother others on the bus trying to sleep.

"Hey, Hoss, are you going to ante or just sit there and look stupid?" asked Seitz.

"Shhhh," whispered Hoss, glancing toward Sullivan in the front seat. "Don't want to get him pissed."

Hoss was reminded of an incident he'd witnessed in spring training. The team was returning on a bus from a game in Lakeland when two Latin players in front of him started arguing. Suddenly, one of the players threw a wild punch. Seated in the front of the bus, Sullivan leaped out of his seat and flew down the aisle. Before either combatant knew what happened, he grabbed one by the nape of the neck and slung him out of the way, and then put the other in a headlock and pinned him to the seat.

"That poor guy had no chance of getting out of that headlock," recalled Hoss. "I thought he was gonna turn purple. Trust me, you don't want to be fuckin' with Sully."

Missing His Wife and Kid

The bus pulled into the parking lot at Rickwood after traveling all night. Hoss watched the married players kiss the wives and kids there to pick them up. He couldn't wait for the school year to end back in Arkansas so that his wife, Madelyn, and their three-year-old son, Parrish, could join him in Birmingham for the rest of the season. He'd already lined up an apartment with a swimming pool.

His off-season made him appreciate a lot of things, but nothing and no one more than Madelyn. That didn't stop his teammates from accusing him of still being the biggest flirt in the league, throwing out endless lines to waitresses or anything that moved in a skirt. He didn't deny it. "No harm in fishing from the pier," he explained, "as long as I throw 'em back in."

He was seventeen when he met Madelyn; she was sixteen. He lived on the tenant farm in Pumpkin Center and went to Stanford High, enrollment fifty; she lived in a huge house in Paragould and went to the high school there, enrollment six hundred. They met when she showed up at one of his summer-league baseball games—her girlfriend was dating one of his teammates. According to Hoss, Madelyn fell for him the first time she saw him driving his dad's tractor.

For Madelyn, it was a little more complicated than that. She did live in a big house, wear nice clothes, and fly in her daddy's Cessna, but what she liked most about Hoss was his close-knit family. There was something endearing about the way they all ate supper together, picked cotton together, went swimming down at Sugar Creek together, and gathered around the radio to listen to Hank Williams and Ernest Tubbs on the *Grand Ole Opry*. Madelyn grew up doted on by her parents, but even as a pony-owning child, she savored the wholesome, down-to-earth charms of the Bowlin family with its six siblings and farm animals galore.

In a county with no black residents, Madelyn had the luxury of growing up in the care of a black servant, Lucinda, who managed most of the domestic chores around the house, including getting her ready for school. Madelyn's mother, a former Miss Jonesboro and Miss Arkansas, belonged to the country club and was the picture of a "Southern lady." Madelyn's father was one of the wealthiest men in the county. He'd inherited some money from an uncle who'd been a big shot with Piggly Wiggly, but he also owned a successful clothing store in town. It was where everybody in the county went to get Tuf-Nut overalls.

What Hoss liked about Madelyn, in addition to her blue eyes, shapely body, and beautiful face, was that despite her family's money, she didn't act like a princess. On weekends and in the summer, she'd pitch in at her dad's store, earning fifty cents an hour to stock the merchandise and wait on customers. He also admired her determination to get a degree and become a teacher. In the four years they'd been married, she had gone to Arkansas State in Jonesboro, and would be awarded a teaching credential in a month. Lucinda helped take care of little Parrish while Madelyn was at school.

Despite Madelyn's family money, Hoss always worked in the off-season, getting up well before dawn to drive a milk truck. He admitted that sometimes he worried that Madelyn might some day "outgrow" him. She came from money, she was better educated, and she knew which fork to use at a fancy dinner party. There was also the fear that her parents didn't completely accept him. He remembered the time when he and Madelyn first started dating and he arrived to pick her up driving his dad's rusty cotton-baling truck. Her father answered the door, saw the truck parked in his circular driveway, and promptly closed the door in Hoss's face. He later claimed it was a joke, but Hoss wasn't convinced.

Madelyn loved being a baseball wife—living in different cities, the games, meeting new people. Although she didn't like the road trips, she'd always been quick to make friends, and used the time to visit with the other wives. She called them "built-in friends."

Birmingham would be the fifth minor-league city they'd lived in, but more than at any previous stop, Hoss was anxious for her and Parrish to arrive. He couldn't wait to show off his beautiful family to Bladder, Campy, Sully, Shaky Joe, Droopsy, and the rest of the team. He'd also couldn't wait to tell Madelyn all about his new friends from the tour bus.

CHAPTER 25

Haywood Sullivan

Shaky Joe Grzenda

If there was any part of the team that Sullivan felt best about, it was his two ace relievers—Joe Grzenda, a lefty, and Ken Sanders, a righty. (The wide acceptance of the term *closer* for a bullpen pitcher who could finish a game was still a few years away.) Both were 2–0.

Sullivan loved Grzenda's resiliency. A few months earlier, his career had been as dead as Babe Ruth. He'd been released in the middle of the previous season, and in February, two weeks before the start of spring training, he was home in Pennsylvania, trying to figure out a way not to spend the rest of his life working in a mine like his dad. His chances of landing with the Barons seemed as remote as having a candy bar named after him.

Compared with the rest of the staff, Grzenda was a moxie veteran. At twenty-six, he was already in his ninth year in pro ball—with his fourteenth team.

Grzenda originally signed a pro contract for $4,000 with the Detroit Tigers after graduating from high school on June 8, 1955, in Moosic, Pennsylvania, a small town ten miles from Scranton in the northeastern part of the state. His father was a strict disciplinarian and tough-as-iron-ore coal miner who didn't hesitate to take the belt to his five kids. ("Today they put parents in jail for those kind of things," he said years later. "If they did that back then, my father wouldn't just be in jail, he'd be *under* it.") Joe never saw a penny of his $4,000 bonus. His father controlled the money.

Grzenda did well his first three years, and in 1958 he was promoted to Birmingham, which at that time was the Tigers' AA team in the Southern Association. At the end of July, his record was 14–2. Fans loved him; he was labeled "the most popular player in Baron history." With his whip-like arm, he mowed down hitters, the speed of his fastball compared with that of the hardest thrower in the game at the time, Herb Score. During interviews, he talked so softly that reporters had to lean close just to hear him.

But the hot, humid summer of 1958 in Birmingham began to take its toll. His weight fell from 175 to 160. When he pitched, people in the stands could literally see the sweat fly off the bill of his cap. Over the last month of the season, he lost five games, finishing the season at 16–7, but still tied for the league lead in strikeouts (with a future Cincinnati Red, Jim O'Toole).

His personal highlight that season happened sitting in the dugout early in the season. His eyes wandered to the stands—as ballplayers' eyes sometimes do—and he spotted a beautiful young woman sitting in the fourth row. He'd always been shy around girls, but—not wanting to let this chance pass—he scribbled a note on the back of a scorecard and handed it to the batboy, instructing him to deliver it between innings and to make sure that the manager, Cal Ermer, didn't see him. A few minutes later, the batboy returned with a huge smile and the girl's phone number. Her name was Ruth; she was one of twelve children and worked as a teller at a Birmingham bank. It was the first Baron game she'd ever attended. Pretty soon they were an item.

After serving six months in the Army National Guard at Fort Jackson in South Carolina following the 1958 season, he showed up late for spring training the next year, hurt his arm, and saw his career take a dive. From 1959 through 1963, he compiled a woeful 20–38 record, bouncing among nine minor-league teams, a poster boy for the journeyman minor leaguer going nowhere. (He briefly got called up to the big-league team in 1961, pitching relief in only four games, with a dreadful ERA of 7.94, but getting a win in his only decision.) His nadir came in 1963 at Syracuse when the Tigers released him. With two babies under the age of three, he and Ruth stared at the barren walls of their small apartment, wondering what to do next. He felt lost, broken. Baseball had consumed him since childhood. He had a high school diploma and not many skills. He knew for certain he didn't want to have anything to do with mining and end up like his dad, an angry old man with black lung disease. He had less than $500 in the bank, didn't own a home, and his '60 Pontiac LeMans needed major work. The career that had looked so promising when he was striking out almost a hitter every inning in Birmingham in 1958 was over, relegating him to the giant scrap heap of "can't miss" prospects that missed.

He was face-to-face with the lunch bucket league, unprepared financially, educationally, and emotionally. But just when his depression sank lower than a canary in a coal mine, Kansas City picked him up for a couple of lumps of coal a week before spring training and assigned him to Birmingham, the city where he'd met his wife and had his greatest season.

He was thrilled to still be in baseball, even when Sullivan told him that he would start the season in the bullpen. Despite not getting to start, Grzenda knew a year in the bullpen was better than one minute in a coal mine.

A Knock at the Door at Four in the Morning

Grzenda had just fallen asleep when he heard the knock at the door of his room at Chattanooga's Choo Choo Inn. The Barons had gotten in late following a two-hour bus ride from Knoxville, where they'd taken two out of three and moved into second place, two games behind Macon. He'd picked up another win.

He rolled over and looked at the clock—4 a.m. Maybe somebody had the wrong room, he thought, ignoring the pounding. It continued.

Groggily, he rolled out of bed and stumbled to the door, peering through the little peephole. He did a double take. It was Sullivan.

What the hell was his manager doing pounding on his door at this ungodly hour? Maybe it was a curfew check. But that seemed unlikely. Sullivan had told the team he wasn't interested in being their warden, and besides, managers rarely checked curfew when the team had just won eight out of nine.

He opened the door. "Put on some pants and come down to my room," instructed Sullivan. "I'm in 202."

Without even taking time to light a cigarette, Grzenda quickly threw on his pants and headed down the hall. Maybe Sullivan was about to tell him something bad had happened to his wife and kids. *Please, don't let it be that,* he hoped.

It didn't make sense. The season had gone great for him so far. Four months ago, he was sitting at home in Pennsylvania, brooding over the prospect of digging coal the rest of his life. Now, along with Ron Tompkins and Paul Lindblad, he shared the best record on the club, 3–0. He was throwing the shit out of the ball, the best his arm had felt in years. Plus, he really liked the guys on this team. Everyone got along, something he'd never experienced on any of the teams he'd played on, including his championship Barons team back in 1958. So, if he wasn't getting his release, what the hell did Sullivan want?

When he got to room 202, the door was ajar. Sullivan was sitting on the edge of his bed, wearing only his skivvies.

"What's up, Skip?" asked Grzenda.

Sullivan paused. To Grzenda, it felt like forever.

"You're going to The Show," announced Sullivan.

Grzenda stared at him, the words not registering. Maybe he didn't hear him right.

"Yep, I just got the call a few minutes ago," Sullivan continued.

At 4 a.m.? Why couldn't they wait until the morning?

"They want you in KC for tonight's game," said Sullivan. "You're flying out in a couple of hours."

Grzenda stared in disbelief. "Are you serious?" he asked.

Sullivan just sat there, flashing his movie-star smile. He knew Grzenda's story. As much as he'd come to rely on having a great lefty-righty combo out of the bullpen, and as crucial as Grzenda would be to the team's pennant hopes, he was happy to be the bearer of such good news.

"I'm stunned," said Grzenda. "I don't know what to say except thank you, thank you, thank you,"

Grzenda had loved playing for Sullivan. Of all the fifteen managers he'd played for, he liked Sullivan the best—the way he treated his players, the way he understood the game, the way he'd given him a chance.

Overwhelmed by the news, Grzenda's mind raced. He thought about being able to finally buy new tires to replace the worn-out ones he had on his LeMans. He wondered if Ruth would be upset about leaving Birmingham and all her friends and family. How would she get to Kansas City with the two kids? If she drove, at least she'd have good tires.

He thought about his dad and how he'd always told him he was worthless, and how he was determined to always treat his own sons like big leaguers.

He thought about how much he wanted a cigarette.

"Thanks for giving me the chance, Skip," he said.

But as Grzenda left the room, a thought occurred to Sullivan: Was Finley just jerking everybody's chain when he promised to do "everything possible" to help Birmingham win the pennant? The A's were in last place, already so far out of the first division, let alone first place, that Joe Grzenda could be Sandy Koufax and Cy Young all rolled into one, and the A's would still be doomed to the cellar. How was calling up Grzenda, the Barons' best reliever, helping Birmingham? Sullivan thought of five pitchers on fifth-place Dallas, the A's Triple A team, who could have just as easily been called up.

CHAPTER 26

Haywood Sullivan

The Knockdown Pitch

Sullivan wasn't going to waste his time and energy fretting over losing Grzenda to the big-league team. Yes, it bothered him, but he reminded himself that the primary purpose of a minor-league team was to prepare its players for the big leagues. He'd done his job. When he was a quarterback in the SEC, if the ref made a bad call against the Gators, or if he threw an interception, he had to block it out and move forward. He was good at it then, and he could call on that training.

As left-handed-hitting Bill Meyer, a twenty-one-year-old outfielder from Southern California, stepped into the batter's box, Sullivan motioned for him to meet halfway between home and the third-base coach's box.

"Be alive up there," Sully warned.

In his previous at-bat, Meyer, nicknamed "the Snake," hit a rocket that cleared the right-field fence by about eight furlongs. There was no love lost between the Barons and Lookouts, a Phillie farm team. In the first game of the series, the Barons roughed up the Lookouts' star hurler, future Hall of Famer Fergie Jenkins, sending him to an early shampoo. The Lookouts didn't appreciate the Barons' raucous dugout celebration.

At six foot one and 160 pounds, Meyer didn't look like a guy who could hit tape-measure homers. In fact, one *News* headline called him "Little Meyer." But he had quick wrists and a sweet swing that generated tremendous bat speed. Balls jumped off his bat. In spring training, Sullivan had not been dazzled, but Meyer was starting to grow on him.

The first pitch from Lane Phillips sailed up and in, knocking Meyer back from the plate. He stumbled to regain his balance, then stared at Phillips. At six foot three and 168 pounds, Phillips wasn't exactly Sunny Liston, either.

The next pitch to Meyer drilled him on the forearm. Everybody in both dugouts moved to the top step, ready to charge the field. (That was a part of the baseball code: If there's a fight, every player in the dugout, bullpen, or same zip code better be willing to throw down for his fellow warrior and charge into the melee…which usually amounts to nothing more than a pair of testosterone-laced scrums, harmlessly circling each other, their collective spikes pawing at the dirt.)

If this was about to turn into a donnybrook, the Barons took comfort in knowing that if they did charge the field, they had a secret weapon—Sullivan. He was the biggest man on the field, and if Hoss's story was accurate, pity the Lookout who found himself in a headlock. Not only was Sullivan an ex–football player, he had played without a face mask. A column about him in the *News* declared: "Behind his easy demeanor, he is an imposing man."

The Snake dropped his bat and slowly started walking. All eyes on the field and in the dugouts were on him. Same with the fans. And the umps. And the batboys. And the guys selling hot dogs. But instead of charging the mound, Meyer trotted to first, ignoring Phillips.

Sullivan applauded. He wasn't a man to back down, but he believed pay-back didn't need to be delivered with a hummer to the ribs or a wild boar charge at the mound. He flashed the steal sign. On the first pitch to Woody Huyke, Meyer got such a big jump that the catcher didn't even bother to throw.

Rattled, Phillips walked Huyke on four pitches. That brought Rosario to bat. Sullivan met him near the plate. "Get a good pitch and make him pay," he said.

Swinging at the first pitch, Rosario drilled a line-shot homer to right, the ball leaving the park faster than a guy could say "statehood for Puerto Rico." As the three Barons circled the bases, Sullivan glared at Phillips. The message was clear: *Don't even think about throwing at our next hitter.*

The next hitter was Wayne Norton. Phillip's first pitch was a low and inside fastball. Phillips swung, golfing it deep and gone—a back-to-back job, on back-to-back pitches—and that, except for the shampoo, was the end of the evening for Phillips. The Barons won 7–2.

The Man

For the Barons, Sullivan was omnipotent. He not only had the power to tell them when to bunt or steal, but he also dictated what time they were supposed to go to bed, whom they hung out with, and what they wore in the hotel lobby. He was their teacher, the person responsible for working with them on improving their sliders or how to choke up and punch the ball to the opposite side. But most important, he filled out the player progress reports to send to the front office. These daily reports determined who had a chance to move up in the organization. He must've written something good about Grzenda.

Although he'd only been in the managing biz a short time, he had already established certain parameters. For one, he wouldn't go out and pound down beers after games with the boys. He wouldn't check curfew unless he suspected the players were taking advantage and staying out too late. ("If you can't get laid by midnight, then give it up.") He wouldn't schedule workouts on days off, unless the team was making more mistakes than a juggler with blisters, and he definitely wouldn't make them show up to the ballpark in the middle of a hot and humid day in July and August when players were starting to tire, and the weather was too hot to even sit on the veranda in the shade of a weeping willow and sip mint juleps.

Sullivan didn't have a pitching coach, hitting instructor, fitness trainer, or masseuse to travel with the team. He didn't drive the bus, but if it broke down, he damn well knew where to go to get it fixed.

As a player, he'd liked the camaraderie of the clubhouse, the feeling of being one of the guys. He missed being able to go have beers with his teammates after a game, but he knew he had to keep his distance. Sometimes that was hard, especially on the road, where he spent most of his time by himself. But he knew that getting too close with his players would land him in the baseball graveyard, already populated with former minor-league managers who had tried to be one of the guys and ended up getting trampled to death by players stampeding to oblivion.

He knew that young players—and even old ones—liked to hit the nightlife and chase girls. It was as much a part of the baseball culture as jock rash. Some players called it the "Neon League." Others called it "the game within the game." He knew it was inevitable. Running the team like a police state wasn't his style. "But don't let me catch you," he warned.

In his original interview with Finley, he said he wanted the game to be fun, as it had been when he was growing up, an era when kids gathered in the street or at the park to play work-up or over-the-line until dark. There was no orga- nized Little League, or coaches, or parents screaming from the bleachers… just kids making up their own rules. But he also made it clear to Finley that he knew baseball was a business, and people's livelihoods were at stake, and the young men wearing the uniforms represented the cities where they played, whether that be Kansas City or Birmingham. There had to be rules, discipline, and a clear sense of order. The manager was the boss. Period.

When Finley was asked whether Sullivan's Alabama roots would interfere with his ability to treat all his players equally, he defended his decision.

"The key to a good manager is his relationships with the players," he said. "People who think Sully won't be fair to colored players have never met him. He's one of the most decent people I've ever met. If I thought for one second that he couldn't be fair, I wouldn't have hired him."

Einstein in the Dugout

With the Barons leading 6–0 in the seventh inning against the Charlotte Hornets at Rickwood, Paul Lindblad gave up a line-shot homer. In the dugout, Sully shook his head, puzzled, detecting something amiss with his starting pitcher. Hornet hitters were suddenly taking vicious cuts, digging in at the plate, like they knew what was coming.

Sully turned to the players on the bench. "I think Lindy's tipping his pitches," he said.

Ever since Ty Cobb was in diapers, hitters and coaches had been studying pitchers in an effort to figure out if they were telegraphing their pitches. A pitcher might grip the ball one way for a fastball, another for a curve; or he might position his feet on the mound one way for a slider, another way for a changeup. If opposing hitters know what's coming, it's like batting practice. Some hitters can pick up these clues by themselves at the plate; others want a signal relayed by the bench or a base coach—a whistle for a fastball or a finger to the bill of the cap for a changeup.

Some hitters want to know, but others don't, afraid that if the alert for a curveball is false, they won't be able to get out of the way if a fastball actually arrives. When he was with Boston, Sullivan played in a game against Jim Bunning, the ace of the Detroit staff, and Del Baker, a Red Sox coach, called every pitch Bunning threw...and Bunning still threw a one-hitter. The only Red Sox hit was by Ted Williams, who refused the information because he was legendary for his ability to make a pitcher throw his entire assortment of pitches his first time up, enabling him to pick the pitch he wanted in subsequent at-bats.

Sullivan nodded to Seitz and Tompkins on the bench. "I want you two guys to watch Lindy's head and see if he's tipping it that way." Then he assigned two others players to watch his feet, and two more to watch his hands.

In the eighth inning after two straight line-shot base hits, Sullivan, Huyke, and Seitz simultaneously noticed the same thing: Lindblad was tilting his head to the left on breaking balls. Sullivan trotted to the mound and conveyed the discovery to Lindblad.

With some pitchers, it might take days or weeks to make an adjustment. Some might never make it. But Lindblad was a quick study. He nodded in agreement with Sullivan, and then he retired the last five hitters in a row, his head held steady. The Barons won 6–1, Lindblad striking out eight and improving his record to 4–0, keeping the team only a game out of first.

CHAPTER 27

Albert Belcher

Doubts

Belcher set down his copy of the *Birmingham News* and shook his head. He wouldn't admit it, at least not publicly, but sometimes Charlie Finley got on his nerves. Today was such a time. He'd just read an article that practically anointed Finley as the James Dean of baseball, the rebel who had the lords of the baseball establishment shaking in their wingtips. Finley was still taking on the Yankees, claiming the other American League owners were its lapdogs. He hadn't given up on the grievance he'd been harping on for weeks—the owners' refusal to let him move in the right-field fence in Kansas City. Belcher had gotten a taste of Finley's provocative style when he demanded that Belcher move in the fences at Rickwood. But Finley didn't own Rickwood—Belcher did. He was glad he hadn't knuckled under to Finley's pressure, especially after he saw that the long ball wasn't going to be the Barons' limousine to the pennant. After the first month of the season, the Barons were seventh (out of eight) in Southern League homers.

Calling up Grzenda had also rubbed Belcher the wrong way. He loved Joe—who didn't?—and he marveled at what a great comeback story it was. But the chances of Kansas City finishing anywhere but last place, with or without Joe, were lower than the Alabama congressional delegation voting for passage of the impending civil rights bill.

"That man sat in my office, right across the desk from me," said Belcher, "and he looked me straight in the eyes and promised he'd do whatever it took to bring Birmingham a pennant. How long did it take him to break that promise? A month."

It wasn't so much that Belcher resented Finley sucking the ink out of the sports page—the man was good copy. But Belcher was a good old boy schooled in the Southern way of doing business: A man's word was his bond. He'd shipped countless train cars filled with his lumber based on just a handshake; he'd ordered the paint for Rickwood on another handshake...and paid it off before the paint even dried.

When Belcher plunked down $150,000 to refurbish Rickwood, it was his own money. What the A's had contributed to the Barons—salaries, equipment, travel—came out of the A's treasury, not Finley's personal pocket. Not that Belcher didn't appreciate the fact that Finley had taken a risk to step up and be the Barons' parent club. But he wondered if he'd done it because he loved his hometown and wanted to contribute something positive to the community— or as just a vainglorious grab at the Birmingham spotlight. Somebody brought up the idea that maybe Finley was looking to open an insurance office in town.

Yes, Finley had made a couple of trips to Birmingham prior to the opener to help promote the team. But instead of getting his picture on the front page for being the batboy, writing a check to help with the paint bill would have given harder evidence of his love of Birmingham. At least from Belcher's perspective.

Belcher hoped that calling up the team's best reliever would be an aberration, not a trend. Maybe Finley's motives were pure. Belcher knew he'd find out quick enough. Finley had made another promise that he'd do everything he could to sign the best amateur talent, such as Blue Moon Odom, Catfish Hunter, Willie Crawford, and Rick Reichardt, and start them all with the Barons.

"Can you imagine all that talent in Birmingham?" said Finley.

Belcher had something else he was worried about—that Finley would fire the A's manager, Eddie Lopat, and replace him with Sullivan. A blind man could see how much Finley admired Sullivan. If Belcher got upset about the A's snatching Grzenda, he would go completely apoplectic if he lost Sullivan. Sullivan was the perfect manager for the return of baseball to Birmingham. Whatever doubt people had about Sullivan at the start of the season had vanished. Everybody loved him—the sportswriters, the fans, the business community, and, most of all, the players. When Sullivan hustled in and out of the dugout between innings, Belcher had watched women in the box seats ogling him as if he were Gregory Peck.

All Belcher could do was cross his fingers and hope Finley would leave his team and his manager alone. But as everyone in baseball knew, that wasn't Finley's customary way of doing business. Belcher just hoped Finley's love of Birmingham would come back and win the day.

White Boycott? Black Boycott?

In May, the Barons were suddenly the hottest team in the league. Sullivan was especially pleased with a complete-game, eight-strikeout victory thrown by Paul Seitz, the Ohio native's first win since coming off the disabled list after his opening night debacle. It was the Barons' fourth straight win and lifted them into a first-place tie with Macon. The key blow was Bill "Snake" Meyer's eighth homer, a drive that cleared the BELCHER LUMBER sign in right field, earning him an extra $50.

The victory moved them into first place. The next morning, in a show of journalistic cheerleading, the headline in the News read: OUR TEAM NO. 1.

Despite the hot streak, Belcher wasn't happy when he counted the gate receipts. Attendance on this night was only 686. The night before it had been 709, and while the Barons were still 8,586 ahead of the 1961 attendance pace, Belcher was concerned. The team had won fifteen of its last twenty games and it had the hottest player in the league in Campy, who had scored thirty-three runs in thirty-three games and was now leading the league in stolen bases and triples, as well as anchoring the best double-play combo in the minors. Meyer was tied for the league lead in homers, and despite a recent mini slump, Rosario was second in the league in batting average. The pitching staff was as good as any in the league, with several potential big-league arms, and the addition of Reynolds had bestowed the team with one of the best hitting prospects in the league.

So why weren't more fans turning out? Belcher had entered the season hoping for one hundred thousand in total attendance for the year, but at this rate wouldn't make it.

Birmingham's influential black newspaper, the World, which had been extremely critical of the city's white power structure, was doing its best to encourage attendance. Sports editor Marcel Hopson wrote:

There is peace and tranquility at Rickwood Field. So, dear fans, let's go out en masse to help set paid attendance records and show our favorite Birmingham Barons that the true sportsmen and lovers of topflight pro athletic entertainment are 100 percent behind them in an effort to make the 1964 season the best ever in this area.

Alf Van Hoose, who covered the Barons for the News, wondered if the lagging attendance had to do with race:

Is pro baseball not well in a town which once boasted of being the capital of the minor leagues? Is this town, as a whole, still in general shock from the various troubles of recent months? Has there been a silent boycott of the old ballyard because Albert Belcher had the courage to lead the future wave of ballplayers here?

And in Other Alabama News

In Birmingham, civil rights activists feared that the passage of a civil rights bill would stimulate a devastating white backlash, not just in Alabama and the South but all across America. George Wallace's success in primaries in the Midwest did nothing to alleviate their fears. Belcher worried about the bill's impact on the Barons and their fans. He did not support the civil rights bill, but he was also pragmatic and saw the inevitability of its passage and the end of Jim Crow's reign of terror in the South.

In the months since Bull Connor had jailed Martin Luther King, the white citizens of Birmingham, including its media, had organized to repudiate the steady barrage of outside criticism leveled at their city. A community affairs subcommittee to "Sell Birmingham" had been formed to paint a "correct and good picture of our city in the minds of people of America." Civic leaders continued to blame the city's problems on outside agitators. They despised the *New York Times* for sending reporter Harrison Salisbury to Birmingham, and insisted that his portrait of a city where "fear stalked the streets" was slanderous, and skewed outsiders' perceptions of their hometown. A lawsuit was filed against the *Times*.

The Birmingham press took special pleasure in returning the fire at New York. A front-page headline in the *News* declared: NEW YORKERS TERRORIZED BY YOUNG NEGROES. The following day, in a column titled "Et Tu, New York City?" Keith Walling wrote that there was enough crime going on in New York "to keep a whole staff of police reporters busy." He wrote about a section of the Bronx being patrolled by "vigilante committees" to protect citizens from "hoodlums, muggers and rapists." He maintained that the people of Birmingham would never stand by in passive silence as a young woman was stabbed repeatedly, as New Yorkers had when Kitty Genovese was murdered. He implied that these cowardly witnesses were the same people who had gotten so upset over events in Birmingham. His conclusion was that the problems occurring in New York needed to be corrected by New Yorkers, and that Birmingham—"which certainly has had more than its share of outside criticism and advice"—should enjoy the same opportunity to remedy its deficiencies.

Although the streets of Birmingham had been relatively quiet in recent months, a battle between police and demonstrators broke out in Tuscaloosa, eighty miles to the west. In an effort to quell the disturbance, Bobby Shelton, Grand Wizard of the Ku Klux Klan, had formed a motor patrol of vigilantes to cruise the streets to keep "Negroes out of white neighborhoods." Police used tear gas and fire hoses, and the mayor of Tuscaloosa proclaimed that further demonstrations would be met with additional force.

Some viewed this renewed tension by whites in Alabama as backlash over a unanimous Supreme Court decision overturning an Alabama court order barring the NAACP from operating in the state. The State of Alabama had ruled that the NAACP, among other things, had illegally "paid Negro students to attempt to integrate the University of Alabama in Tuscaloosa," although the Crimson Tide's football team under coach Paul "Bear" Bryant remained all white.

Albert Belcher was worried: "I've lived around here too long to think there won't be another explosion."

CHAPTER 28

Hoss Bowlin

Money for the "Next Willie Mays" but None for Hoss

Lindblad approached Hoss's locker. "You look upset," he said.

"Sort of."

"Is it because your mother named you Lois? Are you wishing she'd named you Betty? That has a nice ring to it...Betty Bowlin. Can I call you Betty?"

Hoss ignored him. "Did you see the story in the paper today about Finley going to California to talk to that high school kid?"

Lindblad nodded.

"That's hogshit," said Hoss. "I couldn't get the tightwads to pay for my cancer surgery last winter, and now they're gonna give this kid more than our whole team makes in a year."

Hoss was referring to Willie Crawford from Crenshaw High in LA. Finley called him the "next Willie Mays." The *News* described the seventeen-year-old Crawford as a "strong-armed Negro boy who bats and throws left-handed, hits for power and runs the 100-yard dash in 9.4." He was also quarterback and captain of the Crenshaw High football team, high-jumped six feet, four inches, and broke all his school's records in basketball and football scoring.

Finley hadn't spared the hyperbole in describing Crawford. "He has everything it takes—splendid coordination, strength and speed. I've never met a boy with greater determination," he said. "The kid gets up every morning so he can work out an hour before he goes to school. He will knock your socks off. This is the most outstanding prospect in the country. And we'll start him in Birmingham."

Finley knew he was competing with every other team to sign Crawford, especially the Dodgers, but he figured he had an advantage because he was willing to spend more money, as well as the fact that Crawford's parents were from Bessemer. Finley had the mayor, a judge, and an influential banker from

Bessemer write letters to Crawford to plead his case and extol the virtues of Birmingham.

"It might as well be public knowledge," said Finley. "Willie Crawford is just what I said he is, the most outstanding high school boy in the country."

All this slobbering, of course, had the Barons rolling their eyes. Between them, Hoss and Lindblad had gotten $4,000 to sign. The bidding for Crawford was expected to start at $100,000.

With the end of the school year approaching, big-league teams, including the A's, were burning high octane to arrange their priorities for signing new talent. There was greater urgency than in years past because starting in 1965, Major League Baseball was instituting an amateur draft. Young players would no longer be able to sign with the highest bidder—they would have to go with whatever team drafted them. No owner was more determined than Finley to go after the top amateur players.

"I'll spend whatever it takes," he said.

In addition to John Odom, Jim Hunter, and Rick Reichardt, his list included: Cotton Nash of Kentucky (also an All-American basketball player); Dock Ellis of Los Angeles; and Mike Epstein and Andy Messersmith of Cal. But nobody had Finley's attention more than Crawford.

"Hoss, you didn't think your cancer surgery was *that* important, did you?" said Lindblad.

Campy and Hoss

Embarking on a road trip to Lynchburg and Charlotte, the Barons were now in first place. Lindblad was 3–0 and Ron Tompkins was 4–0, leading the league in strikeouts ahead of Chattanooga's Fergie Jenkins and Lynchburg's Manly Johnston. But Sullivan told reporters that he thought the key to the team's improved play after its crummy start was his keystone combo—Campy and Hoss. It wasn't just their excellent defensive play—Campy was now hitting a respectable .270, while Hoss was up to .230, and second on the team in RBIs.

The Birmingham press had fallen head-over-ink in love with them. Alf Van Hoose of the *News* called Hoss "gutsy," "courageous," and "possibly as good as any second baseman ever to wear a Baron uniform."

Van Hoose was even more effusive about Campy:

Eye-catching.

Rifle for an arm.

A Rickwood favorite.

The quickest feet and reflexes in baseball.

He hasn't hit a double so far this year because his singles are so hard hit that he has to stop at first and anything that gets between the outfielders is a triple.

Surprising power packed into his little frame.

Touring Lynchburg

Hoss was up at the crack of nine in Lynchburg, climbing on the tour bus with his fellow tourists. Located in central Virginia, Lynchburg was nicknamed "Hill City" for the seven hills the town spread across. Hoss wore Sta-Prest trousers and a charcoal sweater he'd bought at his brother-in-law's store back home.

The bus rolled along a short stretch of the eastern edge of the Blue Ridge Mountains near the Appalachian Trail, and then returned to town, crossing over the James River. Hoss learned that Lynchburg was the only Confederate town not to fall to Union forces, but even more interesting to him was that it was the birthplace of ChapStick and the first "disposable small-volume enema."

What the tour guide neglected to mention to Hoss and the others was that Lynchburg was stubbornly resisting *Brown vs. Board of Education*'s mandate to integrate its school. With the support of Virginia senator Harry F. Byrd Sr., city and state leaders had created "segregation academies" as a form of massive resistance. This defiance spread even to the churches. An influential young minister in town, the Reverend Jerry Falwell, was preaching that segregation was the "Lord's will." He criticized Martin Luther King Jr., declaring that "preachers are not called to be politicians but to be soul winners," a declaration bathed in irony given Falwell's role in the culture wars looming on the political horizon.

The tour guide also neglected to tell Hoss and his new friends that Lynchburg's fans were as verbally abusive as any in the Southern League and that they would make trips to their city a living hell for Tommie Reynolds.

In the Barons' game that night, Hoss got two hits and drove in a run, just as he had after taking the bus tour of Asheville. "It's my good-luck charm," he proclaimed.

"I suppose it's better than wearing the same pair of underpants just because you got a hit," countered Lindblad.

Calling Home

Hoss called home after the Lynchburg game to talk with Madelyn. He told her about the Barons being in first place, his improved hitting, the nice grandma he met touring Lynchburg, and how he'd felt a little tired after a couple of recent games, but not bad enough to ask Sullivan to take him out of the lineup. In return, Madelyn told him how relieved she'd be to finally get her degree and to start looking for a teaching job for next year.

"God knows we can use the money," she said.

Hoss listened as Madelyn told him that her dad had offered to fly her and Parrish to Birmingham in his Cessna. Hoss had never been one to dwell on the inequities of life—growing up on a tenant farm and spending long hours in the hot sun picking cotton didn't afford him much time for wallowing in self-pity—and he wasn't going to start now. Still, he couldn't help but be aware of some of those inequities all around him, such as Finley dishing out six-figure bonuses to high school kids but not paying for his cancer surgery, or his father-in-law flying around the countryside in his Cessna when Hoss didn't even have a car to get to and from Rickwood.

But as long as he kept hitting, none of that mattered.

CHAPTER 29

Haywood Sullivan

A Baseball Ritual

No sport embraces its eccentricities as much as baseball, with its seventh-inning stretch, ubiquitous spitting, interminable statistics, and the time-honored skirmish between manager and umpire, aka the rhubarb: two grown men face-to-face, jaw-to-jaw, chest-to-chest, mere inches apart as they unload verbal tirades and sprays of spittle, the veins in their necks pulsing with rage. They kick dirt, madly gesticulate, and throw hats, performing the signature gestures of ritual tantrums whose sum effects are zero.

Should behavior such as this happen in a corporate office, a courtroom, or a university lecture hall, the involved parties would be unemployed the next day, if not arrested. Yet within baseball, a failure to argue against any perceived injustice is seen as a sign of weakness, revealing a lack of passion for the game. Fiery managers and players are beloved by hometown fans. With children, temper tantrums beget scoldings, time-outs, and in the days of yore spankings. In baseball, they are celebrated, encouraged, demanded. If a player pitches a fit at the ump, he needs to know the skipper has his back. Sullivan was about to state his case.

A tension had been building between the Barons and Lynchburg, the team Sullivan was on record as saying would be the Barons' toughest competition, even though the Lynsox trailed second-place Macon by three games. In the first game of the series, won by the Lynsox, there had been an episode near the end of the game. Lynchburg's pitcher, Manly "Shot" Johnston, hit Tommie Reynolds in the ribs with a pitch. Nobody on the Barons' bench thought it was by accident. Johnston, an Alabama native who had starred at Auburn in football and baseball, was six foot five, 220 pounds, and a very intimidating figure on the mound. He was also imposing at the plate. In a previous outing against Asheville, he hit *three* homers, including two in one inning. After he drilled

Reynolds, Sullivan approached umpire Nick Colosi. "Somebody's going to get hurt," he complained. Colosi turned his back.

In the second game of the series, with the Barons trailing 4–2 in the third inning, Dick Kenworthy of Lynchburg hit a grounder to deep short. Ranging to his right, Campy made a backhand grab and gunned a bullet across the diamond to Rosario. The throw pulled him off the bag. Rosario turned and tagged the sliding Kenworthy.

"Safe!" yelled the ump, Nick Colosi.

"I tag heeem," shouted Rosario.

Colosi ignored him.

"Buuullllsheeeet!"

Colosi glared, waiting for more, like a parent ready to ground a teenager if she dares utter another word. Instead, Rosario turned and bounced the baseball off the ground, snatching it barehanded. Colosi thought he'd just been shown up.

"You're gone!" he snapped, pointing Rosario toward the dugout.

As Rosario rushed in to protest, Sully paused briefly at the top of the dugout's steps. Normally a calm, deliberate man, he now dashed toward Colosi. He hadn't forgotten how Colosi had summarily dismissed him the previous night, and although the incident hadn't escalated into a beanball war, Sullivan thought Colosi had failed to take charge.

He edged Rosario to the side, and then moved to within a foot of Colosi, towering over him. Colosi turned and walked away again.

Sullivan quickly circled, getting in his face. "That was a bullshit call. You've been out to get us for two days."

Colosi whirled and thrust his right thumb into the air. "You're gone, too!" he bellowed.

With that, Sullivan exploded, his veins popping, his head snapping from side to side. Colosi didn't give ground, and for the next thirty seconds the two men barked at each other from point-blank range. Finally, Sullivan turned and retreated, leading Rosario into the dugout, the Lynchburg fans booing.

For the Baron players, however, it sent a message: Their manager would have their backs. Not that he needed it, but Sullivan had just gained another arrow of respect for his quiver.

The Barons eventually rallied to win the game 8–6, sparked by seven strong innings of relief by Stanley Jones, allowing them to maintain their one-game lead over Macon. They also won the rubber game of the series, although Lynsox pitcher Cisco Carlos hit Reynolds with another fastball to the ribs. It took everything in Reynolds's considerable self-control not to charge the mound.

Larry Stahl Tries for the Cycle in Charlotte

Coming to bat in the top of the ninth against Charlotte, Larry Stahl had a chance to pull off one of the most difficult feats in baseball—hitting for the cycle. And what would make this even more unusual was that it would be in order—starting off with a single, then a double, followed by a triple. Now all he needed was a homer.

For Stahl, a left-hand-hitting outfielder, it had been a slow absorption into the Barons' fold after serving six months duty in the army reserve during the off-season. He'd missed spring training, and Sullivan had used him mainly as a pinch hitter in his first two weeks. To help him regain his hitting stroke, Sullivan had come to the park early almost every day to pitch him extra batting practice. At six feet, 175 pounds, Stahl wasn't a brawny, muscle-bound guy, but he'd shown in BP that he was capable of hitting the long ball—a couple of his shots traveling over 450 feet. He'd been itching to play regularly, but with outfielders Reynolds, Norton, and Meyer all swinging the bat well, it was hard for Sullivan to squeeze him into the starting lineup. This game against Charlotte was only his third start since joining the team. In his first two, he'd gone 2 for 7—not bad, but not enough to convince Sullivan to play him full-time.

Signed by Kansas City out of high school in Belleville, Illinois, in 1960, Stahl had never played above A ball in his first four years, hitting a total of only nineteen homers and doing little else to distinguish himself. He'd played with only a couple of the guys on the team previously, so his teammates were still trying to assess how much he could take of the razzing and locker room barbs that were so much a part of the baseball fraternity's way of life.

On almost every team there are players who, because of temperament, or slumps, or other personal quirks, excuse themselves from the daily give-and-take. On the Barons, Campy was clearly not participating in the tête-à-tête, partially because he spoke so little English, but also because others were leery of his temper even though he hadn't really had any serious blowups. With Stahl, the players were also taking a cautionary approach. He'd arrived accompanied by rumors that he had a bad temper as well. Lindblad, who liked to hang nicknames on teammates, was itching to call him Dumbo because of his large ears, but so far had refrained.

As sometimes happens in the evaluation of players, the scouting reports on Stahl gave conflicting pictures. For example, one year under "hitter type" he was listed as a "pull hitter." The next year he was "a spray hitter." Under the category of "team leader skills," one year he was rated "a great leader," but the next year his rating found he possessed "none at all." These reports didn't exactly paint the most positive picture. Under the category "desire for winning," he was given back-to-back ratings of "minimal." And even worse, one year his "morale" was listed as "angry."

Sullivan had read these scouting reports, but fortunately for Stahl, he preferred to draw his own conclusions. As a player, Sullivan had witnessed managers who had it in for certain players—didn't appreciate their skills or thought they were a negative influence in the clubhouse—and were predisposed to turn in less-than-satisfactory evaluations. With the competition to make the big leagues so intense, getting on the wrong side of a manager could jeopardize a player's future, especially a borderline prospect like Stahl.

As Sullivan watched him step to the plate in the top of ninth against Charlotte, he knew a home run off Hornet reliever Hal Stowe would give him the cycle.

Stahl stepped out to adjust his helmet. Batting seventh in the lineup, he eyed Rosario and Reynolds standing on first and second following consecutive singles. With the Barons leading 8–0, and Nicky Don Curtis working on a three-hitter, the game, along with the team's thin hold on first place, was secure.

The crowd—or what was left of the 642 who had originally shown up at Clark Griffith Park—yawned.

The first three pitches from Stowe were all balls, not even close. Anxiously, Stahl stepped out of the box to check if Sullivan would have him taking. If he walked, there went his chance to hit for the cycle.

Sullivan gave him the green light.

From his stretch, Stowe delivered, a waist-high fastball right down Main Street. Stahl's eyes got as big as a kid at the county fair.

For a batter, a crippled fastball down the middle can be a gift from the baseball gods. Good hitters, and even bad ones, usually crush it. But sometimes those same baseball gods will turn their backs on the hitter, and he'll pop it up, or line to short, or swing and miss. The lucky pitcher will take a deep breath and genuflect to those baseball gods.

On this balmy night in North Carolina, Stahl's swing was perfect and the ball rocketed off his bat, soaring deep over the right-field fence—a three-run blast. As he trotted around the bases, he couldn't contain his smile. He'd just joined an elite group of professional baseball players who'd done the nearly impossible—single, double, triple, homer...the cycle...in order.

Sully and the Bear

Prior to a series opener against Asheville at Rickwood, Sullivan sat alone in the Barons' clubhouse, filling out the lineup card. On the field, the players loosened up, many of them half awake from the all-night bus ride from North Carolina. Suddenly, a familiar face and an even more familiar hat entered the clubhouse. Sullivan stood to greet the visitor. It was Alabama football coach Paul Bear Bryant and his legendary houndstooth hat. If George Wallace was the governor of Alabama, Bryant was the king.

In past years, Bryant had been a regular attendee of Barons' games, but this was his first game of the '64 season. It wasn't the first time he and Sullivan had met, however. When Sullivan was the state's outstanding quarterback recruit at Dothan High, Bryant tried to recruit him for the University of Kentucky, where he was coaching at the time, but Sullivan chose to go with Coach Bob Woodruff at Florida. In the two games Sullivan quarterbacked for Florida, Bryant's Kentucky teams prevailed, 40–6 and 14–6.

Sullivan inquired about Alabama's chances for the coming season. "Depends on how Namath's knee holds up," replied Bryant. "How about you? Got any good prospects?"

"Keep an eye on the second baseman," said Sullivan. "I'm not sure he's a big-league prospect, but he's got more guts than just about anybody I've ever come across. He had surgery for cancer in the off-season."

"Wow."

"And check out our shortstop," continued Sullivan. "You ought to see this kid stripped. He's really something. Strongest little guy I've ever seen. He's not even grown yet. From the waist up, he's a big man."

"Where's he from?"

"He escaped from Cuba. All he ever knew before baseball was swinging two machetes in a cane field. Swish, swish, swish…all day long."

"Bet he's happy to be here."

"I've been sitting back expecting some guy on another team to jump him," continued Sully. "He's so little-looking. I think we'd see something. He's so doggone quick and strong. I'll guarantee you, I wouldn't want any part of him."

With Bryant and his wife watching the game from behind the first-base dugout, the Barons defeated Ashville 7–3. The star of the night was Campy, putting an exclamation point on Sullivan's pre-game praise with a three-run double off the 375 mark in left center, followed by a towering home run over the 407 mark in straightaway center. It was only the sixth time in Rickwood's long history that a player had cleared the green ten-foot fence at that spot. The last to do it had been American League home run champ Harmon Killebrew. Campy and Hoss also turned in two eye-popping double plays.

As Sullivan walked off the field, he caught the Bear's eye and issued an I-told-you-so smile.

The speed of the legs, the dexterity of the body, the grace of the
swing, the elusiveness of the slide, these are the features that
make Americans everywhere forget the last syllable of a man's
last name or the pigmentation of his skin.

—Branch Rickey, Brooklyn Dodgers general manager

PART V

THE SEASON

June

League Standings, June 1			
	W	**L**	**GB**
Birmingham	27	16	
Macon	25	16	1
Chattanooga	23	17	2½
Lynchburg	22	19	4
Knoxville	19	22	7
Charlotte	16	22	8½
Columbus	16	25	10
Asheville	15	26	11

CHAPTER 30

Blue Moon Odom

A Sleepover to Remember

Inside the red-brick duplex on E Street in Macon's housing projects, Charlie Finley sat across the dining room table from John Blue Moon Odom and his mother, Florine. Also at the table was Blue Moon's high school coach, Robert Slocum, as close to a father figure as he'd had since his own father died when Odom was five. This was the first leg of Finley's mission to sign America's best amateur baseball talent.

"Well, whattya think?" he asked.

Finley had just slid a bonus contract in front of Blue Moon. It called for a payment of $75,000 up front and a first-year salary of $900 a month (the second most of anybody on the Barons).

"That's a lot of money," said Mrs. Odom, wide-eyed.

Indeed, it was the biggest bonus ever offered to a black athlete in America in any sport, and a larger amount than any Georgia athlete had ever received. It was substantially larger than the offers of the two closest bidders, the San Francisco Giants and the Boston Red Sox. Finley had helped his cause by being the only owner to personally show up to make his pitch for Blue Moon. And this wasn't his first trip to Macon. He'd paid a visit to Odom's house two weeks earlier, armed with the same persuasive powers that had earned him millions in the insurance business.

"Mr. Finley," said Blue Moon, "I got a special request."

"What's that?"

"I want you to take $5,000 out of my bonus and give it to my mama's church."

Finley explained that Blue Moon would have to take out the money himself. "It'll be a nice tax deduction," he said.

"I'll take your word for it," said Blue Moon, glancing at Coach Slocum to make sure it was okay.

Shaking Finley's hand, Blue Moon and his mother agreed to the deal. In addition to the $75,000, Finley had made three other promises that helped seal the deal. He'd fly Blue Moon up to Kansas City with him so he could spend a week working out with the big-league team. Finley wanted Manager Ed Lopat to personally observe his pitching motion and see if he could figure out how to get Moon to come more over the top on his curveball. It would be Blue Moon's first time ever on a plane. Finley had already arranged for a reporter and a television crew to follow Blue Moon around Kansas City for a day.

Another promise was that Blue Moon would get to make his professional debut in his hometown of Macon. The Barons were due in next week. Finley explained that even if Lopat thought Blue Moon was ready for the big leagues immediately, he'd pitch that first game in Macon.

"It'll be the biggest crowd in Macon history," guaranteed Finley.

The last promise was that Finley would arrange for the purchase of the new Ford Galaxy that Blue Moon wanted, right down to the four-on-the-floor transmission and candy-apple-red paint job.

Technically, Blue Moon couldn't sign the contract until after his graduation from Ballard-Hudson High the next day.

"I'll be there," promised Finley.

They celebrated by eating a fried chicken dinner, complete with collard greens, corn bread, and black-eyed peas. The *Macon Telegraph* reported the next day that Finley had cooked the dinner, but that wasn't true. He did, however, help set the table and do the dishes. And just to make sure another team wouldn't sneak in and steal the deal, he spent the night on a couch in the living room, outbidding by $2 the general manager of another big-league team who'd offered to pay Blue Moon's mother $8 for the sleepover rights.

Let the Hype Begin

Even though it was over a week until Blue Moon's debut, the media hype was already raging, especially in Macon. His signing had been a front-page headline, with the $75,000 figure right there in bold print for all to see. He'd been variously described as "a flame-throwing right-hander," "a young man with a golden arm," and a "hard-throwing young Negro." Macon fans had already dubbed his debut "Blue Moon Night." A photo of him standing between his mom and Finley, all of them smiling wide, went out over the wire services. For his arrival in Kansas City, a "horde of news media will be waiting for him when he steps off the plane." The *Kansas City Star* was planning a full-page feature headlined JOHNNY ODOM'S FIRST DAY.

In the *Macon Telegraph*, a column by Harley Bowers titled "Sudden Fame and Fortune" expressed concern about how he'd handle all the pressure:

By the time all the TV, radio and newspaper guys are through with him, he might not even remember his name. One can only imagine the effect all this is likely to have on a boy who has never known luxury before. Odom may weather the deluge of publicity but this type of buildup and the sudden accumulation of some degree of wealth has ruined many a bonus baby.

If there has ever been a youngster under great pressure, it will be Odom on the night of his debut June 11. There is little doubt that his appearance on the mound for Birmingham against Macon will fill Luther Williams Field.

Odom's future really depends on his own ability to keep his feet firmly on the ground and not let all this sudden fame go to his head. If he can stay on course, his natural ability may take him on to major league stardom.

Oh, No, You're Not

Standing by the front door, his suitcase packed, Blue Moon waited for his mom to come out of the bathroom. It had all come so fast and furious for him in the last twenty-four hours—signing a $75,000 contract; walking across the stage at Ballard-Hudson High to receive his diploma; saying good-bye to Perrie, his high school girlfriend, and brushing away her tears. His mother warned him about getting too big a head. Later that morning, Finley would be coming to the house in a limousine to pick him up and take him to the airport for their flight to Kansas City...where a TV crew would be waiting.

Mrs. Odom walked into the living room wearing the same dress she always wore, the one to clean the white family's house. Blue Moon moved in front of the door.

"Where you going?" he asked.

"To work," she replied.

"Oh, no, you're not."

"Why you acting crazy?"

"Mama, you get on that phone right now and call those people and tell them you're not coming today. Or tomorrow. Or any other day."

"I can't do that."

"You saw that contract, didn't you? It means you don't have to never scrub no more floors. Not as long as I'm your son."

A few minutes later, Florine Odom called the white family and said she wouldn't be coming in today. Or any other day.

"And as soon as that money's in the bank," said Blue Moon, "I want you to go out and start looking for a new house for yourself."

CHAPTER 31

Haywood Sullivan

A Lot Riding on Tonight's Performance

Full of confidence, pitcher Ron "Stretch" Tompkins bounded out of the dugout and headed toward the mound at Rickwood. He was a perfect 5–0, and was leading the league in strikeouts, averaging almost one an inning. Sportswriters had voted him the Southern League's player of the month for May. With a win in the series finale against Asheville, he could extend the Barons' winning streak to seven and their league lead to four.

He also had another big incentive. Pat Friday, Kansas City's general manager, had made a trip to Birmingham specifically to see him. To accommodate Friday's schedule, Sullivan had moved Tompkins up a day in the rotation. With an excellent outing, the tall Californian could be joining Shaky Joe in the big leagues.

For Sullivan, the notion of losing the ace of his pitching staff was unsettling.

The Pride of Chula Vista

When Tompkins ran wind sprints, he looked like a giant stork. At six foot five and 180 pounds, he was all knees and elbows. He threw three-quarters sidearm like Don Drysdale, and when he brought his right arm back behind him and then unfurled it, it was like Lash LaRue's crackling whip. And he threw the hell out of the ball. (These were the days before the radar gun, so velocity was an estimate.)

Labeled another one of those "can't miss" prospects as a senior at Chula Vista High just south of San Diego, Tompkins seemed destined to be a star. His father built a regulation pitching mound, complete with a rubber and a home plate sixty feet, six inches away, in their backyard. He also coached all of Ron's summer-league teams, and had Ron take piano lessons, not only to help

163

him become a more well-rounded young man, but also to help his hand-eye coordination for baseball.

Ron was an average student, not motivated in school, except for sports. He had a sister, but she was six years older, so they weren't particularly close. They did have something in common, however—they both stuttered. Badly. Embarrassingly. Ron worked hard to overcome it, and in his senior year he even ran for student body vice president and won, giving a speech in front of the entire student body. By comparison, pitching in front of the A's general manager with a possible trip to the big leagues on the line was a breeze.

A Shaky Start

Standing on the mound at Rickwood, Tompkins could see Pat Friday sitting right behind home plate. He walked the first hitter on four pitches.

The second hitter lined a double in the gap, scoring the runner, sending Tompkins hustling to back up home. Sullivan called time and walked slowly to the mound.

"You're rushing your pitches," he said. "Take your time. Relax."

Tompkins settled down and retired the side, leaving the runner stranded.

Walking off the mound, he wished he could tell Friday to forget what he saw with those first two hitters and to just judge him on the rest of the game. He also wanted to look to the wives' section and let his wife, Sherri, know that he'd be okay. She knew a possible trip to The Show was at stake.

Young Love

They met at Chula Vista High, and Sherri—tall, good-looking, and on track to go to San Diego State—had been with him through all his baseball highs, including when Ron signed a letter of intent to play for Rod Dedeaux, the legendary coach at USC. But then he changed his mind and signed a $20,000 bonus contract with the A's the day after graduating from high school in 1962. His dad had scheduled the eight interested teams, giving each scout an hour to make his pitch. Four days later, Ron kissed Sherri good-bye and boarded a plane to Florida to start his career. When he walked through the airport at Daytona, he was surprised to find restrooms marked COLOREDS. He'd never paid any attention to the fact that California had its own de facto segregation, a reality that Tommie Reynolds, also from San Diego, would soon explain to him.

In that first pro season, he had an impressive 2.48 ERA, striking out 131 in 122 innings. After the season, he returned to Chula Vista and he and Sherri, now a student at San Diego State, took up where they left off. She went with him when he picked up his brand-new '62 Corvette, his big purchase from his bonus money. He gave the balance of it to his parents, who bought a family cabin east of San Diego.

In December, Sherri got pregnant. They got married in January. For Ron, it was all happening so fast—seven months earlier, he and Sherri were the prototypical carefree, good-looking Southern California high school sweethearts, walking down center hall to senior comp, double-dating to Oscar's Drive-In, and making out in the front seat of his '55 Chevy—and now they were married with a baby on the way. They were both still eighteen. Ron traded in his Corvette for a more family-friendly '64 Bonneville. And now, twenty-five hundred miles from home, Sherri sat in the stands at Rickwood with her ten-month-old son in her lap and watched Haywood Sullivan come to the mound in the sixth inning and pull her husband from the game, while a few rows down, Pat Friday jotted in his little notebook.

A Happy Clubhouse...Almost

In the clubhouse after winning their seventh straight game—a come-from-behind 7–6 victory—the Barons were whooping it up. But not Tompkins. He'd just had his worst outing—six innings, five earned runs, four walks, and only one strikeout. He'd been wild, falling behind almost every batter. His record was still a perfect 5–0, but he'd bombed miserably in front of Pat Friday. His chances of getting called up had just taken a serious nosedive.

He found little solace in the Barons' most exciting win of the year—in the bottom of the ninth, Campy had led off with a single, stolen second, and scored on a base hit by Hoss. Tompkins looked up and saw Pat Friday enter the locker room and stop to congratulate Ken Sanders, the winning pitcher, and then shake hands with Campy, who was now hitting .296. After that, he passed right by him and didn't say a word, disappearing into Sullivan's office and closing the door behind him.

For Sullivan, it was a good night. His team won its seventh straight game, increasing its league lead to four...and he would not be losing his star pitcher.

Head down, Tompkins was the first to leave the locker room, walking out into the warm evening air, Sherri and his son waiting in the Bonneville.

CHAPTER 32

Blue Moon Odom

Catfish

Two hours before Blue Moon's debut, the grandstands at Macon's Luther Williams Field were already filled, with black fans spilling into the segregated seats formerly occupied only by whites. In the Barons' locker room, Blue Moon was sitting alone, a stranger still to his teammates.

The clubhouse door opened and in walked Charlie Finley, grinning like he'd just won the lottery. He headed straight for Blue Moon, shook his hand, wished him good luck, and then walked into Sullivan's office.

Blue Moon's heralded debut wasn't the sole inspiration for Finley's smile. He'd just garnered another of the top prospects that he'd vowed to sign—Jim Catfish Hunter—again shelling out $75,000, this time to a right-handed pitcher fresh out of high school. At Perquimans County High in Hertford, North Carolina, Hunter had won twenty-six games and lost only two, with five no-hitters and two perfect games. But his most remarkable performance was striking out twenty-nine in a twelve-inning game.

"He's a real farm boy," Finley told Sullivan. "A handsome kid and one of the most determined youngsters you'll ever see."

Hunter seemed a perfect complement to Blue Moon—two Southern fireballers with great nicknames and interesting backgrounds. Hunter got his nickname because he supposedly disappeared once when he was eight and had the whole town looking for him until they finally found him down by the riverbank, reeling in a big catfish.

Despite signing the big contract, Hunter would have to wait to start his pro career. Prior to his senior year, he and his older brother had gone hunting and the brother's gun accidentally discharged, hitting Catfish in the foot. When the brother saw all the blood, he fainted. Catfish crawled to a pond, took off his shirt, wet it, and then crawled back to revive his brother, who then went for help. Doctors had to amputate Catfish's big toe and part of his foot, but he was still able to blow away the hitters in his senior season.

Finley was sending him to the Mayo Clinic to have his foot reexamined, and then he would assign him to a minor-league team.

"Sully, I want him to start with you in Birmingham," said Finley. "Wouldn't that be great? A Blue Moon and a Catfish on the same team. You gotta love it."

Pre-Game Jitters

Sullivan had been in the game a dozen years, and he couldn't remember a player starting his career with so much hype as Blue Moon, not even with his own career back in 1951 when he signed for a whopping $45,000 with the Red Sox.

The *Macon Telegraph* had run three front-page stories about Blue Moon's debut, plus a wire-service photo of him during his visit to Kansas City sitting next to A's manager Ed Lopat. During that week with the big-league team, Blue Moon had worked with Lopat on having his legs wider apart when he finished his follow-through, as well as coming more over the top in his curve. Lopat also had Odom do a lot of running, worried he wasn't in baseball shape.

Blue Moon was confident. "I've seen the Peaches play this year," he said in one of the front-page stories. "I can beat 'em."

He'd returned to Macon only the previous day, and had spent the night with his mother. The only Baron name he knew for sure was Sullivan's. He didn't know that the Barons' league lead was still at four over Lynchburg, either, following their wins in the first two games of the series against Macon. In the second game, Tompkins had rebounded from his disastrous start in front of Pat Friday and thrown a complete game, six-hit victory, improving his record to 6–0.

The crowd, predicted to be a record turnout, was even bigger than expected—7,005 fans cramming into a stadium with a capacity of 5,000. It was standing room only, fans lining the foul lines and spilling out into the outfield behind roped-off areas. And they were noisy. There were even fans sitting at the edge of the Barons' dugout.

Initially, Finley went upstairs to the press box behind home plate, where he let the hyperbole ring. "Blue Moon will be the best athlete in the organization," he said.

But after fidgeting in his seat for a couple of minutes, he left the press box for a seat along the third-base side, the only white face in an all-black section. If this was to be the most ballyhooed sports event in Macon's history, white or black, he wanted to be in the middle of it.

Originally, Pat Friday was scheduled to join him, but the previous day Finley dispatched him to Massachusetts to dole out another $100,000 to Skip Lockwood, an outfield phenom just graduating from high school. Friday was supposed to make it to Macon in time for Blue Moon's debut, but at the last minute Finley dispatched him back to Kansas City to fire Manager Ed Lopat and replace him with Mel McGaha, the manager of Kansas City's AAA team in Dallas. Some speculated that Finley preferred Sullivan—McGaha had never played in the big leagues—but surmised that he had decided to let Sullivan finish the season in Birmingham in order to gain a full year's experience before taking over the A's.

Bigwigs had also shown up for the game, including the mayor of Macon, Southern League president Sam Smith, and Barons' owner Albert Belcher. Extra security was also on hand. Macon had always had segregated baseball and segregated seating, and this would be the town's first experience with a totally integrated crowd. More than half of the patrons were black. Normally, fewer than a hundred blacks showed up for Macon's games.

Also in the stands were Blue Moon's mother and his girlfriend, Perrie. Like everyone else, they fanned themselves to keep cool. The temperature at game time was ninety-one degrees, down from a sweltering ninety-six earlier in the day.

Waiting for the pre-game introductions, Blue Moon wiped the sweat from his forehead. Having played countless games in sweltering Southern heat, he was no stranger to the dripping humidity. But it had been three weeks since he had pitched in a game, and Finley shared Lopat's concern that he wasn't in baseball shape.

In the pre-game introductions, the stadium announcer made the call: "And pitching for the Barons, number 13, Johnny Blue Moon Odom."

The stands shook so hard that several Baron players grabbed their gloves and retreated from the dugout steps. In the dugout, Tompkins held a fungo bat between his legs just in case. In the stands, fans held orange baseballs, a pre-game giveaway from Finley. (He owned a surplus of these orange balls, his proposal for using them in big-league games having been unanimously rejected by the other owners.)

"These people are nuts," observed Hoss. "I'm not sure giving them orange balls was such a good idea."

Blue Moon's First Inning

With the count one ball and two strikes on Teo Acosta, Macon's leadoff hitter, Blue Moon snapped off a hard-breaking curve, freezing Acosta in his spikes. "Steeeerike!" bellowed the ump.

The crowd went completely and totally nuts, stomping, screaming, whistling.

Blue Moon didn't smile, he didn't pump his fist... he just bent down, picked up the resin bag, and waited for the next hitter to step in. Wasn't this why he got all that money?

The next hitter, second baseman Bill Oplinger, lined a single to left. The crowd groaned.

The third hitter, Len Boehmer, one of the best contact hitters in the league and currently second in the league in batting average, worked the count to two and two, and then Blue Moon, working from the stretch, struck him out with a sinking fastball.

If the first strikeout brought thunder from the stands, this one brought delirium, with black fans yelling in celebration as if Ty Cobb himself had gone down swinging. It was so loud that players in the Barons' dugout covered their ears.

Facing Macon's cleanup hitter, Jerry Kushner, Blue Moon quickly got ahead of the count, no balls, two strikes. Baseball wisdom, he knew, said that the pitcher should not give the hitter anything too good to hit in this situation, but with his adrenaline running wild, and with the crowd going bananas, he fired a fastball low and away. Kushner swung... and missed.

Blue Moon Odom, the richest bonus baby in Georgia history, had just struck out the side in his very first inning.

The fans went stark, raving bonkers, his girlfriend, Perrie, jumping up and down, hugging Blue Moon's mom. Sullivan stood on the top step of the dugout, congratulating Blue Moon as he walked off the field. Players on the bench shook their heads in disbelief. Blue Moon issued only the slightest hint of a smile.

In the stands, Finley stood shoulder-to-shoulder with black fans, whistling, applauding, and beaming. For him, it was a moment of vindication and validation. His recent spending spree—over half a million dollars—on untried young players had raised eyebrows throughout the baseball world, with accusations that he was trying to use his money to change the baseball landscape, accusations he scoffed at.

He had made Blue Moon a rich young man... and now Blue Moon had just made him the happiest man in baseball.

The Rest of the Game

In the bottom of the second, Blue Moon gave up a line single to Lee May sandwiched between two walks. With the bases loaded and two outs, he struck out the next batter, sending the crowd into another frenzy.

And if the crowd weren't delirious enough, he jacked them even higher when he came to bat in the third inning and laid down a perfect bunt for a base hit, beating the throw by two strides. The Barons scored two in the inning, taking a 2–0 lead.

Standing on first base after a hit to drive in a run, Tommie Reynolds turned to Macon first baseman Lee May and gestured to the screaming crowd. "These people are crazy," he said.

"If they decide to rush the field, I've got my exit all picked out," replied May.

"I'm right behind you," said Reynolds.

In the bottom of the third, the Grand Debut began to unravel a bit. Blue Moon gave up three singles, a wild pitch, and a balk as the Peaches tied the score. He breezed through the fourth, but then in the fifth, with the Barons back on top 4–2, he gave up two more runs, one of them on a wild pitch. Sullivan sent Hoss to the mound to calm him down and to get him to take more time between pitches.

"When I got to the mound, all I could see were the whites of his eyes," Hoss recalled after the game. "He was so amped up."

In the bottom of the sixth, Blue Moon came all the way unraveled, giving up four runs, hurting himself with three walks, one of them with the bases loaded. He also hit a batter and wild-pitched in another run. Finally, mercifully, Sullivan came and pulled him from the game. His totals for the evening: five and a third innings pitched, seven hits, eight earned runs, seven walks, and seven strikeouts.

As Blue Moon dejectedly made his way to the dugout, the black fans stood and cheered, not the deafening roar from before, but still plenty loud. Then they turned and headed for the exits en masse, with three innings still left in the game.

Post-Game Spin

The post-game analysis was mixed. A headline in the *Birmingham News* read: MOON SHOT FIZZLES OUT. But the *Macon Telegraph* declared: ODOM LOOKS IMPRESSIVE. Finley had come down from his earlier exaltation to tell a reporter: "I was very impressed with Blue Moon's performance, considering the tremendous pressure he was under and the fact that he was not in top physical condition. He might be in good shape for a high school kid, but he still needs a lot of conditioning for pro ball. I'm not worried. He will help us win a lot after he gains some experience."

Sullivan also expressed satisfaction with Blue Moon's first game: "Johnny has a good, moving fastball and his curve will come around. He threw a lot of pitches—124 in only five innings—and that tired him out a bit."

For his part, Blue Moon showed his inexperience in dealing with the media and that he still needed to learn how not to give the opposition quotes for the bulletin board. "I really don't think there is a lot of difference between pitching in high school and pitching in the Southern League," he said. "Maybe the players are a little better and don't swing at many bad balls, but I'm not worried. I'll do all right in this league."

Tearful Good-Bye

After the game, as the Barons boarded the bus for the four-hour drive back to Birmingham, Blue Moon stood off to the side, trying to console his seventeen-year-old girlfriend, tears streaming down Perrie's cheeks. It wasn't the eight earned runs he'd given up that had her so upset.

"I don't want you to go, Johnny," she said, loud enough for others to hear. "I know you're gonna meet somebody..."

Worried that his new teammates were watching this tearful farewell, he gave her a quick kiss and then turned and boarded the bus, leaving her crying in the parking lot as Iron Lung pulled out into the warm Georgia night.

CHAPTER 33

Haywood Sullivan

An Orgasmic Experience

Coming into the season, Sullivan told himself he wanted to communicate with his players. As a player, he appreciated knowing what his role was, even if it meant being told he was just a big, handsome stiff and his only job was warming up pitchers in the bullpen. But the managers he'd played for—Pinky Higgins, Hank Bauer, Joe Gordon, and Eddie Lopat—were all old-school guys who didn't think players needed to be mollycoddled. These were managers who'd lived through the austerity and hardship of the Great Depression and World War II. They were, as sportswriters of the 1960s liked to call them, "grizzled old vets."

As a new manager, he was determined to keep his players informed. Maybe he wouldn't try to explain why he had called for a bunt or changed pitchers, but he was determined to at least be approachable. That was his personality. When players didn't know their roles or weren't told why they'd been benched, they could become cancers in the clubhouse. He hadn't been on a championship team since high school, including his football days, and the common thread in the losing, he realized, was poor communication.

Two months into the season, he'd figured out that the job was more complicated than he'd imagined. Managing was more than just filling out the lineup card or arguing with umps. He also had to be a disciplinarian, teacher, evaluator, mediator, counselor, and bearer of bad news—all roles he was happy to take on. He didn't want to be a babysitter, friend, confidant, or jailer. Nor was he going to buy beer for the underage guys.

Since the start of the season, he'd already had to serve as the "Turk" to five players—Danny Greenfield, Gary Sanossian, Mike Maloney, Freddie Velázquez, and Brice Smith. He remembered the times he'd been sent down and how much it hurt. In cutting these players, he tried to soften the blow, to provide a positive spin by assuring them that with a little more experience, they could make it back... even though the chances of a guy who's getting sent down from AA making it all the way to the big leagues were low. Ending the dream was the worst part of his job.

The challenge and the responsibility of managing had convinced him to abandon any thoughts of playing. He missed the challenge of stepping into the batter's box with his Louisville Slugger to face a pitcher determined to make him look like a fool. He missed the almost orgasmic feeling he got when his bat connected perfectly with the ball and the vibrations sent a shiver all the way to his toes.

Molding a group of twenty-two young men of diverse backgrounds into a team who could put differences aside in the name of harmony and a Southern League championship, he decided, would be even more orgasmic.

The Question of Racism

In the 1964 world of pro baseball, there were no psychological evaluations or background checks. So how did Finley know that Sullivan, a man with no managerial experience, would have the right stuff? And how did a man from Dothan, by way of the segregated SEC and the most racist organization in baseball—the Red Sox—learn to treat everybody with respect?

In Sullivan's case, there was no special moment, no epiphany, no thunderbolt from above. Sullivan didn't see Pumpsie in the Red Sox clubhouse one day and suddenly realize, hey, I like this guy. It was more a case of his being the genetic beneficiary of the decency gene. And it probably wasn't random. He grew up in a home where the parents, Ralph and Ruby Lee Sullivan, believed all humans should be treated with dignity and respect, whether they owned the store or swept the floors.

Even though most of Haywood's life was spent in the company of whites, and he had very little interaction with blacks, he held to the tenets of fairness that he'd learned from his parents and all those Sundays spent in church with them. (His dad was Methodist, his mom a Baptist; they usually attended the Methodist church.) Churches, of course, can be refuges for racism, but not in the Sullivan family. They truly subscribed to the gospel of "do unto others."

In partnership with the common moral decency he'd learned at home and in the church was his understanding of the dynamics of a team. For as far back as he could remember, he'd belonged to a team. On each of those teams there existed the collective notion, usually unspoken, that the players needed to get along. Sullivan intuitively understood that this wisdom applied as fully to an integrated team as a segregated one. For reasons no analysis or questionnaire could easily explain, some whites grew up respecting blacks, and some blacks grew up respecting whites, regardless of any geographic, political, or generational obstacles. Sullivan didn't need a black roommate in college to teach him how to treat people fairly—his instinctual sense of fairness guided him.

A shared passion to win was a powerful adhesive for a team. He knew that teamwork and camaraderie helped give birth to victory. And vice versa. Neither a fart on the bus nor a game-winning hit possessed color. Baseball was fun to play. It's hard to hate, Sullivan understood, when you're having fun.

He wasn't so Pollyannaish, however, to claim that color didn't matter. He understood that Bert Campaneris, Blue Moon Odom, Tommie Reynolds, Woody Huyke, Stanley Jones, and Santiago Rosario faced challenges he could only imagine. He felt empathy when he heard a fan howling like a monkey at Reynolds. He also felt rage. But from the teachings of his youth, he knew how to control that rage. He subscribed to the old adage that deeds, not words, described a person's true character and convictions.

If he had just been putting on a charade, and pretended to respect Campy, Reynolds, and the others based only on what their success could do to advance his career, he would've been labeled a phony the first week of spring training. The game would not have been fun. And teams that don't enjoy the game or teammates' company don't win.

Hoss, Reynolds, Campy, Stretch, Droopsy, and all the other Barons didn't give two hoots how Sullivan's essential decency was formed. It didn't matter to them if it had been family, church, or the experience and ethics of teamwork that formed his character...they were just happy to play for him.

CHAPTER 34

Albert Belcher

A Fat Lady Is Stuck in the Turnstile

With all the publicity surrounding Blue Moon, Belcher was counting on a big crowd for the newest Baron's debut at Rickwood in a couple of days. Despite the team being in first place, the Barons were now only sixteen hundred ahead of the 1961 attendance figures.

Belcher was also counting on another factor to boost attendance—if the Barons were in first place on July 5, they would get to host the Southern League All-Star Game on July 12, a contest pitting the first-place team against the league's best players. In 1951, Birmingham had hosted a Southern Association All-Star game that drew an overflow crowd of nineteen thousand.

Belcher knew that the days of minor-league baseball drawing that kind of a crowd were gone forever, but by his estimate, if an All-Star Game could draw six thousand fans, the gate receipts would put another $12,000 to $15,000 in the coffers, plus concessions...which could be the difference in the team's turning a profit in 1964. As much as he loved baseball, he wasn't in this thing to lose money.

July was just around the corner and that meant hotter weather, which used to mean improved attendance. The theory was that as the temperature rose, people went to ball games to help take their minds off the heat. They could refresh with ice-cold beverages. But that was before air-conditioning and television. People now preferred sitting home in their climate-controlled living rooms watching *Gunsmoke* on a hot and humid Saturday night.

Belcher joked about hoping that television and air-conditioning manufacturers would go out of business. Although the days of ESPN and fourteen televised games every night were still years away, the reality was that the *Game of the Week* with Dizzy Dean and Buddy Blattner on Saturday afternoons was pulling people right out of the seats of minor-league parks, including

Rickwood. Although he didn't say it publicly, Belcher also worried that the hotter weather could mean more racial disturbances.

"But we'll be all right if we can just get that fat lady stuck in the turnstile to stop blocking our fans," he said.

The Clown Prince of Baseball

On the eve of Blue Moon's Rickwood debut, Sullivan pulled Belcher aside. "Is there any possibility of pushing back Max Patkin to the next night?" he asked. "I'd rather not have him here the night Blue Moon is pitching."

"I seriously doubt it," replied Belcher. "Patkin is booked almost every night."

With attendance declining in minor-league cities, teams were adopting new marketing strategies and promotional gimmicks to attract fans to the ballparks—family night, ladies' night, Little League night, fan appreciation night, farmers' night. Almost every minor-league franchise featured a night with Max Patkin. The Barons had scheduled him way back in January.

Billed as the "Clown Prince of Baseball," Patkin had been a minor-league pitcher until an arm injury ended his career. He joined the navy during World War II, and while pitching for a service team in Hawaii he gave up a home run to Joe DiMaggio. In mock anger, Patkin threw his glove down, and then trotted behind DiMaggio as he rounded the bases, much to the delight of the fans—and a career was born.

For two decades Patkin had been barnstorming the country, performing at a different minor-league ballpark almost every night. He could contort his rubbery face into a thousand shapes. He wore a baggy uniform that hung loosely on his skinny body, and instead of a name or number it had a big question mark stitched on the back. His hat was always on sideways (before it was fashionable); he spewed endless geysers of water in mock exasperation. Performing his antics mostly between innings, he would also coach third base for an inning or two for the home team. Fans loved him. Teams that ran into him at three or four different ballparks during a season, however, grew weary of his act. Vulnerable to Patkin's commotion, pitchers sometimes got distracted and thrown out of rhythm.

"Blue Moon doesn't need any more distractions than he's already got," said Sullivan.

"I'll see what I can do," said Belcher.

Mixed Feelings

Prior to Blue Moon's Rickwood debut, Belcher revealed to reporters a conversation he had on opening night. It wasn't the secret about the bomb threat—it would be years before he'd reveal that—but rather the story about Finley coming to him after that first game and telling him he believed the Barons were in for an "ugly season" if he didn't send them help.

"We talked about the importance of giving the city a winning team to help keep a lid on things around here," said Belcher. "I should give Finley credit for sending us some talented players."

The addition of Reynolds, Stahl, and now Blue Moon gave support to Finley's promise. Losing Joe Grzenda didn't.

"I guess the proof will be what happens the rest of the season," Belcher said. His biggest concern was that Finley would call up Campaneris, who was now hitting .301.

Praise for Belcher

While the Birmingham press continued to fall all over itself in praise of Finley (who was coming to town again for Blue Moon's game), they also took note of Belcher's role in bringing back baseball. Benny Marshall, sports editor of the *News*, put it this way:

Albert Belcher had the audacity to become a pioneer around here.

Let it be said loud and clear for all to hear . . . the new Barons have added a great deal to the summer of 1964 in Birmingham. It's difficult to find a long face, any place around Rickwood most nights now.

Thank you, Mr. Belcher.

Vietnam

Sitting in his office, Belcher hung up the phone and shook his head. He'd just talked to Pat Friday, the A's general manager. Friday had called to see if Belcher could help find a National Guard unit in Alabama that would have an opening for Blue Moon.

In recent months, major-league teams had become nervous about losing players to the military. As long as Blue Moon had been in school, he received a student deferment, but now that he'd graduated, a notice from the Selective Service Board was as certain as sunrise. Two years of military service would be required . . . or six months of active duty in a reserve unit, with an additional six years of two-week summer duty.

All over the country, sports teams were scrambling to find openings in these reserve units for their athletes. Players who had already completed their military obligation, such as Larry Stahl and Tommie Reynolds, were valued commodities. So were married men. Because married men were exempt, weddings were being rushed as a way to avoid the draft. Blue Moon and Perrie had even talked about it. But she still had a year left in high school, so that option seemed premature.

In the previous week, Vietnam had leaped from a small, back-page story to banner headlines, casting a dark sense of foreboding. On consecutive days the *Birmingham News* ran headlines about Vietnam that bumped the stories about Wallace's campaign and the ongoing battle over the passage of the Civil Rights Act to the bottom of the page. One headline in all caps read: McNAMARA DISCLOSES: BLANK CHECK FOR VIET NAM WAR.

The editorial page also reflected this mounting concern. A column titled "Darkness in Vietnam" stated: "To put it bluntly, it becomes more and more apparent that the situation there is going to hell."

In another story, syndicated columnist William F. Buckley Jr. called the situation "a nightmare." A poignant, full-page ad simply listed the names of the 130 Americans killed in the line of duty so far in Vietnam. The ad was paid for by parents, relatives, and friends of the dead Americans, and was posed as an open letter to President Johnson, simply asking: "Why?"

Belcher promised Pat Friday that he'd make some calls to Alabama National Guard units, but from what he'd heard, openings were scarce. The reality was that Blue Moon, despite his new career and sudden wealth, was nineteen years old, out of school, and in excellent health—just the sort of young man the military wanted. Belcher knew that it could be only a matter of weeks, maybe days, until that notice from the Selective Service arrived in the mailbox...and his new box-office draw could be gone.

CHAPTER 35

Blue Moon Odom

Confident or Cocky?

The headline the day of Blue Moon's home debut against Chattanooga read: BLUE MOON VOWS RICKWOOD WILL SEE A SHOW. He brashly told a reporter that he hadn't seen a Southern League pitcher yet with "a fastball as good as mine."

Given that he'd been in the league less than a week, his boast was about to be put to the test. His pitching opponent for the Lookouts would be Fergie Jenkins, currently leading the Southern League in strikeouts.

Blue Moon's boast had raised eyebrows with two of his own teammates— Ron Tompkins and Paul Seitz—who didn't believe he even threw harder than they did. Tompkins, who was second in the league behind Jenkins in strikeouts, was coming off a nifty four-hitter the previous night, boosting his record to 7–0 and putting his flop in front of KC's general manager behind him.

Upon first meeting Blue Moon, Bob Phillips of the *Birmingham Post-Herald* described him this way:

> The 19-year-old Negro has an easy smile and there is a touch of dimples in his face. His demeanor makes you wonder why he ever was dubbed Blue Moon.

Phillips asked Blue Moon what he liked to be called.
"Blue Moon or Moon, it don't matter," he replied.
Phillips let on that he knew Blue Moon had a girlfriend back in Macon.
"What's she call you?" he asked.
"Johnny."
"How come you asked to wear number 13?" Phillips asked.

179

"That was my number in high school. I had good luck there, so why change?"

Pumped

Blue Moon hadn't adjusted yet to baseball player time—stay up late, get up late. Eager to atone for the poor showing in his first start, he was up at 8 a.m. The Barons had found him a room to rent in a modest house on West 1st Street, only a couple of blocks from Rickwood. The owner of the house, Mrs. Polk, a grandmotherly black woman, had already taken to treating him like a son. On this morning, she had bacon and eggs waiting for him on the kitchen table.

After inhaling breakfast, Blue Moon drove his new Ford Galaxy the two blocks to Rickwood, arriving ten hours before game time. General Manager Glynn West spotted him and told him to go home and rest, which was like ordering a lion to purr. He returned to the park at three o'clock, still two hours ahead of his teammates.

When he finally walked down to the bullpen to warm up, he received the same advice from Sullivan that managers had been handing out to pitchers since before Babe Ruth left the orphanage: Keep the ball down, get ahead of the hitters, and don't rush yourself. Sullivan also had one more piece of advice: "Don't let Max Patkin distract you."

A New Moon

Belcher surveyed the crowd. Paid attendance was 5,536, not as large as he'd hoped, but almost three times bigger than they'd been averaging. Unsuccessful in getting Patkin to change the date, he was at least glad he was paying him a set fee ($200) rather than a share of the gate.

Belcher spotted two gentlemen in houndstooth hats seated in the box seats behind the Barons' dugout—Charlie Finley and Bear Bryant. This was already Finley's fourth trip to Birmingham in 1964; Bryant had driven up from Tuscaloosa specifically to check out Blue Moon.

With the crowd cheering on every pitch, Blue Moon got off to a shaky start, unable to get his curve over. But a Campy-to-Hoss double play bailed him out in the first inning, and a great backhand stop by Rosario ended a Lookout threat in the second.

In the third, two walks and a single brought in a run for the Lookouts to tie the score, 1–1, and then in the fourth, another pair of walks and a single put

Chattanooga in the lead, 2–1. After four innings, Blue Moon had given up five hits and four walks.

In the fifth, he walked the leadoff hitter. In the stands, Finley shifted uncomfortably. Sullivan hustled to the mound.

"Use your fastball more," he instructed.

Blue Moon knew his fastball was his money pitch, but thought he needed to use his curveball more in the pros against better hitters than he'd faced at Ballard-Hudson High. Unfortunately, he was falling behind in the count to almost every hitter.

Heeding Sullivan's advice, he started to settle down and rely on his fastball. Over the next five innings, he gave up no runs and only one hit and one walk. Meanwhile, the Barons were figuring out Jenkins. Led by Hoss's three hits and four RBIs, they won the game 8–2, Blue Moon pitching a complete game for his first win as a pro, so focused that he barely noticed Patkin's antics or the highest decibel level at Rickwood in years.

Is There Such a Thing as Too Much Praise?

Finley gushed. "I've got to admit that I was a little shook last week when I saw Moon get roughed up pretty good in Macon," he said. "But I feel a lot better now. I'm not worried about the 75K I gave him. In fact, if I see anybody else with an arm like that, I'll write another check, same amount."

Sullivan was impressed, too. "Blue might not have been as quick as he was against Macon, but he was a better pitcher," he said. "Much better."

The stats bore him out. Against Macon, Odom threw 124 pitches in only five innings. On this night he threw 118 in nine innings, with 56 fastballs and 18 curves for strikes. Fifteen of his outs came on ground balls. He struck out six.

"Don't forget, this is just a kid," added Sullivan. "He's got things to learn, lots of them, but he's got a good head on him. He'll pick it up quickly. He's going to make quite a pitcher. I think Charlie will get his money's worth."

Also adding praise was Patkin, a man who'd seen more than a thousand pitchers over the years. "If he keeps throwing like that, he'll be plenty successful," he said. "He's got a bit of Satchel Paige in him. Colorful. It could make him a lot of extra money, and fans, too."

And another voice joined the chorus. "He won, that's what I like the most," said Bear Bryant. "He looks like a winner. I like the way he pitched in the fourth quarter. After he got the lead, he got tougher. I'm not a baseball man, but I've got some ideas about folks who get tougher in fourth quarters."

Probably the least impressed was Blue Moon. "My curve wasn't behaving like it oughta," he said. "But my fastball was all right. When it's getting right, it tails off and drops. Batters don't get to it fat."

Later that night, his good fortune continued when he was pulled over by a burly Birmingham policeman, then let go with just a warning.

The next morning, he called his mom back in Macon. She listened to his account of the game, and then offered her two cents. "John," she said, "I didn't raise you to go getting yourself a big ol' head."

CHAPTER 36

Paul Lindblad

Slump

Back on the road, the Barons lost the series opener to Knoxville, 4–2. In the locker room, Sullivan noticed the slumped shoulders of Lindblad, the losing pitcher.

"Your arm okay, Paul?"

Lindblad nodded. After starting the season winning his first five games and pitching his way into the regular rotation, he had now lost four straight. In this game, he'd given up nine hits in six innings. The loss cut Birmingham's lead over Lynchburg to only one and a half games.

Earlier, Sullivan had stressed the importance of the Barons' leading the league on July 5. With his four straight losses, Lindblad worried he'd be responsible for blowing the lead and the chance for Birmingham to host the Southern League All-Star Game. Or even worse...cost his teammates a trip to Hawaii.

Despite Lindblad's assurance that his arm was okay, Sullivan knew that arm troubles had cut short the left-hander's first pro season and earned him a free trip to the Mayo Clinic. As a player with the Red Sox and A's, Sullivan had seen players tell the manager that the arm was fine when it wasn't. These players worried that they'd get tossed onto the disabled list and end up peddling used cars by the end of summer. But judging from Lindblad's velocity, Sullivan thought his arm was fine.

So what was it? How could a guy go from winning five straight to losing four straight? Part of it was simply bad luck. Pitchers often complain of getting no support, but in Lindblad's case it was true. A blundering defense had saddled him with sixteen unearned runs in six games. (By comparison, during that same period Tompkins suffered only one unearned run.)

Sullivan took comfort in knowing that of all the pitchers, Lindblad was the most solidly grounded, the one best suited to weather bad breaks.

Sullivan understood the ebb and flow of a locker room—a player riding an emotional high one week, and then wallowing in the discarded peanut shells of self-pity the next. In baseball, newspapers carry a daily log of successes and failures, amplifying the toll on the psyche.

The next morning, Lindblad didn't pick up a copy of the *Knoxville News-Sentinel*. It was hard enough to have experienced his fourth straight loss up close and personal—he didn't want to read about it, too.

His New Teammate

It was as hot as a Tennessee tar road as Lindblad and Blue Moon finished their tenth and final wind sprint after batting practice in Knoxville. Sweat poured off them.

"Let's run a couple more," said Lindblad.

"Sure," replied Blue Moon.

Lindblad was impressed with Blue Moon's work ethic. With all the money and hype he'd gotten, it could've been easy for him to play the role of pampered bonus baby. But he hadn't. He ran his wind sprints hard—as well as fast—and didn't try to cut it short as some pitchers did.

Lindblad also appreciated the way Blue Moon was trying to fit in. Or maybe he wasn't trying; maybe it was natural. Joining the team in the middle of the season, when bonds and friendships had already been forged, wasn't easy, especially for someone coming straight out of high school. But since he'd donned the green-and-gold uniform of the Barons, Blue Moon hadn't isolated himself…except after the games…and it wasn't his fault that he wasn't allowed to stay in the same hotel or eat in the same restaurants as Lindblad and the other white players.

Lindblad had overheard whispered grumbles from a few teammates about all the money Blue Moon had gotten, and how Charlie Finley had flown in to watch his first two games, and how he peeled out of the Rickwood parking lot in his brand-new fire-engine-red Galaxy as if he were some sort of Barney Oldfield. But to Lindblad, that kind of petty jealousy seemed like wasted energy and bad juju for the team. He was glad to have Blue Moon on the Barons, and if Blue Moon could help the team get to Hawaii, then Lindblad would be the first to put on a grass skirt and do the hula. Blue Moon had been with the team for only ten days, but Lindblad was ready to pay him the high compliment: "He's a good teammate."

As it was with pitchers in any minor-league system, the competition for Lindblad to make it to Kansas City came mostly from the pitchers within the organization. This created a funny dynamic—pitchers secretly rooting against their own teammate. Nobody would admit it, but down deep where the competitive current flowed the strongest, most pitchers hoped their teammate out on the mound would get roughed up just a bit—not bad enough for the team to lose, but bad enough to go in the manager's report to the front office.

But Lindblad was imbued with the same decency gene Sullivan possessed. By Lindblad's reckoning, he and Blue Moon weren't in competition, because Blue Moon was right-handed and he was a lefty. And it wasn't as if Kansas City had a staff full of Koufaxes and Drysdales.

Lindblad's attitude was simple: Focus on being the best pitcher his talent would allow. If that meant changing his grip on his curve, or running more wind sprints, or—God forbid—going to the bullpen, then that's what he'd do. Everything else was out of his control. Otherwise, the curse of sixteen unearned runs in a month would've had him slamming walls. So would've Blue Moon's $75,000 bonus compared with his $2,000.

A Baseball Wife's Job Skills

In his hotel room, Lindblad called home. Kathy always seemed to have the knack of lifting his spirits. It was part of the job.

"I threw like crap last night," he said.

"Your daughters and I still love you."

In high school, Kathy hadn't dreamed about going to college or becoming a stewardess or any of the other things most teenage girls in Chanute thought about. She wanted to be married and raise a family...with Paul. He was polite and thoughtful back then, and nothing about him had changed. She'd always been skilled at accommodating and adjusting. When he gave her his senior class ring to go steady, it was so big that she wrapped it with white medical tape to fit on her finger...and let all the other girls know he belonged to her. When he got his picture on the front page of the *Chanute Tribune* for chasing down the thief who'd broken into the gas station, she cut out the article and framed it. She often left choir practice early or skipped a Future Homemakers of America meeting just to be with him. Now, three years later, she washed his clothes, served him meals, and kept a baseball scrapbook.

She loved being a ballplayer's wife. It felt like her destiny. Already she'd been to places she'd never imagined—Iowa, Florida, and now Alabama. But of course it wasn't perfect. There was the constant struggle to scrape together enough money for diapers or groceries, and the embarrassment of having to take out a loan. When Paul was on the road, she hated being alone, living in a town where her only friends were other baseball wives. She didn't like hearing the rumors about players bringing girls back to their hotel rooms. But worrying about that, she told herself, was a good way to go nuts, much in the way that thinking about the abuse she'd suffered at the hands of her stepfather, and whether she'd ever get up the courage to tell Paul, was as well.

"Don't be discouraged," she said. "I'm sure Sully has faith in you."

For as long as she'd known Paul, he'd been upbeat, even when his arm went bad in Burlington and they didn't know if his career was over. The only time she could remember him being really down was once after he'd come home from visiting his father. That night, she sat across the kitchen table from him and heard an honesty and vulnerability she'd never heard before. "I hate him," he'd said. It was just before spring training and he'd told his father he needed a loan to tide them over until the season started. That's when his dad told him he was worthless.

One Step Forward, Two Steps Back

After getting off the bus in front of the hotel, Lindblad watched Blue Moon and the other black players ride off together to their separate accommodations in a part of Knoxville he would never see. He didn't have to be an activist to appreciate the irony of black players being good enough to play ball with whites and to entertain white fans, but not good enough to stay with them in the same hotel. In Birmingham, he'd heard the claim: "Things are better than they used to be."

But were they?

It had been nine months since the bombing of the 16th Street Baptist Church, and Birmingham still found itself at the epicenter of America's long journey toward racial reconciliation. Many residents of the city felt ashamed for what had happened, and in the months that followed they steadfastly chronicled the progress they'd been making.

At the top of the list of improvements was the ease with which Rickwood had been integrated, both on the field and in the stands. Aside from an occasional racial taunt at an opposing player, the grand experiment was lending proof to Dr. Martin Luther King's notion that given a common goal, blacks and whites could work together.

There were others signs of progress. Blacks now sat on nine of ten subcommittees of the Community Affairs Committee, the biracial group set up to study the city's racial problems.

Three black students graduated from previously all-white high schools, with their parents in the audience. There were no incidents.

A previously all-white local bank hired two black tellers.

Even the 16th Street Church was showing signs of revival. Blond-wood paneling had replaced the somber mahogany in the balconies and choir box. Flooring had been replaced, and walls and ceiling were repainted with brighter colors. New stained-glass windows had been installed to replace the ones blown out in the blast.

The tension that stalked the city the previous year, especially at night, had lessened. There'd been no new demonstrations or bombings.

And perhaps best of all, Bull Connor no longer ruled the police force.

The *World*, the city's black newspaper, told a different story, however, wondering whether any real progress was being made. The paper ran editorials decrying the absence of black police officers in Birmingham and the fact that Mayor Albert Boutwell had done little to enact any of the recommendations made by the black leaders on the Community Affairs Committee, and seemed to have gone out of his way to ignore them. Hotels, motels, and restaurants remained segregated, and only token integration had taken place in the schools. How could it be considered progress when only three black kids had graduated from previously all-white high schools? When the U.S. Circuit Court of Appeals ordered the desegregation of the city's schools, mandating that grades one, ten, and eleven be integrated in the fall, rather than adhere to the mandate, disgruntled whites threatened to close the schools. How was that progress?

Perhaps nothing angered black leaders more than the fact that nobody had been brought to justice for the church bombing, despite a massive investigation by the FBI. The suspicion was that FBI director J. Edgar Hoover was stonewalling because of his animosity toward Martin Luther King Jr. and the civil rights movement.

At times, the mainstream Birmingham media fanned the flames, especially regarding the impending passage of a civil rights bill. In one of his columns, Keith Walling of the *News* expressed the attitude of many in the city:

One of the tragedies of the so-called civil rights measures is that they simply cannot be enforced in a manner that would affect the hopeless dream of so many misguided people.

Still, "so many misguided people" with the "hopeless dream" continued to fight for passage of a civil rights bill. Efforts by Southern senators to block such a bill now appeared doomed, despite heated debate. But the impending passage of the bill didn't silence these Southern senators, such as George Smathers, a Democrat from Florida:

In most places in the South, blacks have never been turned away at drug stores or other places of public accommodation.

Evidently, he hadn't been traveling with the Barons.

Because of the fear of the passage of the civil rights bill and the impending arrival of anti-segregation volunteers across the South—or, as Senator John Stennis of Mississippi called them, "agitators"—the Ku Klux Klan was experiencing a dramatic increase in its membership—reportedly, the Klan now had over fifty thousand active members, with Birmingham having more than any other city.

CHAPTER 37

Hoss Bowlin

On the Tour Bus Again

For Hoss, the highlight of each road trip was the local bus tour and the chance to learn some little tidbits of history about the cities he visited. Knoxville, he discovered, was the home of the Dempsey Dumpster and Mountain Dew, which was originally sold to mix with whiskey and had a hillbilly and an out-house on its label to appeal to the moonshine folks in the hills of Tennessee. He also found out that in a book titled *Inside USA*, published in 1934, John Gunther described Knoxville as the "ugliest city" in America. According to the brochure, that sparked a downtown rejuvenation.

As the bus passed the landmark Tennessee Theatre, Hoss was surprised to see blacks standing in line with whites for tickets to a matinee. In 1963, the theater had been desegregated after demonstrators pointed out the hypocrisy of Knoxville billing itself as an "All-American City" while maintaining sepa-rate public accommodations. Knoxville's downtown lunch counters were also integrated, and it was one of the first Southern cities to hire black policemen.

Hoss enjoyed riding up to Sharp's Ridge, where he could see the Great Smoky Mountains in the distance. But his favorite part of the tour was getting out and walking through the campus of the University of Tennessee. Located in the heart of Knoxville, the university was slightly ahead of other Southern insti-tutions in admitting blacks. Its first black student was enrolled way back in 1952, more than a decade ahead of the University of Alabama (although it was not until June 1964 that a black completed a four-year undergraduate degree at Ten-nessee, and the school's first black athlete did not arrive on campus until 1967).

Of course Hoss wasn't as interested in campus history as he was the coeds hurrying to their summer school classes. An ardent admirer of attractive young women, he thought Knoxville girls were pretty, but not quite as good-looking as the two girls from the Ice Capades who rode with Hoss and a couple of

teammates on the same elevator at their hotel. If he was to believe these teammates, they got lucky with the skaters, and could've gotten free tickets to the
show except that it was at the same time as the Barons vs. Smokies game.

Guess Who's Coming to Dinner

Sullivan walked out of his office and glanced at Hoss, who gave him the
thumbs-up sign, letting him know he was okay to play again that night. It had
been over two months since he'd sat out a game, but no way would he take
himself out of the lineup. His batting average, which had barely jiggled the
meter back in April, was now up to .270. According to Alf Van Hoose of the
News, he was a solid candidate for the Southern League All-Star team...if
the Barons weren't in first on July 5 and hosting the game.

Hoss eyed Stanley Jones approaching his locker. Jones had been pitching
well lately, mostly out of the bullpen, and with a 5–2 record was second only
to Ron Tompkins in wins. Hoss didn't know Jones all that well—they stayed in
different hotels, ate in different restaurants, and didn't chat much at the ballpark or on the bus—but he thought he seemed like a nice quiet guy, who had a
wife and three little kids, and every time he pitched at Rickwood the black fans
cheered like crazy for him.

"I was wondering," said Jones, his voice barely above a whisper, "if you'd like
to come over to my place for dinner on Sunday? My wife's a great cook. My
mom and dad and a few aunts and uncles will be there, too."

The invite caught Hoss totally off-guard. He prided himself on trying to get
along with everybody on the team, but he didn't figure that one of the black
players would extend him such an invitation.

"I don't know if you know that my wife and son got in town last week," said
Hoss. "Are they invited, too?"

"That's why I'm asking," said Jones. "My wife got to talking with your wife
the other night, and thought she was real nice."

Kid Magnet

It was Camera Day at Rickwood—anybody bringing a camera could get into
the ballpark for fifty cents and take pictures of his or her favorite ballplayers
before the game. Judging from the swarm of kids draped over the railing and
clamoring for Hoss, he was the most popular.

Six months earlier when he was lying on his back in the oncology ward
at the Memphis hospital, and the doctor had told him his baseball days were
over, he did a lot of thinking about what the future might hold. With less than

a year's worth of college credit on his transcript, his options were limited. Getting up at 4 a.m. to drive a milk truck, as he'd done in a couple of off-seasons, wasn't appealing. Maybe he could go to work selling shirts and underwear in his father-in-law's clothing store in Paragould, but he knew enough about himself to think retail sales wasn't his calling. Or he could go back and help his dad with the farm, but there again, picking cotton and feeding the pigs held little appeal. What he really wanted to do, other than make the big leagues, was coach. He loved working with kids. In his third year of pro ball in Billings, Montana, he organized a baseball clinic and spent most mornings during home stands working with local kids. His efforts didn't go unnoticed. The Billings City Council awarded him the Youth Inspirational Award for 1962.

"Hey, Hoss," yelled a freckle-faced eight-year-old, "make a funny face."

Hoss made a funny face.

"Mr. Bowlin, can I get a picture of you next to my son?" asked a young mother.

Hoss posed with the youngster, nudging him with his elbow to get him to smile.

And so it went, the rest of the team fulfilling their Camera Day obligation and retreating to the clubhouse, but not Hoss.

"Who else wants a picture?" he asked.

This time he flexed. If it had been Halloween, he probably would have pulled up his shirt and showed the kids the Frankenstein scar running up his stomach.

What a Second Baseman Won't Do for $100

After infield practice, Hoss heard somebody call his name. He turned around, surprised to see Albert Belcher motioning him over.

"Young man, how'd you like to make an extra $50?" asked Belcher.

Given his $600-a-month salary, and the money he owed the hospital in Memphis, he liked the sound of it. "What do I have to do?" he asked.

"It's simple," replied Belcher. "Ride Miss Baron around the park."

Miss Baron was an old mule that Belcher had bought, partially to be the team's mascot but also to poke fun at Finley and his mascot for the A's, a palomino mule named Charlie O.

"When?"

"Tonight, just before the game starts."

"Sign me up," said Hoss.

He figured this would be an easy fifty bucks. He'd been around horses growing up, and used to hop on the family's workhorses and ride out into the fields.

"There's no saddle," said Belcher. "Think you can do it bareback?"

"Piece a cake."

"Wanna make another fifty backs?" asked Belcher.

"How?"

"When, or should I say *if*, you bring Miss Baron back to home plate, I'll be up on the roof of the grandstand. The PA guy will make an announcement, and then I'll throw a baseball down to you...and if you catch it in a popcorn box, it's another $50."

"While I'm still on Miss Baron?"

"Yep."

"Cash on the barrelhead?"

Belcher showed him a roll of hundreds.

"What if you make a bad throw?"

"I won't."

A few minutes later, Hoss mounted Miss Baron and whispered in her ear. As the crowd roared, off he rode...down the third-base line to the foul pole, across the outfield, and then clippity-clomping back to home...just as he'd said...a piece of cake.

He waved to the cheering crowd.

As the PA announcer directed everyone's attention to the rooftop, the batboy handed Hoss an empty popcorn box. Belcher inched toward the edge of the roof, waved to the crowd, and peered down. Hoss signaled he was ready.

Belcher gave it a toss, and the ball arched downward toward home plate. Raising the popcorn box, Hoss reached out, his eyes fixed on the flight of the ball...as it sailed right into the box.

And the crowd went wild...especially Madelyn.

After the game, Belcher hand-delivered to Hoss a crisp $100 bill. He put it toward his hospital bill.

CHAPTER 38

Tommie Reynolds

Idiots

After the final game of the series in Knoxville, Tommie Reynolds had a funny feeling about leaving the locker room to walk to the bus. The race-baiters in the crowd had been riding him hard all night. Just to be safe, he grabbed a Louisville Slugger model K55.

Sensing something wasn't right, Sullivan stopped him near the door. "Wait," he instructed. "We'll all go out there together. It'll be safer."

As the team headed out the door, a small mob of white fans stood between the players and the bus. Reynolds clutched his K55 to his chest, exactly as he'd held his M1 rifle during an army inspection.

"Do all those nigger-loving teammates of yours let you sit up front?" one hollered.

Nobody on the team responded.

"Are they taking you back to the zoo, Monkey Boy?"

The platoon of Barons eased past the mob, and then climbed on board the bus, a melee averted. In a few minutes, they would leave Bill Meyer Stadium for the two-hour drive through the sultry Tennessee night to Chattanooga.

Settling into a seat next to Blue Moon, Reynolds glanced out the window. A guy in a T-shirt that looked as if it hadn't been washed since the Great Depression was jumping around and scratching himself like a monkey. Blue Moon and Reynolds ignored him. Maybe it was the same guy who'd thrown olives at Reynolds in left field after he'd hit a home run. A couple of olives had bounced off his side, but he'd kept his eyes focused on home plate . . . just as he'd been instructed.

The Barons had won the last two games of the series, Reynolds hitting homers in both, giving him five for the year, all on the road. At this point in the season, all of the team's players of color—Reynolds, Jones, Campaneris, Rosario, and Huyke—were making significant contributions. Reynolds had no doubt that as soon as Blue Moon settled into the life of pro baseball, he'd be a big help, too.

As the bus pulled out of the parking lot, the dirty-shirt guy was still jumping around like a monkey. "Idiot," mumbled Reynolds.

Pregnancy Test

As Iron Lung rolled south on Highway 11 toward Chattanooga, Reynolds shoved thoughts of the idiot from his mind, thinking instead of his girlfriend, Penny, in Daytona Beach. He hadn't seen her since the end of spring training, and when they'd talked on the phone a couple of nights earlier, she'd told him that she still hadn't gotten her period and was going to the doctor for a test.

He would call her tomorrow from Chattanooga.

If she was pregnant, he knew what they'd do—get married. They were in love. Plus, it was "the right thing to do." But when would they get married? Where?

They both had raised the question of whether they were ready. There'd been all the letters and phone calls during his first season in pro ball at Burlington, as well as the two adventures she'd taken to Bradenton to see him, first when he was there for Instructional League, and then again during spring training. She hadn't told her mother back in Georgia of either of those trips. Proper young women weren't supposed to do that kind of thing.

Sometimes when he was lying in bed, trying to get to sleep after an 0 for 4, he thought about the fact that they barely knew each other. They hadn't even met each other's parents or spent a holiday together. Would it be an issue that she was on her way to earning a college diploma and he had only a high school education? Was she cut out to be a baseball wife? Could she handle all the nights alone? Could she handle moving from town to town as he pursued his career? Would she fit in with the other wives, most of whom were white and not as educated as she was?

When it came to women, Tommie wasn't going to put Rhett Butler out of a job. He'd never had a steady girl, not in high school back in San Diego, and not during his three years in the army. It wasn't that he wasn't good-looking, or smart, or caring. It just hadn't happened. And now that the possibility of jumping headfirst into marriage was as close as a pregnancy test, he wondered if marriage appealed to him because he didn't like being alone every night, and just wanted a wife to take care of him, somebody like his mother, who always had dinner waiting for his dad when he got home from another tough day of picking up other people's garbage. Or was it because he was now living in the

Deep South and felt so disconnected from the world around him? He couldn't even eat in the same restaurants as his teammates, and he'd just had to carry a bat simply to get on the bus. Was all this isolation making him think he needed to be married?

If he did get married, he wouldn't be the only Baron who'd gotten his girl-friend pregnant and leaped into marriage. But he didn't know that. Ballplayers didn't talk about that kind of stuff, at least not Birmingham Baron ballplayers.

It was funny. Despite all the time players spent together—on the bus, in the hotels, in the locker room, in the dugout—their level of communication was superficial. They talked about hitting and pitching and movies and cars and the hot babe sitting behind third base. But in the same way that the dirty-shirt idiot jumping around like a monkey didn't know the first thing about Tommie Reynolds—such as the fact that if those Russian ships hadn't turned around before they got to Cuba, he would have been on the front line, laying his life on the line so idiots could have the right to jump around like monkeys—his teammates didn't know much about him, either. Players didn't talk about the arguments they'd just had with their wives, or the overdraft notice from the bank, or how much they hated their fathers.

Unequal Playing Field

Reynolds slept most of the ride, but approaching Chattanooga he stirred, awak-ened by the conversation in the seat in front of him. Lindblad and Hoss were complaining about their accommodations back in Knoxville—bad TV recep-tion and a broken air conditioner.

Reynolds bit his tongue. He liked Lindblad and Hoss, but he was sure they had no clue about how lousy the accommodations were that their black team-mates had to endure. In the Knoxville boardinghouse where they'd stay, there were no televisions or air-conditioning units...or bathrooms in their rooms. In Macon, they stayed in a flophouse with holes in the walls. In Charlotte, all five black players shared a single room in a boardinghouse.

But in Washington, DC, the U.S. Senate was getting very close to passing a civil rights bill.

The Disabled List

Penny was pregnant. After discussing the options, they decided that she would take a bus to Birmingham as soon as the Barons got off the road. They would get married as soon as possible.

The next day, Reynolds woke up unable to keep anything down, feeling chills and fever. As much as he wanted to suit up that night—he was on a hitting rampage, smashing two towering homers in his last two games—he called Sullivan and told him he was sick and couldn't play. Sullivan got him a doctor's appointment. The diagnosis was pneumonia.

Told by the doctor that Reynolds shouldn't play for at least a week, Sullivan placed him on the ten-day disabled list. Stress-related illnesses and diagnoses were not in vogue in 1964, but a pregnant girlfriend and racial taunting probably hadn't helped him stay healthy. It would be eighteen days before he would play again, not good news for a team struggling to score runs and hold on to their lead.

CHAPTER 39

Bert Campaneris

Don't Get Campy Pissed

In Chattanooga, the Barons and Lookouts split the first two games of the series. The bright spot for the Barons was Campaneris, who collected five hits and three stolen bases in the two games. The pitching, however, wasn't good. In the series opener, Blue Moon gave up seven hits and five runs in only four innings before Sullivan pulled him. (In his first three starts as a pro, Blue Moon had not generated $75,000 of return on Finley's investment: 18 innings pitched, 20 hits, 15 runs, 13 walks, and 18 strikeouts.) Fortunately, the Barons rallied, knocking Fergie Jenkins out of the box again, winning 8–7 in thirteen innings and preventing Blue Moon from taking the loss. In the second game, Lindblad's woes continued—he yielded nine hits and seven runs in only four innings, suffering his fifth straight loss.

In the bottom of the eighth in the series finale, the Barons trailed 6–5. Chattanooga's John Upham, a third-year player from Windsor, Ontario, led off with a single. The next hitter was shortstop Mike Marshall, who was third in the league in batting average. (The next year, he would convert to pitcher and go on to win the Cy Young Award as a reliever for the Dodgers.)

On the mound, reliever Ken Sanders checked Upham at first, and then delivered. Marshall swung, hitting a sharp grounder to Hoss, who momentarily bobbled the ball but recovered in time to flip it to Campy for the force-out just ahead of the sliding Upham.

With no chance to double Marshall, Campaneris leaped to avoid Upham… but it was too late. Coming in high, Upham's spikes caught him just above the knee, ripping his pants and sending him crashing to the ground.

Both players quickly jumped to their feet.

Words were exchanged—and they weren't church-approved words—and at six feet tall, 175 pounds, Upham had a four-inch, twenty-pound advantage over Campy.

Campy took one step back, and then before Upham could react he threw two lightning-quick punches, both shots landing solidly, dropping Upham to his knees...confirming Sullivan's prediction to Bear Bryant regarding the outcome if someone challenged Campy.

Both benches emptied, players sprinting to the middle of the field. Before Campy could hit Upham again, Hoss bear-hugged him from behind, and then they were smothered under a sea of Baron jerseys, protecting them from the swarming Lookout players.

Order was finally restored and the players retreated to their benches. When the umpires ejected Campy, Sullivan argued in vain that Upham had intentionally tried to spike him.

In the top of the ninth, with the Lookouts still leading by one and tempers still on a jagged edge, the Barons took notice as the Lookouts' ace, Fergie Jenkins, came on in relief, despite having pitched two nights earlier. This was his first-ever relief appearance. Not only was he one of the hardest throwers in the leagues, he was also one of the biggest, a six-foot-four, 220-pound specimen. He and Upham had both grown up in Windsor, Ontario.

The Barons' first batter, Santiago Rosario, knew he was about to catch a heater in the ribs...or worse.

Instead, Jenkins struck him out on three pitches. He also struck out the next two hitters, ending the game.

A Fastball to the Head

The Barons returned to Rickwood for a series with the Columbus Yankees. Stepping into the batter's box in the third inning of the second game of a twi-night doubleheader, Campy had all but sewn up the Southern League's player-of-the-month award for June. His batting average was now up to .328, and he was leading the league in five categories—hits, stolen bases, runs, triples, and hit-by-a-pitch. For the month of June, he was hitting .410.

"He's the best prospect in the minor leagues," observed Alf Van Hoose.

The Barons had won the first game of the doubleheader 5–0, Rich Allen pitching a dominating three-hit shutout. On the hill for the second game was Blue Moon, hoping to find his groove.

The Yankees' pitcher, Don Semon, a right-hander who threw as hard as anyone in the league, got his sign from the catcher—fastball. The book on pitching Campy, who leaned out over the plate with a crouched stance, was hard stuff, up and in, and to try to jam him and not let him beat the ball into the ground—with his wheels, he'd beat it out.

Because he crowded the plate, Campy frequently got hit. During his first two seasons, he'd been beaned twice, the second one sending him to the hospital, although he was back on the field the next day. His attitude was that he'd survived an escape from Castro's Cuba on a fishing boat, so he knew that playing baseball in America held few genuine perils.

When he'd first arrived in Birmingham, he admitted to being scared. Teammates had told him about Birmingham's reputation. During the first month, as he faltered at the plate, he also struggled emotionally. After games, afraid of getting attacked, he ran the five blocks from Rickwood to his boardinghouse. He missed his family back in Cuba, his heart filled with the aching loneliness of a stranger in a foreign land, forced to deal with a language he hadn't mastered. If he tried to go home to Cuba, he knew he risked imprisonment. He worried about his parents and brothers and sisters, and whether something bad was happening to them because of him. But as his batting average began to rise, so did his spirits. He liked playing for Sullivan, and it helped that he had two Spanish-speaking teammates. It also helped that he was a fan favorite at Rickwood. Every night, fans chanted when he stepped to the plate:

"Campy...Campy...Campy."

Semon went into his windup and let fly. As soon as the ball left his hand, he knew it was off-target—too high, too inside. Campy froze.

"Ohhhhh!" screamed Semon, his voice echoing throughout the park.

The ball slammed into the left side of Campy's face, inches from his eye. Down he went, writhing in the dirt.

By the time Sullivan and the Baron trainer, Fred Posey, reached him, he was unconscious.

As teammates huddled around him, an eerie silence filled the stands.

Campy quickly regained consciousness, moaning. The pain was excruciating. "Somebody call an ambulance," ordered Sullivan.

Semon peeked his head through the crowd of players. He was ashen-faced. Everybody knew it wasn't intentional. Seeing Campy's bloodied face, he retreated.

In minutes, an ambulance arrived. Campy was eased onto a stretcher and lifted into the back. General Manager Glynn West climbed in with him. More than anybody else, it had been West who had gone out of his way to make Campy's stay in Birmingham as comfortable as possible, taking him shopping, giving him rides, helping him with his English.

"Where shall we take him?" asked the paramedic.

"University Hospital," replied West.

The paramedic issued a puzzled look. "They don't take Negroes there," he said.

"I don't give a damn," retorted West as the ambulance left the field. "Take him there anyway."

Hospital Visit

Approaching Campy's room in the University of Alabama–Birmingham Hospital, Sullivan carried a white paper bag in his big left hand.

For the first time ever, the hospital had admitted a person of color. When the ambulance carrying Campy had arrived at the emergency entrance, General Manager West summoned Dr. Joseph Hosford, the director of emergency services at the hospital and a friend. Dr. Hosford explained that the hospital didn't accept blacks.

"But we're going to break that rule," he said.

Slowly, Sullivan entered Campy's room, holding the white bag behind his back. He was surprised to find his star shortstop sitting up and smiling. Diagnosed with a hairline fracture of the cheekbone and a mild concussion, Campy had been lucky. Baseball, as they say, is a game of inches, and so, too, was Campy's fate—if the ball had hit him an inch higher, he would've lost an eye...or worse. As it was, Campy would be leaving the hospital the next day.

"I play mañana," he declared.

Those weren't exactly the doctor's orders—he'd prescribed a week's rest.

With Tommie Reynolds already on the disabled list, Sullivan did want Campy back in the lineup mañana, but he had to follow doctor's orders. He knew how tough his little shortstop was, and that when he did return, he'd still crowd the plate, he'd still slide hard stealing bases, and he'd still hang tough on double plays.

Glancing at the tray of uneaten hospital food, Sullivan pulled the white bag from behind his back and handed it to Campy, who quickly opened it and smiled wide.

"Bueno, bueno!" he exclaimed. "Hamburgee."

In Birmingham they love the governor.

—Lynyrd Skynyrd, "Sweet Home Alabama"

PART VI

THE SEASON

July

League Standings, July 1

	W	L	GB
Birmingham	45	27	
Lynchburg	42	33	4½
Macon	39	32	5½
Charlotte	38	34	7
Knoxville	37	38	9½
Chattanooga	36	38	10
Columbus	31	42	14½
Asheville	25	49	21

CHAPTER 40

Birmingham

Belcher Concerned

Albert Belcher was worried. Even though there still had been no incidents at Rickwood, a racial tension still blanketed Birmingham. With the civil rights bill expected to be passed by Congress within days and signed into law by President Johnson, a backlash in Birmingham was feared . . . and predicted.

He wasn't foolish enough to believe that the Barons' first-place standing had dissuaded the Ku Klux Klan or any of the thousands of people in his city who believed with everything in their hearts that integration was wrong. In speaking at Rotary clubs and chamber of commerce breakfasts, Belcher heard their anger. He heard it when he talked to his friends on the Mules; he heard it from Birmingham's old-money gentry in Mountain Park. He worried that a backlash would erupt in Birmingham, where editorial after editorial criticized the impending passage of the bill—and what better symbol was there than the Barons, the new model for how integration was supposed to work? A few well-placed sticks of dynamite could blow everything he'd worked for to smithereens. He ordered extra security.

Governor Wallace Stirs the Pot

Bull Connor had been the face of segregation in 1963, but with Bull's removal from office, George Wallace took over that distinction in 1964. In his surprisingly successful presidential campaign, Wallace repeatedly accused the Johnson administration, including Attorney General Robert Kennedy, of cramming its agenda down the throats of "the will of the people." He predicted a quick repeal for the bill.

He promised that as governor of Alabama he would do nothing to enforce the Civil Rights Act, and that included any attempts to desegregate schools. The "racial mixing" of children, the Jim Crow crowd believed, would eventually lead to interracial marriage and the "ruination of society." Threats to block this integration when school resumed in late August were endless.

Wallace also vowed to close all of the state's parks if attempts were made to integrate them. The closure of Alabama's parks, however, wouldn't impact the Barons—Belcher owned Rickwood. But more than the fear of integrated parks was the concern that passage of a civil rights bill would lead to integrated rest-rooms…which would lead, according to the Jim Crow theory of hygiene, to the spread of venereal diseases.

Missing Civil Rights Workers

The disappearance of three civil rights workers in Mississippi—Andy Good-man and Michael Schwerner of New York, and James Chaney of Mississippi—was headline news in Birmingham. A large search party, including FBI agents and a hundred sailors from a base near Meridian, was organized to comb the bayous, gullies, swamps, and red hillsides near Philadelphia, Mississippi, where they were last seen. But so far, all the searchers had gotten for their efforts were bad sunburns and a few encounters with copperheads and rattle-snakes. To cover the story, the *Birmingham News* sent reporter Don Brown to Mississippi. He compared what was happening in Mississippi to Birmingham:

> Like Birmingham last summer, Philadelphia has been caught with an ugly face in the world spotlight. Birmingham need only put itself in their place for a moment. Those who know something here in Philadelphia—if anyone does—are afraid of a few, just as those Bir-mingham people are who might help solve the church bombing. But you can't blame them. Their homes might be burned, their children run down in the streets.

Residents of Philadelphia, borrowing a page from the Birmingham play-book, blamed the disappearance on outside agitators. A local insurance man, who chose to remain anonymous, wrote:

> All these "righters" came here trying to save us. Funny, we've been getting along fine for a long time. I supposed if someone would lose his temper and kill three or four of these Negroes, that would keep them in their place.

Mississippi politicians also weighed in on the missing "righters," including Senator James Eastland:

I think those people are voluntarily missing. I'm pretty sure we'll eventually discover this is all a Communist plot to stir up trouble.

The events in Mississippi did not go unnoticed by Tommie Reynolds. In a way, he and all of the Barons, black and white, were civil rights workers. They hadn't volunteered to work for the cause, but it wasn't a stretch to think that whatever hatred inspired the locals in Mississippi to cause the disappearance of the three young men could work in similar ways in Birmingham against the Barons. Reynolds and his teammates were part of the perfect symbol—the great American pastime—and by the reckoning of the segregation hard-liners, they were defiling the purity of America's game.

Reynolds understood that next time, instead of howling like a monkey and jumping around like an idiot, the dirty-shirt guy could bring a rifle to the park. If these people had been vicious enough to bomb a church in broad daylight, and blow up a preacher's house on Christmas night, what would stop them from dynamiting a baseball grandstand? Or what would prevent them from snatching a couple of the black players off the street and making them disappear like those three missing civil rights workers in Mississippi?

The New Law of the Land

Belcher worried that the disappearance of the civil rights workers in Mississippi was a harbinger of a more violent resistance to the dismantling of segregation, a campaign that could eventually have a direct impact on the Southern League. With all the certainty of a life spent in Alabama, he believed that the enactment of a civil rights bill could exacerbate the violence.

On July 2, the House joined the Senate and gave its approval of the bill; all that was needed now for it to be enacted into law was President Johnson's signature. Across the South, calls went out for flags to be flown at half-mast. Staunch segregationists worried that Johnson would sign the bill on July Fourth, and to them, that was treason. An editorial in the Birmingham News expressed the view of many:

The president should not tie his signature of the bill with the day commemorating establishment of this as a free nation. The two events—the signing of a civil rights bill and Independence Day—have nothing in common.

Sensing a potential problem, President Johnson signed the bill on the afternoon of July 3 rather than the Fourth, thus avoiding any conflict with traditional celebrations across the country. Reaction was immediate. The NAACP urged blacks to test it as soon as possible—to go into hotels and restaurants and demand to be served. Opponents wasted no time in declaring they would challenge the bill's constitutionality. In Montgomery, Governor Wallace refused to participate in a conference on implementing the bill. In Washington, DC, Republican presidential candidate Senator Barry Goldwater warned of a "civil rights explosion."

Initial Reaction in Birmingham

Mayor Albert Boutwell dodged giving his approval of the law. "The city has made no recommendation, either for compliance or non-compliance," he said. "This is a Federal law and there are private businesses involved. It is not our business to enforce the law or to tell private businesses how it must operate or whom it must serve."

The immediate reaction in Birmingham was better than many expected. No incidents were reported at any of the nine restaurants and four downtown movie theaters that blacks entered around noon in small groups. The Birmingham Hotel Association issued a statement that its hotels would comply.

This unexpected compliance earned kudos, sort of, in a *News* editorial titled "A Good Beginning":

> This newspaper opposes the Civil Rights bill as a measure of invasion of individual rights far too sweeping in scope. It is the product of political pressure unparalleled in recent years. We can only hope that in time public opinion will bring changes. In the meantime, let us keep the peace.

The Backlash Begins

A few days after the passage of the Civil Rights Act, six black men entered McClellan's, a variety store in Bessemer, not far from where Stan Jones grew up. They took a seat at the lunch counter and ordered sandwiches. The assistant store manager told them they wouldn't be served.

When the men refused to leave, the assistant manager called the police, as well as a couple of his friends. Within minutes, eight white men, all carrying baseball bats, entered the store. The assistant manager locked the door behind them. For the next ten minutes, as a loudspeaker across the street blared "Dixie," the men with bats flailed away as the black men tried to fend off the savage attack. The melee knocked merchandise to the floor. Blood flew. The police finally arrived, but remained in their cars, parked outside.

When the attack was finally over, two black men were in the hospital. No arrests were made. The next day, a dozen blacks attempted to register to vote in Birmingham but retreated after being threatened by a group of angry whites. Although these attacks received scant coverage by the local media, a flurry of letters to the editor unanimously opined that the bill was not worth the paper it was written on. A. C. Brasher of Birmingham wrote:

The bill has been passed, but the right to be respected has to be earned.

The passage of the bill brought Bull Connor out of the woodwork. He promised that he would attend the Democratic National Convention and, just as he'd done in 1948, lead Alabama delegates in a walkout to protest the bill's passage.

One indirect impact of the bill's passage on the Barons was a complaint filed by the white owner of Ollie's Barbeque in Birmingham, a popular restaurant where blacks had always been refused service even though the restaurant was located in a black neighborhood. Several times Lindblad had stopped in to pick up an order of ribs for his black teammates. When ordered to be in compliance with the law, the owner sued.

"It makes no sense that Negroes can't even eat in their own neighborhood," concluded Lindblad.

Ollie's wasn't the only restaurant refusing to comply with the law. Defiance quickly spread. Restaurant owners and innkeepers across the South refused service to blacks... just as they always had. In Atlanta, restaurant owner (and future governor) Lester Maddox defiantly stood in front of the front door of his restaurant, Pickrick, holding an ax handle to block entry. When a lower court reiterated the order to integrate, he continued to refuse. With tears streaming down his cheeks, he handed out ax handles to supporters, read from the Bible, and vowed to take his fight all the way to the Supreme Court.

And then he padlocked his restaurant.

President Johnson vowed to enforce the new law. In response, Maddox turned his restaurant into a Goldwater for President campaign office.

The backlash intensified. On a rural highway in northern Georgia, a carload of whites drove up behind a car carrying three black men and fired two unprovoked shotguns blasts through the rear window, killing Lemuel Penn, the director of five Washington, DC, vocational schools. A lieutenant colonel in the army reserve, Penn was returning home from a training session at Fort Benning. (Arrests were eventually made, but an all-white jury acquitted the defendants.)

On the same day of that shooting, a rabbi in Mississippi was attacked walking down a street in Hattiesburg, while in Greenwood, a black Baptist church used for meetings by activists in the Student Nonviolent Coordinating Committee was burned to the ground as a fire truck called to the scene stood idly by.

In Birmingham, Jonathan McPherson, a chemistry teacher making $522 a month at Mills College, passed the physical and written tests for certification to become the first black police officer in Birmingham, a job paying $380 a month. He was quickly ruled ineligible because a background check revealed he lived in Hueytown, a community outside the city limits, even though several white officers didn't live within the city limits, either.

Birmingham Responds to the Backlash in the North

As race riots spread in the North, the Birmingham press seemed—if not to gloat—to at least find a measure of redemption in publicizing the demonstrations. The latest riot in Jersey City was greeted with a large, bold headline in the *News*: MOB OF NEGROES ATTACKS WHITES AND POLICE IN JERSEY RACE EXPLOSION.

Whites in Birmingham believed that the Johnson administration's sympathy for the civil rights movement had somehow authorized black people to take the law into their own hands and deny the civil rights of "innocent citizens." An editorial in the *News* accused the Johnson administration of not understanding the effects of the bitterness and resentment sweeping the country. City after city, it noted, was being subjected to mob violence and riots in the name of "civil rights demonstrations," and allowing the "civil rights to be taken away from white people by means of riots or mob violence."

As proof of this hypocrisy, an editorial in the *News* pointed out that the FBI was now offering a substantial reward for information about the three missing civil rights workers in Mississippi, and yet providing no assistance for help in apprehending blacks allegedly "responsible for the lawlessness burning American cities."

The *News* did not report that thousands of black "rioters" had been arrested.

CHAPTER 41

Haywood Sullivan

First Place Every Day of June

June had been a good month for Sullivan and the Barons—they'd led the league every day, and still held a three-game lead on July 5, giving them the right to host the Southern League All-Star Game. Several players were playing at an All-Star clip: Campy was on pace to be the league's MVP; Ken Sanders was 7–0 and almost automatic coming out of the bullpen; Hoss had turned into a clutch hitter, and no second baseman in the Southern League had better hands or could turn two quicker; Stan Jones was a surprise, now leading the team with eight wins as a long reliever; and at the plate, Reynolds, although he was still on the disabled list, was hitting over .300; with Rosario, Meyer, Norton, Stahl, and Huyke also providing, if not Murderers' Row power, punch in the middle of the order.

Still, Sullivan had concerns—mainly his pitching. Lindblad had lost five in a row; Seitz was struggling to keep the ball in the county, let alone over the plate; Tompkins seemed to have lost something off the fastball that had struck out thirteen in a game in May; and Blue Moon was a mess. In his five starts in June, he'd averaged a walk per inning. The swagger he'd arrived with had been replaced by a droopy-shouldered shuffle. Sully worried that all the hype had put too much pressure on him. In a conference call with the A's brass, the idea was floated that the best option would be to send him down to Lewiston.

"I think we should at least give him a couple more starts here in Birmingham before we do anything drastic," said Sullivan.

It was decided that Bill Posedel, the A's minor-league pitching instructor, would meet up with the team and see if he could figure out Blue Moon's problem.

Nobody doubted his talent. But even the reporters covering the team were questioning whether he belonged in AA. Alf Van Hoose of the *News* wrote:

209

His performance has got to cast a distinctive shadow on his future career as a Baron. He has been too wild recently to be a winner. With nine other pitchers available, Manager Haywood Sullivan cannot afford to keep starting him if he can't find the plate consistently.

Nervous About Finley

Haywood Sullivan appreciated Charlie Finley for giving him a start to his managing career, and for generously assigning him to AA Birmingham, where he was the youngest manager in the Southern League by almost ten years. He also appreciated that Finley was serious about turning Kansas City into a winner—the signings of Blue Moon and Catfish Hunter were evidence of that. But Sullivan was an old-school kind of baseball man, and shook his head at some of Finley's gimmicks—orange baseballs; Charlie O the mule; sleeveless uniforms; stints as a batboy.

Still, he could live with all that. What bothered him was the nagging suspicion that Finley was going to come swooping in again, just as he'd done with Grzenda, and take away the heart of his team, specifically Bert Campaneris and Ken Sanders. If he did, then it would speak volumes about whether Finley's proclaimed intention of supplying Birmingham with a winning team was honest.

Logically, at least from Sullivan's viewpoint, it wouldn't make any sense to raid the Barons and put a dagger to their pennant hopes. If Finley needed players in Kansas City because of injuries, which was always a possibility, he had players available on the AAA team in Dallas. Already twenty-five games out of first, Dallas was in last place in the Pacific Coast League. If they lost a player or three, it would have no impact on a team going nowhere. And if Finley didn't like what Dallas had to offer, he could dip down to any of the A's four A-league teams. All of them were either in last place or next to last. Of all the teams in the A's organization, from top to bottom, only the Barons were in a pennant race.

They were also the only team playing in a city as potentially explosive as Birmingham.

But maybe Sullivan was just being a little too paranoid. The A's were also in last place, twenty-one games out of first and plunging deeper. Surely Finley wouldn't jeopardize the Barons' chances just to decorate the A's coffin.

A Victory for Budweiser

With the score tied 3–3 in the bottom of the ninth against Columbus, Ron Tompkins was due up with a runner on first, no outs. He glanced at Sullivan in the third-base coach's box, expecting him to signal for a pinch hitter. In the bullpen, Sanders was warming up. Instead, Sullivan motioned for Tompkins to meet him halfway between third and home.

"How do you feel?" asked Sullivan, knowing that in the history of the game, no pitcher had ever admitted to the manager that he was exhausted and wanted out of the game.

"Still feel strong," replied Tompkins, who'd struck out six and retired the last twelve hitters in a row, his best outing in a couple of weeks.

"Must be the beer," said Sullivan.

Tompkins grinned. Earlier that day, on Sullivan's advice, he'd drunk a couple of Budweisers at home with his lunch—not exactly standard training procedure. Over the last month, the heat and humidity had taken a toll on the string-bean Californian. He'd lost ten pounds, weight he didn't have to lose. Sullivan thought that beer might help prevent the weight loss. (The era of team nutritionists and health trainers was still far in the future.)

"Okay, sacrifice him to second," Sullivan whispered.

Returning to the plate, Tompkins felt good. Few things bolster a pitcher's confidence as much as a manager's faith.

Settling into the batter's box, Tompkins tried to stay loose. He'd bunted thousands of times in practice; he knew the proper technique—get square to the pitcher, extend the bat, elevate the meat end slightly above the handle, grip it loosely, and then, on contact, give with the pitch. But in practice, the pitcher was usually throwing lollipops. In a game, with the ball blazing toward home, it wasn't so easy.

On the first pitch, just as he'd done all those times in practice, Tompkins laid down a perfect sacrifice bunt, advancing the runner to second.

Two hitters later, Larry Stahl drilled a single to left, scoring the runner to win it for the Barons.

With the victory, Tompkins's record now stood at 8–1 ... and 1–0 on Bud. He wondered if he could get Sullivan to recommend a Budweiser clause in his next contract. Probably not ... he was only nineteen.

Snake Power

Sullivan's report to the front office on his twenty-three-year-old center fielder, Bill Snake Meyer, was positive. Now in his fourth year of pro ball after signing out of high school in Hawthorne, California (an LA suburb), Meyer was a pleasant surprise for Sullivan. The previous year, when Sullivan had been a player-coach at Portland in AAA, Meyer had been a teammate. But he hit an anemic .191 with only two homers, and seemed overmatched. The high hopes the organization had held for him in 1962 when he hit .289 with eighteen home runs in only a hundred games at Lewiston had withered.

Going into spring training, Sullivan doubted if Meyer was even ready for AA. But then he hit shots all over the yard in Daytona and earned a spot with the Barons. Still, Sullivan didn't insert him in the lineup on opening day. But now, with two months left in the season, Meyer led the team in homers with eleven. Two nights earlier, he had earned himself the $50 bonus from Mr. Belcher, the fourth time he'd hit a homer over the BELCHER LUMBER sign atop the right-field grandstands at Rickwood. With his wife expecting their second child, the money would come in handy.

Sullivan had worked with the slender-built Meyer on developing a short, compact swing. It helped that he had great coordination and strong wrists, and he attacked the ball.

"But we need to put about ten more pounds on him," he said. "It'll make him stronger and not as prone to injuries as he has been in the past."

Sullivan wasn't the only one impressed by Meyer's power. In an article titled "The Thin Man Is a Slugger," *News* sports editor Benny Marshall labeled his long blasts as "distinctive" and "rockets." He predicted a bright future:

Meyer is tall and thin, a frail-looking sort of boy who seems to have no place at all in the homerun business. He ought to be beating out bunts, which he is swift enough to do. But he isn't a bunter. He's a boomer. Fans need to be advised to get out and see him soon. The Southern League can't keep him.

Sullivan knew that Finley subscribed to the Birmingham papers. He just hoped that Finley didn't take this column as his cue to call up Meyer.

CHAPTER 42

Blue Moon Odom

A Last Chance to Shine?

With home games against Asheville and Lynchburg slated before for the All-Star Game, the Barons had a chance to pad their lead. They would start the home stand with a doubleheader against last-place Asheville, with Blue Moon scheduled to start the first game, Lindblad the nightcap. With only one win between them the whole month of June, Odom and Lindblad knew that their performances would be critical in determining their fates for the rest of the year, if not their careers. Pitching coach Bill Posedel was in town to watch.

In the first inning, Blue Moon walked the first two hitters. After a quick trip to the mound by Sullivan to settle him down, he served up a hanging curve to Asheville's first baseman Dave Kwiatkowski, who bombed it deep over the left-field fence—and just like that the Barons trailed 3–0.

Blue Moon gave up another run in the third, and then was finally relieved in the fourth after issuing two more walks, giving him a total of six bases on balls in four innings. He also hit a batter and committed a balk.

Returning to the dugout, he took a seat at the end of the bench and stared off into space. Less than a month earlier, he was the talk of baseball, the poster boy for cockiness and a grand future. Every article written about him played up the fact he'd received the largest bonus ever given a black athlete, and in his first pro game, his hometown fans had gone totally nuts when he struck out the side in the first inning.

But his control had vanished like a morning mist. Whether it was because of the pressure, or flawed mechanics, or the fact that pro hitters wouldn't swing at pitches that Georgia high school kids flailed at hopelessly, Blue Moon was on the cusp of an eclipse that might conclude with an embarrassing trip to Lewiston, Idaho.

Fortunately, for the fourth time in a row the Barons rallied after he was pulled from the game. Down to their last out, the Barons watched Rosario drill a two-run homer to lift them to a dramatic win.

The other good news was that Campy was back in the lineup, taking up right where he left off before the beaning, legging out a triple and turning two spectacular double plays.

In the second game of the doubleheader, Lindblad hurled a complete game four-hitter, his first win after five straight losses. His performance boosted the Barons' lead to six games, the largest of the year.

In the victorious Baron clubhouse, Blue Moon sat in front of his locker, trying to put on a happy face. Sullivan sat down next to him.

"Keep your head up," he said, and then informed him that Posedel would start working with him the next day.

Blue Moon nodded. Until a month ago, he had experienced nothing but success. Everything had come naturally. At Ballard-Hudson High, Coach Slocum had basically just turned him loose. Why tinker with success? But now he'd just been told he needed special instruction. He'd already lost three more games in a month than he had in his whole high school career. He missed home, his mother's cooking, and the sweet kisses of his girlfriend, Perrie. Perhaps more than anything, he couldn't stand the thought of letting down Mr. Finley, the man who'd shown all the faith in him and made him "a rich young man."

Pitching School

Bill Posedel stood next to Blue Moon on the bullpen mound, providing a crash course on the pitching fundamentals normally taught during spring training. While his teammates had been endlessly drilling on the art of the follow-through and covering first base in Daytona, Blue Moon had been sitting in math class back in Macon, daydreaming about his pro career.

Posedel's plan was not to make any major overhauls with Blue Moon's mechanics. The young pitcher had the one attribute that not even a great pitching coach can teach—a cannon for an arm. Fundamentally, his motion, release, and follow-through were all fluid and sound. During the week he'd spent with the big-league team prior to joining the Barons—something no other player in the organization had gotten to do—the organization decided the best strategy was to basically leave him alone the first month, to let him sink or swim with the obvious talent he possessed.

But Posedel knew that lots of kids entering pro ball had great tools. The difference between those who made it and those who didn't was often what was between the ears and inside the heart. Nobody doubted Blue Moon's competitive fire. But some now questioned whether he could handle the mental strain.

Posedel and Sullivan agreed that at this early stage of his career, Blue Moon was a thrower and not yet a pitcher. In high school he didn't have to worry about setting up a hitter—how to come inside and then go away, how to change speeds, how to attack a hitter's weakness. All he had to do in high school was rock and fire.

Sullivan's experience as a big-league catcher had exposed him to the craft of pitching, but he was under instructions from the front office not to tinker with Blue Moon's delivery, and to let him do things naturally . . . at least to start with. The A's also wanted a consistent voice in working with him . . . they didn't want Sullivan telling him one thing and then Posedel something else. Breaking into the game was hard enough—being away from home for the first time, meeting new people, learning how not to overindulge, figuring out how to sleep on a bus. Loading down a nineteen-year-old with seventy-three techniques for holding a curveball, on top of everything else, could overload his circuits.

On this day, Posedel started with a few of the basics. The first drill required Blue Moon to go through his motion and then prepare to field his position.

In his first five games, he had failed to field several balls hit back toward him.

The next drill was designed to teach him how to hold a runner on first and to improve his pickoff move. Having pitched eight no-hitters in high school, Blue Moon had never had to worry too much about holding runners on. Now, in thirty-seven innings pitched in pro ball, he'd had forty runners reach first by hits or bases on balls. Out of those forty, eleven had tried to steal, and ten succeeded.

After watching Blue Moon work on the drills he'd shown him, Posedel shared his observations with Sullivan. "Geez, what an arm," he said. "I'm not going to suggest anything that will take away any of the confidence he has throwing the ball. I might be able to help him a little on the finesse things, but considering his background and the limited competition he's had, he surprised me with all the things he does so well already. He's got that great competitive drive. I truly believe he's going to be okay. No . . . better than okay."

What's a Brother Have to Do?

While Posedel was working with Blue Moon, Stanley Jones wandered across the outfield, shagging balls during batting practice. Out of the corner of his eye, he spotted Posedel finishing up with Blue Moon and signaling for Paul Seitz to join him in the bullpen. Jones couldn't help but feel jealous. This was Posedel's second visit with the team, and he still hadn't said word one to

Jones...and there was no indication he planned to work with him before leaving town. For minor-league pitchers in the A's farm system, parsing comments from Posedel was a peek into what the future held.

Jones thought he deserved attention. He was tied for the most wins with Tompkins, while Blue Moon had only one win and had stunk up the joint in his last four starts. And in Seitz's last appearance, he had given up four runs in only one inning. Between them, Blue Moon and Seitz had seventy-three walks in eighty-nine innings, throwing with all the finesse of a cement mixer. Jones had thirteen walks in seventy-eight innings.

Jones knew he didn't have the overpowering fastball that Blue Moon and Seitz possessed. But he had control and a ball that moved. And from a marketing standpoint, his hometown connection brought cheers every time Sullivan summoned him from the bullpen.

But he felt underappreciated.

Red Davis, his manager the previous year at Rocky Mount in the Carolina League and now the manager at Macon, didn't skimp on praise for Jones. "I wish I had him on our team," he said. "If I did, we'd be in first place instead of Birmingham."

No player on the Barons was more connected to Birmingham than Jones: His mother had worshipped at the 16th Street Baptist Church as a child; he'd sat on the other side of the chicken-wire fence watching the Barons as a boy. He wanted to be treated fairly. Why wasn't he starting? Why hadn't Posedel said jack to him?

Although Jones didn't think of himself as a civil rights pioneer in the manner of Montgomery bus boycotters or Freedom Riders, he was aware of the importance of his role as a Baron in rolling back the tide of prejudice. When his family and friends came to watch him play, they didn't have to sit behind the chicken wire. Although his people had never enjoyed the guarantees of the Constitution and the Bill of Rights, at Rickwood they now glimpsed how the benefits of genuine citizenship could work.

He felt proud of his contribution. With the Barons in first place, boosted by the efforts of Campaneris, Reynolds, Rosario, Huyke, and himself, Birmingham's black community, which for years had abandoned the team, felt a nudge back toward America's national pastime. Unmistakably, baseball was the most visible of Birmingham's attempts to free itself from its racist past.

But as Jones watched Posedel put his arm around Seitz, he wondered if the A's considered him nothing more than a token offering to the black fans in Birmingham. He liked Blue Moon personally, and was happy he'd gotten all that money, but considering their contributions to the team it didn't seem fair. Not even close.

A Manly Opponent

Blue Moon's opponent for his next start against Lynchburg would be Manly Johnston, who along with Campy was the leading candidate for MVP of the Southern League. He led the league in wins with ten, including two victories over the Barons. But it wasn't just his pitching—he also had five homers. Nobody would've been surprised if he'd been discovered selling Cracker Jack between innings.

Blue Moon remained undaunted. "Nobody is going to harm my fastball," he proclaimed, confident his extra work with Posedel had cured his control problems. "I'll be buzzing 'em."

If he needed added incentive, he got it in an article in the *News* headlined NEW BLUE MOON FACES JOHNSTON. It talked about his work with Posedel, but added that there'd been "cynical whispers that Charlie Finley paid $75,000 for a wild softballer."

Every pitcher in the league knew about Blue Moon's big money, and every pitcher in the league wanted to show him up. That was especially true for Manly Johnston, an Alabama native who'd already been named the starting pitcher for the Southern League All-Stars against the Barons in four days. Now in his seventh year of pro ball, he'd signed with the White Sox out of Auburn University, where he also played football. Initially signed as a hitter, he played his first three years as an outfielder before the White Sox decided to make him a pitcher. Now, at the age of twenty-five with a wife and kids, he was at a crossroads in his career. Seven years of riding crummy buses and scraping by on $5-a-day meal money had grown tiresome. In the off-seasons, he had continued his schooling at Auburn, and was now within a semester of a degree in business administration. With the year he was having, he figured that if he didn't get called up, it would be time to hang 'em up. He hoped a victory over the highly touted Blue Moon would compel the White Sox to call him up. As far as the Barons were concerned, it would be good riddance. To a man, they thought Johnston was a big, obnoxious bully. In his previous start against them, he'd knocked down Tommie Reynolds every time he came to bat. Reynolds suspected it was racial. But he could not test Manly now because he was still on the disabled list.

Another Flop

Once again, Blue Moon walked the first hitter, who scored the first of two Lynchburg runs in the inning. Then it got worse. The Lynsox sent him to the showers after six innings—seven runs, eight hits, six walks, and only two strikeouts.

Manly Johnston pitched a six-hit, complete-game victory, 7–2, moving Lynch-burg back into second place and cutting the Barons' lead to four and a half.

After the game, Sullivan and Posedel huddled, discussing Blue Moon's immediate future. Once again, the idea to send him down to Lewiston was on the table. His record was now 1–3, and if the Barons hadn't rallied in his other failed starts, it would have been 1–6. The bases on balls troubled Sullivan most.

"Let's give him one more start," he lobbied.

Posedel reluctantly agreed. "But this has to be his last chance," he said.

Look Out for Lynchburg

The next night, Lynchburg swept a doubleheader, moving to within two and a half games of the Barons. In the first game, the winning run was driven in on a pinch-hit sacrifice fly by—who else?—Manly Johnston. In the second game, the Barons managed only two bloop singles, giving them a total of eleven hits in their three losses to Lynchburg. Tompkins, named to start the All-Star Game against Johnston, suffered his third loss in his last four decisions.

"I've been saying it for a couple months," said Sullivan after the game. "I think Lynchburg is our toughest challenger. But we're not pushing the panic button. It'll help when we get Tommie Reynolds back tomorrow."

Reynolds did come back for the series finale, and the Barons won 4–2 behind a complete game by Lindblad, his second victory in a row. Although Reynolds went 0 for 3 in his first game after an eighteen-day layoff, he hit the ball hard twice. He was also hit by a pitch. Campy continued to show he was fully recovered, too, lining two more hits and stealing a base.

But for Blue Moon, the world that had seemed so impossibly delicious a month ago was souring fast.

CHAPTER 43

Hoss Bowlin

A Risky Prank

"Quick, Droopsy, here he comes," whispered Hoss. "Hide it."

Three hours before the opening pitch of the All-Star Game, Paul Seitz fumbled to hide a letter to Blue Moon from his girlfriend back in Macon. Hoss knew it was from her because of the Macon postmark and the lipstick imprint on the envelope.

Blue Moon strode briskly to his locker and searched for his mail. "Has the mail arrived yet?" he asked.

"No," answered Hoss. "You expecting something?"

"Maybe."

Blue Moon was anxious to hear from Perrie. With no phone in his room at the boardinghouse, he depended on her letters as a lifeline home. Blue Moon hadn't seen Perrie since she'd bid him that tearful good-bye in the parking lot of Luther Williams Field in Macon five weeks before. Her parents had steadfastly said no to her visiting Birmingham, and it was still another couple of weeks before the Barons were scheduled to play in Macon again.

His shoulders sagged. It was hard enough to be pitching worse than a bad haircut, but to get shut out at mail call only added to his blues.

As the players dressed for the game, Hoss and Seitz hovered near Blue Moon's locker. They began to sing an off-key rendition of "Blue Moon."

Blue Moon studied them. Were they making fun of him? If so, they might regret it. He'd said it many times in high school: Disrespect me and you better be ready to go to fist city.

He was still trying to figure out the give-and-take of baseball's banter. He was also trying to figure out white-guy humor. Until he'd joined the Barons, he'd lived exclusively in a black world. So now, with everything else going on in his new universe, he was trying to get a handle on the nuances of an alternative culture.

Hiding Blue Moon's mail was a risky prank. Even though Hoss and Seitz had been around him every day for five weeks, they barely knew him. Away from the ballpark, they went their way and he went his. They'd heard Stanley Jones talk about a jazz club in town...maybe he went there. Or maybe he went back to wherever he was staying and counted his money. Or maybe he got behind the wheel of that candy-apple-red Galaxy and went looking for trouble. They'd watched him spray rooster tails in the gravel as he zoomed out of the Rickwood parking lot. They knew he had a girlfriend because they'd been sitting on the bus after his first game in Macon and witnessed the tearful good-bye scene.

Hoss knew that messing with a teammate in a slump could be as dangerous as hammering blasting caps. On the other hand, maybe it would loosen him up and let him know they wanted him to be one of the guys. They continued their off-key "Blue Moon" duet:

Blue Moon continued to ignore them.

After waiting a few seconds, Hoss pulled the letter out of his locker. "Oh, look what I just found," he said, dangling the envelope in front of Blue Moon. "Looks like it's from a girl. Do you know any girls?"

Blue Moon reached out and snatched it. "You peckerwoods," he blurted, tearing opening the letter and devouring every word.

An All-Star Buzz

The newspapers were brimming with pictures and stories about the All-Star Game. Even the editorial page hopped on the bandwagon, encouraging fans to attend.

But Albert Belcher, a chronic worrywart, was concerned the crowd would be held down because the game was competing with the televised opening of the Republican Convention in San Francisco.

On the sports page, editor Benny Marshall added his bid for fans to forsake the convention and attend the game, trying to put it into a Birmingham historical perspective:

> Some people might want to station themselves in living rooms to listen to orations opening a Republican Convention, and look at all the funny people. But Rickwood's for me simply because professional baseball of the first-place type is here again, and prospering. Who'd ever have thought it a year ago?

Sitting in the clubhouse after batting practice, Hoss couldn't wait for the game to begin. His brother Jimmy, who'd driven him home from the hospital in the snowstorm, was in town. His father-in-law had flown over in his Cessna, and Madelyn had bought a new dress for the occasion. All the team presidents and league dignitaries would be there. So would the opposing players from the All-Star team. Maybe he'd go up to Manly Johnston and remind him of what a horse's ass he was. But probably not.

All-Star MVP

The crowd arrived early, entertained by a jazz band. Decked out in red, white, and blue bunting, Rickwood had a party-like atmosphere. In the pre-game ceremonies, Southern League president Sam Smith stood at home plate and introduced the assembled presidents of the Southern League teams, each greeted with smatterings of polite applause. He saved Belcher for last.

"...and the man who made all this possible, ladies and gentlemen, Albert Belcher of the Birmingham Barons."

The smattering turned to the thundering sound of a cavalry charge. After the cheering for Belcher died down, Smith continued:

"And now, ladies and gentlemen, please welcome one of the truly great coaches of all time, your own Paul Bear Bryant."

The crowd of 7,252 went nuts. Seated right behind Pat Sullivan and Hank Peters, the Kansas City farm director, Bryant stood and waved, then sat down and resumed devouring his hot dog. The crowd kept cheering, getting even louder when the band behind home plate struck up "Yea, Alabama, Crimson Tide." A line of autograph seekers snaked from the concourse all the way down to Bryant's row.

In the top of the first, the All-Stars scored a run off Tompkins. Coming back to the dugout, he was surprised when Sullivan stopped him and told him that he was done for the night.

In the bottom of the first, Campy led off with a single and stole second. Hoss, who had not gotten a hit off Johnston during the three games he'd faced him in, lined the next pitch into the gap in right center for a stand-up double. He glanced up into the stands where his brother, Madelyn, and her dad were seated. They were jumping around as if John Beresford Tipton had just slipped a million bucks under their door. Hoss scored on a base hit up the middle by Meyer, giving the Barons the lead, 2–1.

Over the next eight innings, a parade of pitchers took the mound (everybody on the staff but Blue Moon and Lindblad), holding the All-Stars to just two more hits and one run. The Barons won 7–2, and although there was no official vote for a game MVP, Hoss got the nod from Van Hoose of the *News*:

Scrappy little Hoss Bowlin showed why he should have been picked to the All-Star team if the Barons weren't leading the league. All he did was get three hits, score two runs, and drive in another two. He and his double-play partner, Bert Campaneris, turned in two twin-killings. This is exactly why the Barons are leading the league and hosted the game.

Big Brother

In the raucous Baron clubhouse after the game, two of the biggest smiles belonged to Tommie Reynolds and Stanley Jones. In only his second game since coming off the disabled list, Reynolds laced two singles and a double. The icing on the cake for Reynolds that evening was knowing that it was also the first Barons' game that Penny, his new bride, had seen him play.

For Jones, it might have been the most fun he'd had at Rickwood since the no-hitter he threw for the Black Barons in 1958. Other than the ovation for Bear Bryant, the loudest cheer came in the seventh inning when he entered the game…and promptly struck out all three hitters he faced, reinforcing his case for promotion back to the starting rotation.

As the players got dressed and headed to the banquet in the Dugout Club under the grandstands, a horde of young autograph seekers waited outside the clubhouse door. Hoss was still inside, taking his time, joined by his older brother Jimmy, a junior at Arkansas State. Eyeing the long scar running up Hoss's chest, Jimmy shook his head in amazement. He remembered helping Hoss to his car after leaving the hospital in Memphis, and how he looked like a ghost. If somebody had asked him what the chance was that Hoss would ever play ball again, Jimmy would've said it was the same as the temperature had been that night—below zero.

The clubhouse door opened slightly and a towheaded eight-year-old shyly peeked inside. Hoss motioned him to enter. Quickly, a dozen other kids swarmed in, too, all of them holding scorecards and scraps of paper, looking as if they'd just snuck into the king's bedroom.

"What position you play?" Hoss asked, signing the towhead's scorecard.

"Pitcher," the boy replied, gazing at Hoss.

"You got a knuckleball?"

The boy looked at him as if he'd just been asked if he'd ever piloted a helicopter.

Off to the side, Jimmy looked admiringly at his brother as Hoss signed all the papers and scorecards thrust in front of him, and then waited patiently for the last boy to file out of the clubhouse, hero-worshipping into the night.

Standing up to leave, Hoss turned to his brother and smiled like a butcher's dog. "That's what makes it great," he said. "It's the kids."

CHAPTER 44

Albert Belcher

The Man

Six-year-old Marc Sullivan, with the same bright blue eyes as his father, sat next to his mom prior to the start of the Barons' game against Charlotte. Pat had driven up from Florida with Marc to spend a few days with Haywood. Their three-year-old twins were staying with Pat's parents back in Lake Worth. Earlier in the season, Pat and Haywood had spent two days driving all over Birmingham looking for an apartment to rent when school was out in June, but when they had trouble finding a furnished three-bedroom that would takes kids and a dog, they abandoned the idea of the family being together over the summer. Instead, Pat would make occasional trips to Birmingham. It wasn't ideal, but after eleven years of married life in baseball, they were used to inconvenience.

Suddenly, Marc started pointing at a man walking down the aisle. "Look, Mommy, look," he exclaimed.

Pat turned, not sure what he was pointing at.

He continued to point. "It's him."

"Who?"

"The man."

"What man?"

"You know... *the* man."

Pat finally figured out that he was pointing at Albert Belcher... *the* man.

A Vote for Man of the Year

When Albert Belcher first started toying with the idea of bringing integrated baseball to Birmingham, one of the first people he contacted was Bill Lumpkin, sports editor of the *Birmingham Post-Herald*. Lumpkin had grown up in

Birmingham and attended the University of Alabama. As a kid, he belonged to the Knothole Gang at Rickwood and spent his summers hanging out at the ballpark. He knew the city, the state, and its people. Not long after the bombing of the 16th Street Baptist Church, Belcher had invited Lumpkin to his woodsy cabin retreat on a private lake east of town. They shared a shot of whiskey, Lumpkin chasing his with water from the lake. After a second shot, Belcher asked Lumpkin for his candid opinion about resurrecting baseball in their emotionally scarred hometown. Lumpkin was a baseball fanatic, but he understood the dangers for Belcher, financially, politically, and personally. He knew most of the Big Mules wouldn't approve. Neither would Bull Connor or the Ku Klux Klan. But he also knew Belcher's determination and his long record of success in business. So he gave his cautious approval. And now that the season was past its midway point, and there'd been no major disturbances, Lumpkin shared his analysis of Belcher's gamble in a column titled "Baron Boss Is a Man of Action":

When year's end comes and honors are being shoveled back and forth, Albert Belcher is the man of action who should stand at the head of the list.

While politicians and committee after committee buried their heads in sand at the sound of anything racial, Belcher went out and single-handedly wiped a blemish off what some called Birmingham's image.

He gets our vote as Man of the Year, Sportsman of the Year, or any other accolade. You name it and Belcher deserves it.

Baseball's Popularity

Through the team's first thirty-six home dates, the Barons had drawn a total of 58,837 (an average of 1,634 per game, not counting the All-Star fray). At the start of the season, Belcher's optimistic goal had been to average 2,000 per game. He could take heart, however, that Birmingham was still leading the league in attendance, with Macon a distant second with 40,783 for forty-one dates (an average of 994). Asheville and Knoxville were barely averaging five hundred per game.

The league's low attendance numbers fueled speculation that the Southern League was in trouble, especially in Knoxville, where rumors persisted that the Smokies might have to fold before the end of the season. But in a meeting of team presidents the morning of the All-Star Game, the Knoxville ownership gave assurances that they were committed to not only finishing the year but having a team in 1965 as well. They had already lowered ticket prices from $1.50 to $1.

None of the owners would publicly blame the smaller crowds on integration, but certainly a reasonable explanation existed that too many whites hated blacks too much to pay to watch them play or, God forbid, sit next to one. Some skeptics maintained that baseball was dropping in popularity compared with football and basketball, and these other sports were stealing baseball fans. But in a recent poll by the *Los Angeles Times* on viewing preferences for televised sports, baseball had dominated: 85.4 percent enjoyed watching baseball; 67.4 percent pro football; 56.7 percent college football; and 35.7 percent pro basketball. And when it came to youth participation in organized sports, baseball leagues had more than twice the number of players enrolled that football and basketball had.

"This is the most enjoyable Baron team I've experienced in the two decades I've been involved in ownership," said Belcher. "I'm confident that the more Birmingham gets to know them and appreciate the way Sullivan has them playing, the more they'll come out to the ballpark."

A Boost to Birmingham's Image

Although the politicians and civic leaders had been slow to warm to Belcher's efforts, there was no shortage of love from the Birmingham press. In a follow-up article to the All-Star Game, Bob Phillips of the *Post-Herald* wrote about its impact:

> That pause in the baseball race shouldn't be allowed to pass without just a mention of the fact that more than 7,000 persons sat there at Rickwood Monday night, heavily mixed racially, and enjoyed an exciting sports event without the slightest trouble.
>
> Short months ago, millions would have said it couldn't happen in Birmingham.
>
> Sam Smith, president of the league, expressed it well: "I wish some of those national magazines had sent a photographer down here to make a color picture of that. But you couldn't expect them to do that. It would make them look bad for some of the stuff they carried about Birmingham in the past."

Although the All-Star game was an artistic and PR success, it was not a financial bonanza for Belcher. The net gate receipts were $8,000, and after the Southern League took its 85 percent off the top, that left the Barons with a profit of only $1,200, plus whatever was earned at the concession stands.

Finley Strikes Out

June wasn't a great month for Charlie Finley. He did sign two of the hottest pitching prospects in the country, Blue Moon and Catfish, but after six games his investment in Blue Moon looked like money down the drain, and doctors at the Mayo Clinic determined that Catfish needed surgery to properly heal the damage the shotgun blast had caused to his foot, so he wouldn't play at all that year. On top of that, the A's were free-falling farther into a last-place abyss.

But the even bigger blow to his ego, as well as to Belcher's hopes for adding another drawing card, was his failure to sign two surefire big-league prospects, Willie Crawford and Rick Reichardt. Finley was certain that he had the inside track on Crawford because Crawford's parents were from Bessemer, and Finley had gotten the mayor and half the bigwigs in the county to write them letters to sell them on the idea of their talented son starting his career in Birmingham. In pursuit of Crawford's signature, Finley went to his house in LA and dined on his mom's Southern fried cooking to demonstrate his down-home credentials. But when it came time to get Crawford's signature, Finley was aced out by the Dodgers. He didn't take it well.

"The boy was trying to play one club against the other," he said. "I got disgusted and walked out."

After failing to sign Crawford, he still thought he had the inside track to Reichardt, the son of a wealthy orthopedic surgeon. A spectacular college athlete at the University of Wisconsin, Reichardt had hit a lofty .500 on the baseball team and played fullback for the Big 10 football champion Badgers. No stranger to hyperbole, Finley called him "the greatest baseball prospect I ever saw." He traveled to Stevens Point, Wisconsin, to make his pitch. He even flew in Mrs. Finley on a private plane, figuring that the mother of his seven children could help sell Reichardt's mom, who had nine children of her own. During this frenzy, an NBC film crew was on the scene to shoot a documentary on Reichardt's signing. In the end, Reichardt chose to take a $200,000 offer from the Angels' owner, millionaire cowboy Gene Autry.

"I wish him well," said Finley.

Finley's willingness to throw money at untried prospects caught the attention of his fellow big-league owners, who publicly disapproved of his open-checkbook policy. Since shelling out $5,000,000 to buy the A's in 1961, he had spent $1,000,710 during the next four years to sign young talent, including $402,410 in 1964. This spending spree had been a bonanza for prospects, forcing every team to bid higher for their services. (It was Reichardt's signing and the money Finley was throwing around that led baseball to adopt the amateur player draft in 1965.) Finley's critics not only questioned his hefty investments but also disparaged his self-proclaimed skill in evaluating talent. Of the 104 players the organization had signed during 1961–63, only one, Lew Krausse, had made the big-league team, and then only briefly. Half of those signed were already out of the game.

It was no secret that Finley wanted to move his team out of Kansas City, and after losing Crawford and Reichardt to the Dodgers and Angels, he wrote a little ditty that didn't endear him to A's fans:

How are you going to keep them down on the farm after they've seen LA. Compared to sunny California and beautiful LA, Kansas City is just a farm.

The A's Are Coming...The A's Are Coming

Belcher was disappointed that Finley hadn't been able to ink Crawford and Reichardt, especially Crawford, but that was quickly forgotten when he and Finley reached an agreement for the A's to come to Birmingham for an exhibition game against the Barons on August 3. (The contract called for the Barons and A's to split the receipts.) It would be the first visit of a major-league team in over a decade. Belcher hoped that A's stars such as Jim Gentile and Rocky Colavito would draw a big crowd to Rickwood, not only providing a financial windfall but also adding to the Barons' impact on the city's image...never mind that the A's were the worst team in the big leagues.

Belcher immediately went to work on the details. He took out large ads in Birmingham's two daily newspapers. The copy read:

It can get pretty lonely at home...when everyone else in the neighborhood is at Rickwood watching the Barons battle the Kansas City A's on August 3rd.
   Box Seats $2.00; Grandstand $1.50; Bleachers $1.00

CHAPTER 45

Paul Lindblad

Put a Shirt on That

Lindblad glanced over at Hoss putting on his uniform, and noticed the scar running down his chest.

"Damn, get a shirt over that," he said.

Lindblad was definitely feeling better than he had after losing five in a row. He was relieved that he hadn't cost Birmingham the chance to host the All-Star Game. Although he and Blue Moon were the only two Baron pitchers not to get in the game—he'd pitched a complete game against Lynchburg the day before— he was gratified that the losing pitcher was the Barons' nemesis Manly Johnston.

"Please tell me you're not going to take your shirt off when we go to Hawaii?" he said.

"Hey, don't jinx it," replied Hoss.

Lindblad issued a thumbs-up and then pulled an envelope out of his locker and opened it.

"Oh, my God!" he exclaimed, his eyes widening. "You can leave your shirt off, I don't care now. This'll buy some sunglasses.

"I can't wait to show this to Kathy," he added.

Kathy Writes Home Again

As soon as he walked into the apartment, Paul handed the envelope to Kathy. She gave him a huge hug and then sat down and wrote a quick letter to her mom sharing the good news:

Dear Mama,

Junior just walked in a few minutes ago and handed me $1,000. I thought he had robbed a bank! But it is <u>ours</u>. He got it for going from A ball *to double A and remaining 90 days. We won't have it long as we are paying our air conditioner off which is $250 and paying $500 on the car and saving the rest in case of an emergency. So, you see there is a place for every bit of it as always.*

I'm also sending you $207 to pay the bank off and $34 for our insurance and Dr. Baker.
Love,
Kathy, Jr. kids

p.s. Jr. won his last game making his record 7–5 so I'll send you the clipping later.

Newspaper Clippings

Paul finished reading the newspaper and shook his head. "I don't get it," he said.
"What don't you get?" asked Kathy.
He showed her the headline: CITY AND FBI KNOW BOMBERS OF CHURCH HERE. He read a paragraph aloud:

The FBI knows who bought the dynamite, who made the bomb, who placed it there, and who engineered the crime. "We know every detail about it," said Lt. Maurice House, chief of Birmingham detectives.

"But they haven't made any arrests," he said.
"Why?"
"That's what I don't get," he replied. "I guess they don't have enough evidence."
"I hope those guys don't come to any of our games," said Kathy.
"Guess we wouldn't know if they did."
"I don't want to even think about."

Stories About Finley

Lindblad had followed the Birmingham press's continued fixation on Finley. It seemed as if there was a story about him every other day. Initially, all the stories were favorable, lauding him for establishing the A's as Birmingham's parent club, or for his promise to supply the Barons with "the best available talent," or for his willingness to spend money on young prospects, or even for his threats to sell the A's if the other owners approved the sale of the Yankees to CBS. The press celebrated Finley as a maverick *and* a native of Birmingham.

But Lindblad could detect that the bloom on the rose had faded slightly.

The way that Finley made the announcement from Kansas City about Blue Moon's assignment to Birmingham rather than let Belcher make it annoyed the Barons' beat writers. Finley's presumption ruffled the feathers of Bob Phillips of the *Post-Herald*:

If I were Albert Belcher I'd issue a cease-and-desist order to Charlie Finley suggesting that he has enough problems elsewhere without disturbing a very successful operation at his Birmingham outpost.

But Lindblad wasn't interested in taking sides in any tension between Finley and the Barons. He was just glad to have gotten his check for a thousand bucks from Kansas City, and hoped that after paying off the bills he'd have enough left over to buy Kathy and the girls new swimsuits for Hawaii.

CHAPTER 46

Bert Campaneris

A Case for MVP

At a press conference during the All-Star gathering, Sullivan made the case for Campy as the league's most valuable player. He raved about his defense—his arm, his range—and how many times he'd cut off an opponent's rally with a spectacular play.

"He makes it look routine," he said.

He also sang his praises offensively—his power, his speed—and how often he had manufactured runs by his foot speed alone, stealing bases, stretching doubles into triples, bothering the pitcher.

"I think it's safe to say he's been involved in half of the runs we've scored," Sullivan ventured.

A reporter brought up Manly Johnston. "Manly's having a great year, no doubt about it," said Sullivan. "But Campy means more to us. Take him away and we're in trouble."

To put an exclamation point on Sullivan's contention, in the crucial series against Lynchburg at Rickwood, Campy got six hits, helping the Barons to take three out of four and hike their lead back to four. He was hitting .323.

Finley's Big Dilemma

Sitting at his desk in his home office on his twenty-acre estate in La Porte, Indiana, eighty miles from Chicago, Finley was faced with a new dilemma— whether or not to call up Bert Campaneris.

Personnel decisions for the A's were usually made collectively by Finley; his general manager, Pat Friday; and the manager, now Mel McGaha. Several times over the last month they had discussed the option of calling up Campy. McGaha had lobbied for it, believing Campy could help Kansas City immediately with his speed and aggressiveness. Friday had demurred, thinking it would be best to leave him in Birmingham until the end of the season, and then call him up for the last month. That left the deciding vote with Finley.

"I wouldn't worry about this decision if I weren't so concerned with Birmingham," he said. "I've got my friends down there. I'm between the devil and the deep blue sea. Betwixt and between."

During the internal debate over whether to call up Campy, Finley took the unusual tactic of keeping the Birmingham press informed of his dilemma. Alf Van Hoose of the *News* made the case for Campy to stay by pointing out that no Baron player called up in the middle of the season for the last twenty years by its big-league affiliate—whether the Yankees, Red Sox, Tigers, or now Kansas City (Grzenda)—had made a significant immediate contribution:

If KC calls up Campy, a guy with the ability of any player called up from the Barons, he'll be missed and mourned. He's as exciting a player as any Baron of recent years. But there will be nothing we can do about it.

From a selfish standpoint, Sullivan didn't think Campy should be called up. Sullivan's reports on Campy to the front office had not only extolled his physical talents but also emphasized Campy's improved temper control. Other than the game he got kicked out of in Chattanooga for decking another player, he had not been thrown out of a game. In his first two seasons, he had acquired a reputation for throwing bats and helmets, and had been suspended by his own manager. But he had toned that way down. Although Sullivan would not take credit for this improvement, his players believed he'd been a big influence. Campy respected Sullivan, and did not want to disappoint him.

After several days of rumors swirling about Campy's status, Finley reluctantly decided to leave him in Birmingham. In the end, the deciding factor was something Sullivan had told him about the Barons' team chemistry.

"Mr. Finley, you hear the term *team effort* overused describing championship teams," said Sullivan. "But with this club, it fits. I've never experienced a squad that has meshed better than this one."

Finley called Belcher and Sullivan to inform them that he had decided to leave Campy in Birmingham. Because conjecture about Campy's status had been all over the news, Finley and Belcher hatched a promotional idea to celebrate his staying. For the Barons' game the night before the exhibition with Kansas City, Campy would play all nine positions. He'd done it before in A ball, only this time when he pitched, he would alternate throwing left-handed to one hitter, then right-handed to the next. He was the only player in organized baseball who could throw with either hand. Finley helped draft the promotional copy.

Reversal of Fortune

After the Barons lost the series opener at Rickwood to Asheville 6–4, Sullivan summoned Campy to his office. In the losing effort, Campy had hit his sixth home run and a double, raising his average to .325. During the game, the PA announcer informed the crowd that on August 2, "our great shortstop Bert Campaneris will be playing all nine positions."

"Campy, I've got good news for you," said Sully, speaking slowly.

Campy stared blankly at him, not certain what he meant.

"You're going to the big leagues," said Sullivan.

Campy raised his eyebrows. With his limited English, he wasn't exactly sure what he'd just heard. Yesterday, he'd been told that he was *not* getting called up.

Slowly, the words sank in and a smile as wide as a machete spread across Campy's face.

An hour earlier, Glynn West had gotten a phone call from Pat Friday in Kansas City. In a game that day in Minneapolis, Wayne Causey, the A's short-stop, had collided with the Twins' Bob Allison and hurt his arm. He would be out indefinitely, and with nobody else to play short, the A's only option, they said, was to reverse the decision made the day before and call up Campy. He would be the A's starting shortstop in tomorrow's game in Minnesota, facing pitcher Jim Kaat.

"Your plane leaves in an hour," said Sully.

After Sullivan informed the team of Campy's departure, teammates quickly surrounded his locker to offer congratulations, pounding him on the back, issuing thumbs-ups. They were happy for him. At the start of the year, they'd been slow to warm to him—his reputation and his reluctance to learn English kept them at a distance. But as the season progressed, he'd become popular with his co-players, not just because he was winning games for them, but also because they'd gotten to know him and appreciate his passion for the game. As happy as they were for him, they were also sad to see him go. They knew his loss would seriously jeopardize the team's pennant hopes.

"He didn't really belong in this league anyhow," said pitcher Nicky Don Curtis.

After showering and getting dressed, Campy tossed his equipment into a bag. There would be no time to go to his boardinghouse and pack. He'd arrive in Minneapolis with only the clothes on his back and his equipment, minus his bats. He'd fetch his belongings when the A's came to town next week.

An hour later, he was on a midnight plane to the big leagues.

A Debut for the Ages

"Campy will be up in a minute," beamed Finley. "Hold on."

Finley was in Chicago, listening to a radio broadcast of Campy's first big-league game via phone from Kansas City and relaying the game by another phone to Benny Marshall, the sports editor of the *News* in Birmingham. This would be Campy's first major-league at-bat. It was a day game, and he'd had only an hour of sleep.

"Here comes Bert Campaneris, leading off for the A's," intoned A's announcer Monte Moore. "He's just up from Birmingham. Lefty Jim Kaat looks in to get the sign."

And then Moore's voice started to climb. "Holy smoke!" he exclaimed.

Campy hit the first pitch thrown to him in the major leagues for a home run to left field.

"How about that!" yelled Finley. "Now, just how about that!"

There was a short pause, and then Finley came back on the line. "Can you hear me all right?" he asked.

"Just fine," said Marshall.

"I'm hanging up now and I'll call you back when Campy comes up again," said Finley. "Man, we should've had that little fellow up here all along."

Thirty minutes later, Finley called back, detailing Campy's second at-bat, a sharp single to right. And then, after reaching first on a fielder's choice in his third at-bat, he stole second. "They didn't even make a throw," extolled Monte Moore.

It was the seventh inning when Finley called back. Campy was coming up against Kaat again, the A's trailing 3–1, a runner on first. Swinging at the first pitch again, Campy drove a shot to left…and over the fence. Monte Moore made the call. "It was an outside curveball, and he pulled it to left. What wrists!"

"This is baseball history!" exclaimed Finley.

The A's won the game in eleven innings.

"Don't you know that Campaneris story feels good?" said Finley after the game. "Don't you know that Charlie Finley feels good? Say, this ought to make quite a story down there in Birmingham. Maybe they won't be so mad at me for taking Campy away, huh? And they can see him again August 3 when we come and play the Barons."

And then he recapped Campy's debut: "Three hits, a stolen base, two homers, including one on the first big-league pitch he ever saw. What a day! What a game! What a ballplayer!"

CHAPTER 47

Blue Moon Odom

Crackerwood Café

In the Rickwood parking lot, the Barons' bus idled as players tossed their suit-cases on board. In a few minutes they'd be leaving for Charlotte, a 390-mile trip that would take them—if they were lucky—ten hours. With a heat wave blanketing the South, it promised to be a sauna on wheels.

Blue Moon climbed on board, his smile masking the dire circumstances surrounding his next start. The headline in the *News* summed it up: ODOM STATUS MAY RIDE ON TOMORROW'S SHOWING.

Of all the big games he'd pitched—high school championships, pro debut in Macon—his next start was the most pressurized. He'd never failed at any-thing, but now he was on the verge.

The supreme confidence that had always been his trademark was showing cracks. He still believed he could dominate the Southern League. Despite his losing record and inability to throw strikes, he was averaging almost a strikeout per inning, and on occasion he made hitters look foolish. But he was almost always behind in the count, and it didn't matter if it was the American League, or the Southern League, or the Appalachia State League: Pro hitters lived for 2–0 or 3–1 fastballs.

As the bus chugged out of Birmingham, the players settled in for the long ride, some playing cards, others trying to sleep, and a couple nursing hang-overs. Blue Moon stared out the window. His teammates knew the situation, too, treading lightly, almost as if he had been physically quarantined.

Four hours later, Iron Lung pulled off the highway onto the gravel park-ing lot of a small hilltop diner surrounded by piney woods and a small fleet of rusted pickup trucks with Confederate flag decals.

"Where are we?" asked Blue Moon, waking from a nap.

They had stopped for lunch somewhere in northern Georgia. On lunch stops on previous trips, the black players usually stayed on the bus and the white players brought lunch out to them. But this time, Sullivan signaled the black players to join the rest of the team. After all, the Civil Rights Act was now the law of the land.

It wasn't as if Sullivan was suddenly a crusader, especially not in the backwoods of northern Georgia. But the Barons were a team, he reasoned. His team. They were in first place; they had won the All-Star Game; they had just traveled 175 sweaty miles in a bus with a broken air conditioner; and they were all decent young men, with a couple of army vets and the best high school pitcher in the history of Georgia among them. None of them had ever been arrested or done drugs; they could all read and write, and didn't cuss at the fans. Why shouldn't they get to eat as a team?

Blue Moon was the first black to enter the café, immediately spotted by the owner. "I'm sorry," he said, "the colored boys will have to eat out back."

Blue Moon froze, delivering an icy glare. Several of the white players had already taken seats in a booth and at the counter. Turning their heads toward Blue Moon, they watched, seeing the same steely-eyed intensity he had when he stood on the mound. Sullivan was still outside, herding the last of the players into the café.

The owner's words settled in on Blue Moon. He wasn't a crusader, either—he'd never tried to test the established order growing up in Macon, never walking through the lobby at the Dempsey Hotel, never disrespecting the white shopkeepers or the cops. But that was then. This was now. Maybe it was because he'd played on an integrated team for six weeks. Or maybe it was because he had more money in the bank than this little owner of a redneck café would ever hope to have. Or maybe it was because he had won only one game in his six starts.

As he spun around to exit, his glare bored a hole in the owner.

The white players stared, not sure how to react. The owner crossed his arms.

At the door, Blue Moon paused, and then motioned toward his teammates, all still seated. "Anyone who don't get back on the bus right now gonna have a problem with me," he said.

In a Georgia minute, everyone was back on the bus as it spewed gravel and pulled back onto the highway.

The Bonus Baby's Place in Baseball's Cosmos

Despite the competitive rivalry among pitchers vying to be the next player to get called up to the big leagues, nobody wanted Blue Moon to bomb again. His success would help them all toward their shared goal—Hawaii.

Sure, maybe in the dark corners of their hearts they might take a small measure of pleasure in knowing he was struggling. Just as girls in high school resent the prettiest cheerleader, baseball players can be jealous of the bonus babies. Blue Moon was the one Charlie Finley slobbered over. The chances were good that Finley wouldn't know the names of half the Barons' pitchers if they sat next to him in the dugout.

There was no personal animosity against Blue Moon among his teammates. When it came down to it, none of them really knew anything about him, any more than they knew about Tommie Reynolds. No one knew that Odom's dad had died when he was five, or that his mom had worked six days a week scrubbing white people's floors, or that his high school baseball field in Macon wouldn't have even been good enough for a junior varsity team in San Diego.

No, this was a roster of twenty-somethings, all of them stars on every team they'd previously played on. Empathy and understanding wandered on the edges of their consciousness. They were members of an athletic cult now, where burping, farting, and gawking at girls were the order of the day. They saw Blue Moon as the antithesis of the world he grew up in—somebody destined to get every break possible. Their contained resentment was as much a part of the clubhouse as Beech-Nut tobacco. The more the team won, the more that resentment shrank. To let it loose again was to submit to the tyranny of the locker room. Winning trumped petty jealousy.

Blue Moon's Last Chance

Blue Moon retired the side in order in the first with—hallelujah—no walks. After a single to open up the second for Charlotte, he got the next hitter to ground into a double play.

With the score tied 1–1 in the bottom of the fourth, Sullivan stirred in the dugout, worried that Blue Moon would start trying to steer the ball rather than just letting it fly.

"Stay focused," he hollered.

For the next three innings, Blue Moon did just that, getting ahead of the hitters and holding the Hornets in check. The score remained tied.

In the top of the seventh, Barons catcher John Stutz homered, giving the Barons a 2–1 lead. After Blue Moon wiggled out of trouble in the bottom of the inning, the Barons scored three more runs in the top of the eighth.

All Blue Moon needed now was to retire six more hitters and his trip to Idaho would be canceled.

In the bottom of the eighth, he retired the first two hitters, but then he gave up back-to-back screaming doubles. Sullivan visited the mound.

"I'm okay," said Blue Moon.

When to pull a pitcher is one of the toughest decisions a manager must make. He has to consider a number of factors—the score, who's warming up in the bullpen, whether the next hitter is a lefty or a righty, the league standings, the fragile nature of the pitcher's psyche, and, most important, what's best for the team. In this instance, Sullivan worried that if Blue Moon got rocked for more hits and blew the lead, he might never recover, even in Idaho. He also knew that he had Ken Sanders, who was 7–0 and arguably the best reliever in the league, ready in the bullpen.

Sullivan didn't hesitate, reaching for the ball. Blue Moon handed it over.

"Great job," said Sullivan.

In high school, Blue Moon had never been relieved.

Sanders got the last out of the inning, and then shut the door in the ninth.

For the first time in a month, Blue Moon was a winner, improving his record to 2–3. It wasn't a virtuoso performance—he'd given up nine hits plus two earned runs, and struck out only three—but the best part was that he walked only two. And for the first time in a month, he was a part of the winning celebration in the locker room. The quarantine was lifted.

Missing Campy

Like all of his teammates, Blue Moon missed Campy. There had been talk on the bus about the wisdom of Finley calling him up and how it could hurt the Barons' pennant hopes, but Blue Moon was more concerned that the team had lost a player of color. There was a bond among them, the bond of brothers within a band of brothers. In the dangerous atmosphere of the South, especially since the three civil rights workers had disappeared, there was safety in numbers and a comfort in being able to walk dark streets together at night and go to sleep in run-down rooms knowing they weren't alone. With Campy gone, Blue Moon had one fewer brother, one less common bond.

Blue Moon was lucky that his initial mentors in navigating the rough seas of pro ball were Campy, Rosario, Reynolds, and Huyke, none of whom recklessly chased the nightlife or courted trouble. In one small way, these men had it better than their white teammates: If they stayed out late or came in drunk, there was no danger of being caught by Sullivan, who was camped out with the white players in their white hotels. There was no chance of Sullivan's venturing into all-black neighborhoods to check up on them. Yet given this freedom, they monitored themselves, mostly behaving, certainly nothing worse than the white players. They were, after all, playing in the Southern League, where options for young black men were limited.

As for Campy, life in the big leagues was good. After five games, he was 9 for 19, batting a robust .473 using a thirty-two-ounce bat borrowed from catcher Doc Edwards. Defensively, he'd played errorless ball. The only negative was that he didn't know if his family back in Cuba had heard the news that he was in the big leagues. Sometimes they could pick up radio broadcasts from Miami, but it was doubtful any of his games had been carried. He'd written a letter, but because it usually took ten days to get there and had to go through government censors, there was no guarantee they had gotten it.

Next Start

Blue Moon's next start was back at Rickwood in the second game of a doubleheader against last-place Asheville. In the opener, Ron Stretch Tompkins improved his record to 10–3 with a three-hit shutout, backed by three hits by Tommie Reynolds.

Taking the field at shortstop behind Blue Moon was Ossie Chavarria, who had been sent to the Barons from AAA Dallas to replace Campy. He was 0 for 10 in his first three games. Also expected to join the Barons was Shaky Joe Grzenda, the veteran lefty who'd been called up earlier in the year. He hadn't arrived yet, supposedly en route with his family by car from Kansas City, although rumor had it that he wasn't happy about the demotion and might be headed home to Pennsylvania instead. Upon hearing the rumor, Lindblad pondered the choice: "Hmmm, let's see," he mused. "Go shovel coal, or go play baseball?"

In the first six and two-thirds innings (of a seven-inning game), Blue Moon set down Asheville with no runs and only four harmless singles, while striking out six and walking none. He was starting to look like he might actually be worth some of that money Finley dished out to him.

Though Blue Moon was mowing down the Tourists, the Barons hadn't exactly torn the cover off the ball, either, getting only one hit, a savage line shot by Reynolds that was hit so hard it ripped the webbing out of the third baseman's glove. The ball rolled down the left-field line, driving in two runners who'd reached base on a walk and an error. It was enough, as Blue Moon recorded the first shutout of his pro career, 2–0.

After the game, Sullivan felt a sense of vindication. More than anyone else in the organization, he'd lobbied to keep Blue Moon in Birmingham. He'd seen the tremendous potential and believed that sooner or later, he'd settle down. Now, with back-to-back victories and a 3–3 record, Odom was rewarding his manager's patience.

CHAPTER 48

Albert Belcher

Courage

As the season wore on, the media celebrated Belcher's decision to resurrect the Barons as an integrated team. Alf Van Hoose fawned over him in a column titled: "Belcher Said His City Was Ready—and It Was."

When Birmingham's morale, and perhaps basic moral standards, had never been lower, Belcher stepped forward to bring back baseball to his city while there were yet echoes of marching feet and lawmen's clubs, and bombs ringing out across a once peaceful valley.

He went to Florida to try to secure a club, and was met with sullen stares that Birmingham people encountered across most of the land at that time.

"Don't worry about colored players in Birmingham," he told the baseball people. "They'll be treated all right. Sure, we've had our troubles. But we need baseball—any city as great as Birmingham needs it.

"It's not going to be easy for us to enjoy a lot of things we'll have to accept, but you watch and see—we'll take what we have to take like men."

He has brought baseball back, and many of us are glad. Some of us will even applaud the courageous, gutsy, rugged individualist who returned it.

But his effort, even as the team was leading the Southern League, had received only token official support from city and state officials. He had received nary a thank-you or congratulation from any official source, including

241

Mayor Boutwell. He had sent an invitation to attend a game to Governor Wallace, but got no response. He knew that some of these same officials would promote what he'd accomplished at Rickwood as "Exhibit A" when they traveled to Washington, DC, or New York to hustle business for Birmingham.

Sheriff Mel Bailey and Police Chief Jamie Moore had helped arrange security at Rickwood, but every other request he'd made to City Hall for help at the ballpark, including improving access roads and fixing a fence on city-owned property behind the park, had been greeted either with no response or rejection. Those repairs had come out of his pocket.

The Crack Widens

A week before the A's visit to Rickwood, Belcher walked into Sullivan's office to discuss Campy's replacement, Ossie Chavarria. "How's he fitting in?" wondered Belcher.

"It's been a tough adjustment," replied Sullivan. "Getting sent down is always hard on the ego, but he's starting to finally hit, so that should help."

Chavarria, a Venezuelan, had started out 0 for 19. He was not only replacing the fans' favorite player, but the team's best player, too. Belcher and Sullivan were both dismayed that Finley had called up Campy because it again raised serious questions about how genuine Finley's convictions were when he was telling anybody who'd listen how much he loved Birmingham, and how he was going to do everything in his power to give the Barons a winner.

Sullivan and Belcher knew that when it came to calling up players, the major-league team had all the control, and that it had always been that way. But they'd thought somehow it would be different with Finley because of his connection to Birmingham, and his sympathy for its problems, and the complete and utter hopelessness of the A's and their journey to nowhere. The two of them had sat in Sullivan's office after the Barons' pitiful performance on opening night and listened to Finley promise to do everything he could to help. They were hard-pressed to figure out how calling up Campaneris benefited either the Barons or the A's.

"But who knows," said Sullivan. "Maybe he knows something we don't."

A Plea to Finley

Sullivan and Belcher weren't the only ones in Birmingham feeling bamboozled by Finley. Following Campy's call-up, Bob Phillips resumed taking Finley to task:

We once more are asking Mr. Finley and the baseball pros he has hired to help him run the Kansas City Athletics to leave our Barons alone until they have the Southern League pennant in the bag.

Once we have won, he is welcome to call up our entire team and bench their big league brothers for the remainder of the season in an all-out effort to beat Washington out of ninth place in the American League race.

Here was the last ever to be seen of Knights and their Ladies Fair, of Master and of Slave. Look for it only in books, for it is no more than a dream remembered, a Civilization gone with the wind.

—*Gone with the Wind*

PART VII

THE SEASON

August

League Standings, August 1

	W	L	GB
Birmingham	58	39	
Lynchburg	58	43	2
Macon	50	45	7
Charlotte	50	47	8
Knoxville	51	49	8½
Chattanooga	46	52	12½
Columbus	44	55	14½
Asheville	37	64	23

CHAPTER 49

Haywood Sullivan

The Trust Factor

Striding to the mound to start the top of the seventh against the Charlotte Hornets, Ron Tompkins was feeling good despite the muggy, oppressive heat. The Barons led 2–0, and he was working on a two-hit shutout, which would be his second whitewash in a row. The Budweiser Rx that Sullivan had prescribed was working.

His first pitch to Charlotte second baseman and future big leaguer Frank Quilici was a called strike at the knees, and was greeted by high-pitched screaming from Rickwood's largest and noisiest crowd of the year—8,137 in attendance for Kids' Night. The din had started in the first inning and hadn't let up.

Also seated in the crowd behind home plate was Hank Peters, the A's farm director. His presence had given Sullivan a funny feeling. He wanted Tompkins to pitch well, of course, but he knew that the A's had just put a pitcher on the disabled list and needed to fill the spot. Given Finley's prevarications over Campy's call-up, Sullivan's trust was evaporating. With Tompkins throwing well again, the Barons could ill afford to lose the big Californian for the stretch run.

Quilici lined Tompkins's next pitch up the middle for a single. Then Quilici got such a big jump stealing second that there wasn't even a throw. Sullivan signaled Stanley Jones to start throwing in the bullpen.

But quicker than a hiccup, Tompkins yielded two more line-drive singles, a couple of walks, and a home run. The Barons trailed 6–2 before Sullivan could yank Tompkins. That would be the final score. It was the Hornets' tenth straight victory, moving them into second ahead of Lynchburg, trailing the Barons by four and a half.

It was the second time Tompkins had bombed when the KC brass had come to see him.

So much for the healing powers of Budweiser.

247

Sullivan Takes Stock

As the season moved into August, the team had now been in first place for over two months. Their lead was the same as it had been when Campy was called up, and as Sullivan had told Finley earlier, he'd never been on a team that got along so well. After a rough patch, the pitching was strong again—Blue Moon and Lindblad had both won their last two starts, but the most reliable hurler was Ken Sanders, who was 9–0. For Sullivan, Sanders had been the biggest surprise of the staff. Although he didn't possess the so-called cannon for an arm, the scouting report was that he had "a shrewd pitching head, an abundance of big league confidence, and good control of all his pitches." (His nickname was "Bulldog," although some players called him Duck because he had a duck-shaped scar on his neck from when he had meningitis as a kid.) Grzenda's arrival from Kansas City after a week's delay—having first been sent to Dallas before being assigned to Birmingham—also boosted Baron pitching. As Lindblad had predicted, Shaky Joe wasn't happy with the demotions but had decided that pitching for the Barons would be better than sledging down into the mines.

Sullivan was happy to have him back. He was also happy with the way Reynolds had been crushing the ball since missing almost three weeks with pneumonia. His average was up to .319, although he was hitting fifty points higher on the road and still didn't have a homer at Rickwood. Lindblad nicknamed him "Roadman." And in a testimonial to the institution of marriage, his average in his twenty games since marrying Penny at the Jefferson County Courthouse was .410. Even with all the games he'd missed, he led the league in being hit by pitches.

Joining Reynolds in the .300 club was Santiago Rosario, his average up to .301. Sullivan was encouraged that he hadn't thrown a bat or a helmet in almost a month.

"I like our chances," said Sullivan in his best coach-speak. "Our boys are accustomed to being in first place. I know Charlotte is hot, but as I've said since early in the year, I think it'll come down to us and Lynchburg."

Finley Strikes Again

The phone rang in Sullivan's office at Rickwood. He wasn't in a good mood. The Barons had just lost the second game of a doubleheader to Knoxville, blowing a lead in the last inning when the normally tenacious Sanders lost his first game of the season.

He answered the phone, listened to the voice on the other end, then said a few words and hung up. "Shit!" he yelled, loud enough that the players on the other side of the door could hear him.

He gathered his composure, and then opened the door. "Ken, can I see you in my office?" he said.

Sanders was sitting in front of his locker, head down, pissed off that he'd just lost his first game.

Slowly, he stood and walked toward the office. One of the things the players had come to appreciate about Sullivan was that he never berated a player in front of others, and rarely upbraided them at all. Sanders hadn't screwed up all year, so he wasn't sure what to expect.

"Have a seat," said Sullivan.

"Sorry I messed up tonight," offered Sanders.

"When you come to the ballpark tomorrow night for the game against Kansas City," said Sullivan, "have your bags packed—"

"What?" interrupted Sanders.

Surely Sullivan wasn't going to send him down just because he lost a game. A week earlier, he had been quoted in the newspaper as saying Sanders was the best reliever in the league.

"And take those bags to the visitors' clubhouse," continued Sullivan.

"Huh?"

"You're going to the big leagues. You'll be leaving right after the game with KC to fly to New York. Congratulations."

Disbelieving, Sanders stared straight ahead, letting the words sink in. "Are you shitting me?" he said.

"Absolutely not," said Sullivan. "I just got the call from Hank Peters."

After Sanders returned to the locker room, Sullivan sat behind his desk, seething, feeling deceived.

Tomorrow, before the game with the A's, he would be posing for pictures with Charlie Finley, while his star shortstop, who was hitting .326 when he left, and his ace reliever, cruising along at 9–1, sat in the A's dugout.

CHAPTER 50

Albert Belcher

Violent Storm Clouds

Advance tickets sales for the A's exhibition had been brisk. Belcher and his general manager, Glynn West, were predicting a crowd of ten thousand. They'd taken orders from Mississippi, Tennessee, Georgia, and South Carolina.

The A's visit would be the first time ever that a major-league team would play a game in Birmingham during the regular season. Finley had chartered a plane for the trip. But three hours before the game, a violent thunderstorm hovered over the city, dumping buckets and causing Belcher to nervously pace and consider the unthinkable—canceling the game.

Also pacing was Ron Tompkins. Sullivan had given him the plum assignment as the starting pitcher and told him to go as many innings as he could, hoping for a complete game. This was Tompkins's big chance to finally impress in front of all the Kansas City brass—Finley, Peters, McGaha, Lopat, and Friday. But for Tompkins, as for any other pitcher, waiting out a rain delay or a cancellation put a wrecking ball through his mental and physical preparation.

Not only would a rainout eliminate his big chance to impress the A's honchos, it would drown Belcher's hopes for a profitable evening.

Finley Arrives and the Clouds Part

To everyone's relief, the storm passed. When the gates opened, the fans of all shades streamed into Rickwood, filling the box seats and grandstands, fanning themselves to stay cool in the muggy ninety-degree heat. As the bleachers filled, ushers escorted fans to roped-off areas in the outfield. Kids clambered over the railings, hollering for balls, autographs, attention.

Extra security patrolled the park, including a Kansas City cop whom Finley had brought in on the charter jet to make sure nobody tried anything funny with the A's players, especially Campaneris.

"It's just to make sure that there are no shenanigans and nobody tries to kidnap my boy," Finley explained. "I'll personally inspect the plane to make sure Campy's on board before we leave."

Belcher was surprised that he hadn't received any pre-game threats. As the fans settled into their seats, they were mannerly and well behaved, blacks and whites sitting side by side, talking baseball. They stood patiently together in line to buy hot dogs and drinks. Nowhere in the South in 1964, or maybe all of America, was integration working better than at Rickwood Field on this night.

Standing in front of the A's dugout, Finley, Belcher, and Sullivan smiled for the cameras.

To the Woodshed

By the time the game started, every seat at Rickwood was filled, with several thousand more fans packed ten-deep around the outfield. They went nuts when the A's leadoff hitter was announced—Bert Campaneris.

As he stepped into the batter's box, Campy smiled and tipped his cap as the long ovation continued. When he grounded out to short, the crowd wasn't sure whether to cheer or hiss. In his three months with the Barons, he had become as popular as any player in the club's history, black or white.

After Campy was retired, Tompkins ran into trouble, giving up two runs on an RBI single by Jim Gentile. Not the start he'd hoped for to impress the KC brass.

The Barons bounced back to score four runs to take the lead and send the crowd to bonkersville, the big blow a ground-rule double by Larry Stahl that bounded into the overflow crowd in left field. But in the fourth, Kansas City tied it, forcing Sullivan to pull a disheartened Tompkins. In four innings, he'd given up four runs, four hits, and a disastrous four walks.

In the middle of the fifth inning, the fans' enthusiasm ratcheted up again, but this time it was for the grounds crew from Kansas City that Finley had brought along on the trip. Headed up by thirty-five-year-old George Toma, widely regarded as the best groundskeeper in the business, they took to the infield dressed in matching green-and-gold outfits with customized gold rakes. The crew, including five brothers of French descent, ages fifteen to twenty, moved with drill-like precision—no dawdling allowed. Accompanied by Chubby Checkers's "The Twist" blaring over the PA system, they shimmied and shook and raked the infield to perfection in only forty-five seconds while the crowd whistled and twisted as Finley beamed.

At Finley's urging, Sullivan brought in Blue Moon in relief of Tompkins, even though he had pitched four innings a day earlier against Knoxville. Nevertheless, in two innings of work against the A's, Blue Moon gave up two harmless singles and no walks while striking out four. The last batter he faced was slugger Rocky Colavito, and with a full count Blue Moon snapped off a curve that Colavito swung at and missed by a foot. The crowd howled and Finley beamed once more.

"Nobody in the big leagues could've hit that curve," observed Eddie Lopat.

In the bottom of the sixth, catcher John Stutz hit a home run to put the Barons up 5–4, and then they added two more in the eighth as Shaky Joe Grzenda, who had let it be known that he wanted to pitch in the game, shut out the A's the rest of the way for a 7–4 victory.

The headline on the front page of the *News* the next day proclaimed: FARMHAND BARONS TAKE PARENT A'S TO THE WOODSHED.

The Day After

The attendance of 16,912 was the third largest crowd in Rickwood's sixty-year history and, according to Belcher, the loudest. Veteran concessionaire Bob Scranton said it was also the hungriest, setting new Rickwood records for eating and drinking: seven thousand hot dogs, twenty-five thousand soft drinks, four thousand bags of peanuts, and fifteen hundred boxes of popcorn. But in the negotiations over the exhibition, Finley had demanded a 60 percent share of the gate, as well as for all of Kansas City's expenses to be covered, including the cost of the charter jet. Belcher had no choice but to agree. But he wasn't happy. When it was suggested in an interview with Bob Phillips of the *Post-Herald* that the game's success had been a joint project between him and Mr. Finley, he bristled:

"Mr. Finley, my eye," he shouted. "What do you mean Mr. Finley? I'm the man who would've been stuck. I guaranteed the cost of the plane, and it would have all come out of my pocket [if it was rained out]. Kansas City took more money out of Birmingham than any big league club ever took."

After hearing Belcher's side of the story, Phillips changed his tune in print:

We had been led to believe that Finley was doing it all out of love for the fans of his old hometown. But Finley wasn't in on the big gamble. If the game had been stormed out, Belcher would have had to cough up the $4,000 along with whatever he had spent in promoting the game.

CHAPTER 51

Tommie Reynolds

Married Life

Tommie and Penny Reynolds walked down the steps of the boardinghouse where they'd been staying in the month since they'd been married—the same place Tommie had lived before the wedding (such as it was). His $35-a-month rent for the room in the two-bedroom house not far from the ballpark included kitchen privileges. The room was not much more than a bed, dresser, and two chairs. Because they'd been married at the courthouse, with no teammates in attendance, there'd been no presents or even a wedding cake.

The morning sickness had passed for Penny. Having grown up in southern Georgia and gone to college in Daytona, she'd spent her whole life in the South. Birmingham didn't feel that much different from the places she knew. She passed her time when Tommie was on the road by reading books, her passion. She usually brought a book to the games at Rickwood, too, and would read a chapter or two between her husband's trips to the plate. Sometimes she sat with the other wives, but other nights she preferred sitting alone. Despite being married, she was still determined to complete her degree and become an English teacher.

On this day, they drove into downtown Birmingham to buy Penny a wedding ring. At the jewelry store they found the ring they wanted, but it was out of Tommie's price range, well above what he could afford on his $600-a-month salary. But the jeweler was a Barons' fan and recognized Tommie. "Maybe we can work out a credit arrangement," he said.

They left with the ring they wanted. Later, Reynolds wondered if he would have been allowed to buy the ring on credit if he hadn't played for the Barons. And when he heard Blue Moon's account of how the Birmingham cop had let him go without a ticket, he wondered the same thing. Being a Baron, he concluded, had benefits not available to all black men in Birmingham.

We're Not in San Diego Anymore, Stretch

In the clubhouse after another Baron victory, Tompkins approached Reynolds's locker to offer congratulations on his collecting two hits.

"My wife said she really enjoys talking with your new bride," said Tompkins. "How about the two of you coming over to our apartment for dinner?"

Reynolds raised his eyebrows. "Are you crazy?" he asked.

"Whattya mean?"

"In case you've forgotten, this is Birmingham, Alabama."

"So."

"Let me try to explain it to you," said Reynolds. "Some folks around here don't take too favorably to Negro folks going into white neighborhoods."

"Doesn't bother me."

"That's nice, but there's also some folks around here who like it even less when white folks cotton to Negroes. Maybe you haven't been keeping up with the news, but three civil rights workers are missing down in Mississippi. I'm guessing they'll probably find 'em hanging from a tree."

They agreed to get together back in San Diego.

A Very Big Gun

Reynolds steered Blue Moon's bright red Galaxy into the parking lot of the University of Alabama–Birmingham Hospital, the same lot where he'd dropped him off the day before. Now he was back to pick him up. Blue Moon had let him drive his car while he was in the hospital. Blue Moon had been admitted for tests to determine what was wrong with him. After his two-inning, four-strikeout performance against Kansas City, he had complained of fatigue and a chest cold that wouldn't go away, similar to what had put Reynolds out of action for eighteen days. Baron general manager Glynn West had made the hospital arrangements for him, making him the hospital's second black patient (after Campy). So far, tests had not revealed what was wrong. This was his second day in the hospital, and unless the doctor gave him a clean bill of health he would miss the team's seven-day road trip to Knoxville and Chattanooga. He was scheduled to pitch the series opener in Knoxville.

As Reynolds shut off the engine and started to get out of the car, he eyed an armed security guard approaching.

"Can't park here, boy," instructed the guard.

"Whattya mean?"

"It's private property."

"The sign there says VISITOR PARKING," countered Reynolds. "I'm here to pick up a friend. He's in room 408."

"This hospital don't take no niggers."

"Did I say he was a Negro?"

"Oh, a smart-ass nigger."

Reynolds was in no mood for this guy's shit, or anyone else's. In last night's game he had come up with the bases loaded and the game on the line in the bottom of the ninth. The situation seemed perfect to play hero—the team had not lost three in a row all season and had won twenty-one of twenty-five one-run games. But he whiffed, adding to the frustration of his continued failure to hit at Rickwood. It was almost as if he were two different hitters—Roadman Reynolds and Rickwood Reynolds.

"You got ten seconds to get your black ass out of here," ordered the guard.

Reynolds eyed the guard resting his hand on his gun. His army training advised him that it was a very-big-caliber gun; common sense advised him not to mess with it.

He climbed back into Blue Moon's car and slowly exited the parking lot.

A few blocks away, he parked on the street and walked back to the hospital, entering on the side away from the guard. Nobody stopped him as he took the elevator to the fourth floor.

In room 408, Blue Moon was dressed, sitting on the edge of the bed. The doctor had just seen him and told him they'd found nothing wrong other than some chest congestion and that he could start pitching again in a week.

"Let's get out of here," he said.

"What did the doctor say?" asked Reynolds.

"Told me I could pitch in Knoxville tomorrow night," Blue Moon replied.

Blue Moon and Reynolds Torch the Smokies

"How do you feel?" asked Sullivan.

"Good," replied Blue Moon. "Let me finish."

It was the top of the ninth of the series opener in Knoxville, and Blue Moon was locked in a 2–2 pitchers' duel. In eight innings, he'd held the Smokies to two runs on seven hits while striking out six.

Sullivan refused to be persuaded by Blue Moon's appeal. "I'm going to pinch-hit Hoss for you," he said.

With a month to go in the season, no Baron had played more games and innings than Hoss. He was exhausted. Since his surgery, he had never totally regained his strength, and he was still ten pounds under his playing weight.

On some nights, his uniform felt as if it were made of Bessemer steel. This was the first game since April that he hadn't started. It would also be his first pinch-hitting appearance.

He walked on four pitches. When the next hitter, Ossie Chavarria, lashed a line drive into the gap in left center, Hoss forgot about being exhausted and raced around the bases to score standing up. By the time the inning was over, the Barons had scored four more runs, the big blow a towering homer by Reynolds...and once again, Sullivan looked like the Einstein of the Southern League. It was Blue Moon's third win in a row.

Starless in Birmingham

With Reynolds continuing his hot hitting on the road, the Barons took three of four in Knoxville. Although Knoxville had integrated a downtown theater and several restaurants prior to the passage of the civil rights bill, the black players still had to stay in separate accommodations, with the motel room that Blue Moon and Reynolds shared so stifling hot that they didn't get to sleep until sunrise. It didn't affect Reynolds's hitting the next night—he stroked two more hits and scored the go-ahead run in a 5–3 win. The Barons won the next night, too, with Larry Stahl extending his hitting streak to ten games. The lead over Lynchburg held steady at three and a half games.

After winning three of four in Knoxville, Reynolds and Blue Moon teamed up again in a 5–1 victory in the second game in Chattanooga, with Reynolds going 2 for 3, stealing a base, and driving in a run as Blue Moon allowed only three hits and struck out ten.

"Moon, that's your best game of the year," offered Sullivan.

Blue Moon's swagger was all the way back, and so was his control. He now looked at each batter stepping to the plate with that you-can't-hit-me glare that he had possessed back in high school.

Despite Blue Moon's and Reynolds's heroics, as well as the Barons leading the league for two and a half months, it was doubtful whether any Baron would be chosen as a league All-Star when the Southern League Sportswriters Association made its picks at the end of the season. Campaneris and Sanders would've been locks, and so would Tompkins six weeks earlier, but now, unless somebody went Babe Ruth in the last three weeks, the Barons would likely be a championship team without an All-Star. Lately, Stahl had been on fire, and he was a good out-fielder, but it was probably too late for him to attract votes. Reynolds had hit some of the longest home runs, but he didn't join the team until May and had spent almost three weeks on the disabled list. Plus, he was only average in the outfield.

Although Barons beat reporter Van Hoose couldn't vote for players on the home team, he believed Hoss deserved consideration based on his excellent defense, grit, and steady hitting:

> Hoss is one of those players you have to see every day to appreciate, so I don't think he'll get the votes.

Fastball to the Face

Even with Finley having snatched away the team's two surefire All-Stars, the Barons kept winning, taking the first three of a four-game set against the Columbus Yankees back at Rickwood.

The next day, they won again, 7–0, behind Lindblad's five-hit shutout, extending Columbus's losing streak on Sunday games to thirteen. The key blow for the Barons was a first-inning grand slam by Reynolds, his first homer of the year at Rickwood.

Sullivan offered a theory on why Reynolds hit better on the road: "Tommie is a serious guy and intense competitor," he said. "He understands what has happened here in Birmingham over the last year. He's married to a Southern girl. He feels the pressure to do well and wants us to win, not just for the team, but for the city. I think sometimes he just tries too damn hard at home."

Neither Sullivan nor any of the Barons could explain how Reynolds, so well respected by his teammates, was the target of so much vile on the road. Over the course of the season, no Baron had been knocked down at the plate more often. Was it because he was the team's best power hitter? Or was it because he had the blackest skin? Reynolds knew that both were plausible explanations. He'd been told before coming to Birmingham that he'd be treated like a dog, and that he needed to ignore the racial slurs and knockdown pitches. And that's exactly what he'd done. Several times after being knocked down, his impulse was to charge the mound. But he knew that would only fuel the haters and the bigots. He'd learned to control those impulses in the army when he listened to "hillybillies" ranting about the "niggers."

In the bottom of the eighth in the series finale against Macon, with the Barons leading 4–1, Reynolds dug in, crowding the plate. The first pitch to him from Marv Fodor was a fastball, up and in. Reynolds tried to duck, but it was too late, the ball hitting him square in the face. He collapsed, blood gushing everywhere.

Sullivan rushed to the plate, certain that Reynolds was seriously hurt. But the baseball gods were smiling on Birmingham that day. Reynolds slowly got to his feet, wiped the blood on his sleeve, and then trotted to first. Later, he received eleven stitches to sew up his lip, but luckily he lost no teeth.

The Barons held on to win, 4–1, taking the series four games to two, increasing their lead over second-place Lynchburg to five and a half.

CHAPTER 52

Haywood Sullivan

Gearing Up for the Stretch Run

In many ways, this had been Sullivan's most enjoyable year in baseball. He loved the challenge of being in charge, making the decisions that won or lost games—who to start, when to pinch-hit, how to motivate, where to position the outfielders. It was rewarding to see players improving and gaining in confidence. Riding on the bus or sitting in the dugout, he liked watching the players interact, and marveled at how well they all got along in a situation that the segregationists had insisted would lead to discord and disaster. There had been no drunken brawls or charging after hecklers to distract from the Barons' accomplishments.

As a native Alabamian, Sullivan took pride in helping to bring to Birmingham something it desperately needed—a boost to its collective self-esteem, and a glimpse of how integration could work. He couldn't count the times a stranger had stopped him at the ballpark or shopping at Piggly Wiggly to thank him for what he was doing.

But it hadn't all been perfect. Maybe the hardest thing was being away from Pat and the kids, although they had visited several times. He loved having his son Marc come to the ballpark, and the way the players went out of their way to play with him, especially Hoss, Lindblad, and Reynolds. Maybe the favorite memory he'd take from the season was watching Reynolds and Hoss toss Marc into the laundry cart and wheel him around the clubhouse, the six-year-old squealing as if he were riding the Matterhorn at Disneyland. The thing Sullivan looked forward to the most after the season was going home and being a full-time dad again.

The other thing that had been hard on him was Finley. In some ways, he respected him, both for what he'd accomplished in business and as an owner. He appreciated that Finley had agreed to make Kansas City the parent club for

Birmingham. If he hadn't done that—when no other franchise would—none of this would have been possible. He also noted that Finley had not only hired him to be a manager but started him in AA.

Yet there was also a part of him that saw Finley as a pompous, meddling phony.

Still Tinkering After All These Games

Sullivan's biggest concern about his starting rotation was Ron Tompkins. He was still throwing as hard as ever, so it was either mechanics or in his head— he'd been wilder than spray paint in a strong breeze. Moving him to the bull-pen was either a possible cure... or a way to seal defeat.

With the loss of Sanders, Sullivan was searching for the right combination of starters and relievers... even though it was late in the season to still be tinkering. He had promoted Rich Allen—the guy who'd taken a line drive to the head—from the bullpen to the starting rotation. Allen had won his last five decisions, and in the twenty-three games he'd pitched since May 22, he had given up only eight earned runs, a stretch of sixty-two and two-thirds innings, with an ERA of 1.13. On the other hand, Seitz, Jones, and Ken Knight had been delivering kerosene, which left Grzenda as the only choice as closer, even though he'd pitched lately as if he were still lost somewhere out on the highway from Kansas City.

Offensively, with only twenty games left to play, Sullivan still needed a reliable cleanup hitter. He'd used Meyer, Stahl, Reynolds, Rosario, Norton, and Tony Frulio in that spot, and none of them had shown the consistency to carry the team. Meyer had for a while, but as Sullivan had feared, his skinny frame had weakened in the heat and he was now out of the lineup with a strained knee. On the bright side, Larry Stahl had hit .560 in the last eight games, and Reynolds was hitting shots all over the yard. If only the Barons played all their games on the road.

A Vote for Manager of the Year

With only three weeks left in the season, Sullivan and the Barons still led Lynchburg by five. As the Barons' magic number—any combination of Baron wins and Lynchburg defeats—fell to nineteen, Albert Belcher dished out the praise for Sullivan: "He's the best manager I've ever dealt with," he said. "His method of handling young players is superior to any we've had. He and those boys have worked together so well. I've been close to the situation all the way and there has never been one ill feeling. He's for them, and they're for him, and that as much as anything is why we're on top."

Van Hoose thought Sullivan was not only a shoo-in for Southern League Manager of the Year, but barring a total collapse down the stretch, he also deserved to win the prestigious minor-league manager of the year award presented by the *Sporting News*.

"It's nice to be considered," Sullivan said. "But we need to win this thing first."

Enough to Make a Guy Want to Gag

Sullivan stared at his boss's photo on the front page of the newspaper. Finley was wearing a Beatles wig and hamming it up with his attractive secretary. Sullivan almost choked on his cornflakes.

When the Beatles arrived in America for their first American tour, Finley thought it would be a grand idea to have them come to Kansas City and play at Municipal Stadium. He contacted their manager, Brian Epstein, in England and offered them $50,000. The response was one word: "No." They were already booked solid. That didn't deter Finley. A week later he upped the offer to $100,000. The response was the same. They were "too busy" was the explanation. But he tried Epstein again, this time at $150,000. "That was talk he wanted to hear," Finley told the *Birmingham News*.

The Beatles accepted his $150,000 offer to play September 17 at Municipal Stadium in Kansas City. It would be the biggest venue of their tour, and the contract was the largest amount ever paid to musicians. The money was paid, in full, up front.

Finley had already begun the preparations. The stage would be at second base, and seats in the infield would go for $8.50, with box seats at $6.50 and grandstand seats for $4.50. Tickets would be printed in wedding-gown white, kelly green, and Fort Knox gold. On the back of each ticket would be the picture of Finley in his Beatles wig.

The part of the story that made Sullivan think, *Okay, maybe this guy isn't simply an egomaniac after all*, was that Finley said he would donate all revenue for the event to his favorite charity, the National Tuberculosis Association, a legacy of his bout with the disease when he was younger.

"I won't keep a nickel," he declared. "I don't want anybody saying I used kids to make money. I'm looking for friends. Some of these young Beatles fans have never seen the inside of a ballpark. Maybe they'll come back. And who knows? Maybe Ringo can play shortstop."

Wouldn't that be nice, thought Sullivan. *Then maybe he can send us back Campaneris.*

Einstein in Green and Gold

Lindblad had taken to calling Sullivan "Einstein," although not to his face. But in the second game of a doubleheader against Macon, the sobriquet would be put to its sternest test.

A few days earlier, Sullivan had demoted Tompkins to the bullpen. In his last start, he had walked six in five innings, his lofty 7–0 record back in May falling to 10–5, his confidence sulking toward its nadir. Sullivan hoped the change would not only get Tompkins's pitching back on track but also shore up a bullpen that in the last two weeks had lost leads handed to it by Blue Moon, Lindblad, and Nicky Don Curtis. Sullivan knew that a good way for rancor and unrest to ferment on a pitching staff was to have relievers regularly snatch victories away from the starters. With Sanders, that hadn't happened. Tompkins had said he understood the demotion and that he wanted to do whatever he could to help the team, although in the minor leagues, all of the rah-rah happy-team incantations were a delicate dance along the fragile fault line separating personal goals and glory from team success.

For the second game of a doubleheader, Sullivan had taken the risk of giving Shaky Joe Grzenda his first start. Grzenda responded, giving up only one run on seven hits, making a strong case to join the starting rotation for the last couple of weeks of the season. But the Barons' bats gave him no support, and they trailed 1–0 going into their last at-bat.

With two out and nobody on, Rosario drilled a triple to right center, bringing up Hoss with a chance to tie the game. Sully called time-out. In his last twenty-three at-bats, Hoss had not gotten a hit. None. Not even a bloop single. His average had fallen twenty points; he looked like Casper the Ghost. If Sullivan had anybody else who could play second, he would have used him.

Sullivan motioned for Hoss to meet him halfway between third and home. Hoss eased toward him, fully expecting to be told he was being pinch-hit for.

"Just relax up there," instructed Sully. "You're due."

Like everyone else, Hoss thought Sully was the best manager he'd ever had. The first pitch was a fastball on the outside part of the plate. Hoss took a rip, making the best contact he'd had in over two weeks, sending a line drive into the gap in right center. It was a stand-up triple, driving in Rosario, tying the game.

Sullivan now faced another decision. He'd moved Hoss to the eight spot because of his slump, so the next batter was Shaky Joe, who hadn't gotten a hit since LBJ was a senator. Figuring Shaky Joe was tired after having pitched twice as many innings as he had in any game this season—a nine-cigarettes-between-innings performance—he decided to go with a pinch hitter and try to win the game right there.

He signaled toward the bench for a pinch hitter—pitcher Rich Allen—surprising everyone on the bench, including Allen. On the season, Allen had gotten only a couple of hits, although in pre-game batting practice for pitchers, which Sullivan sometimes pitched, he was Harmon Killebrew. Lots of line drives. Batting practice, however, was not the real thing.

Sullivan knew this was a risky move, and not just because there was no evidence that Allen was a clutch hitter. The riskier part was that he was sending up a pitcher to hit when he still had two position players on the bench—Woody Huyke and Bill Meyer—hitters who would not be happy to have a pitcher chosen to pinch-hit over them with the game on the line, even if they were nursing nagging injuries.

Allen struck out on three pitches.

Sullivan decided to roll the dice again, summoning the beleaguered Tompkins, who'd been warming up in the bullpen. Tompkins had never relieved before. Not at Chula Vista High, not in Legion ball, not in his two years in the minors. Star pitchers didn't relieve. Now his whole mind-set had to be different. As a starter, he had four days to think about his next appearance. On this day, he had five minutes. Usually, he took fifteen minutes to warm up before a game; on this day, he was throwing full speed after only a minute. It had been only two days since his last ill-fated start, but he'd lasted only three innings in that one, so his arm felt fine.

He walked the first hitter on four pitches.

Glancing toward the dugout, he expected to see Sullivan racing out to yank him. But nobody was warming up.

The next batter, doing Tompkins a big favor, swung at the first pitch, hitting a sharp grounder over the mound. Chavarria raced to his left, swooped it up, stepped on second, and then threw to first for an easy double play.

The next batter flied out to center, ending the inning.

The Barons didn't score in their half of the inning, but Tompkins also retired the side in order again, whiffing two.

With one out in the bottom of the ninth and nobody on, Ossie Chavarria lashed a shot into the gap in right center. As he steamed into third with a stand-up triple, the second baseman momentarily bobbled the relay.

"Go, go, go," yelled Sully, waving him home.

Chavarria, whose churning legs looked like a hamster's on an exercise wheel, shifted back into high gear, racing toward the plate. The catcher waited, crouched and ready. As Chavarria started his slide, the catcher reached out for the ball as it came in a little up the line toward first. At the same time, inexplicably, the pitcher also made a desperate lunge for the errant throw, his head colliding with the catcher's head as Chavarria slid in safely.

"Barons win!" screamed the announcer.

The Barons players, led by Tompkins, rushed out of the dugout to mob Chavarria. As they danced and celebrated, the pitcher and catcher lay in the dirt nearby, both out cold. (They recovered.)

The Barons' magic number was now fourteen.

Finley Strikes Again

The day after Blue Moon notched his fifth straight win—a 5–1 gem that would've been a shutout except for his own error on a throw to first—he was summoned to Sullivan's office. In those five wins, all complete games, he'd walked fewer than two a game.

"What's up, Skip?" asked Blue Moon, stifling another one of his lingering coughs.

"We want you to go back to the hospital and get checked out again," answered Sullivan. "You need to be healthy."

"When?"

"Right now."

Blue Moon turned to leave.

"Before you go, I've got something else to tell you."

"What's that?"

Sullivan explained that he'd just gotten off the phone with Charlie Finley.

"You're going to the big leagues," said Sullivan.

"No, for real?"

Sullivan explained that the plan was to have Blue Moon pitch two more games for the Barons, and then as soon as they clinched the pennant, he'd leave to join the A's, most likely for their series in Kansas City against the Yankees.

"You could be facing Mickey Mantle in your first game," said Sullivan.

"It don't bother me," replied Blue Moon. "It don't bother me t'all. The Yankees? They don't scare me. They look just like any other club to me. You just go out there and throw strikes. My fastball been movin' real good. They either hit it or they don't."

The Barons' magic number was down to twelve.

CHAPTER 53

Haywood Sullivan

As Good a Hitting Performance as I've Ever Seen

Batting in the eighth inning for the Barons in Asheville, Tommie Roadman Reynolds stepped into the box, pretty sure the first pitch was coming at his head. In his two previous trips to the plate, he had homered, each blast traveling well over four hundred feet. Prior to this three-game set in Asheville, he had homers in three of the last four games at Rickwood.

"Be alive up there," warned Sully.

Sure enough, the first pitch was up and in, sending him sprawling to the dirt. He glared out at the pitcher; players on both benches readied to charge the field. Slowly, he picked himself up, dusted his backside, and then stepped back into the box.

The next pitch was a hanging curve. His eyes lit up, and he swung from his ass, the ball rocketing off his bat, a majestic drive. It cleared the left-field fence, the light tower, and possibly the Blue Ridge Mountains.

He didn't stand at the plate admiring his work; that was an arrogance still years in the future, possibly because hitters knew that pitchers of the era—the Don Drysdales and the Bob Gibsons—would deliver them a horsehide sandwich every at-bat for the rest of their baseball lives if they tried to show them up. Reynolds simply dropped his bat and trotted around the bases. He would've cracked a smile, but he still had the stitches in his lip from getting drilled in the face.

Despite his three prodigious blasts—all tape-measure jobs—the Barons lost, their magic number remaining at twelve.

"That was as good a hitting performance as I've ever seen," said Sullivan.

A Change of Heart

Sullivan's concern about the Barons' lack of power in the heart of the order had been assuaged a bit with Reynolds's recent power surge. Larry Stahl was also on a base-hit binge.

If the term *scrappy* applied to the Barons, then nobody better personified it than the twenty-three-year-old left-hand-hitting Stahl. When he joined the team in May after finishing his military obligation in the army reserve, Sullivan questioned if he had the skills to help the team. But upon arriving in Birmingham, something clicked. Maybe it was the maturity of having served his hitch in the military, or the benefit of his recent marriage, but Stahl had a different explanation: Haywood Sullivan. There was an unspoken bond between the two men—Sullivan had been hard-nosed as a player, in both baseball and football, and appreciated the same trait in Stahl, a player not afraid to crash into a fence chasing down a long fly. In the month of August, he was 31 for 81 (.383), raising his average thirty-two points, and was now hitting exactly .300. In Asheville, he'd gone 4 for 10, with two homers and six RBIs.

"I didn't think so a couple of weeks ago," said Sullivan, "but I'll take the middle of our order—Reynolds, Stahl, and Rosario—over any in the league."

Three Shots at Glory

With only two weeks left in the season, the Barons were set to open their last home stand—five games against Charlotte followed by a crucial three-game showdown series against Lynchburg. Sullivan predicted that by the time the team left town for the final week of the season—three games in Charlotte and a season-ending three games in Lynchburg—the pennant would be clinched. In the bottom of the ninth in the first game against Charlotte, the scene was set for another patented Barons' comeback. Trailing 3–1, they were in danger of their third loss in a row, matching their longest losing streak of the year. It would also waste an excellent outing by Blue Moon, his first since getting the word he was being called up—eight innings, two earned runs, and only two walks, his sixth game in a row walking two or fewer.

Five days earlier when Finley had called to break the news that Blue Moon was being called up, Sullivan had lobbied not to tell Blue Moon until a day or two before he departed, worrying that informing him too soon could get him too excited and he'd lose his concentration in his final starts. Finley overruled him. He wanted to get the publicity rolling for Blue Moon's debut in Kansas City against the Yankees...never mind that there would still be a week left in the Southern League schedule.

When the Barons got two runners on in the ninth, the crowd of 1,256 was on its feet. But Rosario popped to short and Huyke hit a feeble grounder back to the pitcher.

The Barons' lead over Lynchburg was now down to four and a half... with thirteen to play.

In a doubleheader the next day, they won the first game, 2–1, behind a four-hitter by Tompkins, far and away his best performance in over a month. Sullivan had taken a chance and moved him back into the rotation after his win in relief.

Trailing 4–3 in the last inning of the nightcap, they loaded the bases with only one out. A base hit and they would widen their lead. But Rosario and Tony Frulio failed to deliver, and the lead over Lynchburg was down to four.

The next night it was Hoss's chance at glory. With the Barons losing in the bottom of the ninth and the tying run on base, he struck out swinging, missing the ball by an Ozark mile.

Three times in their series against Charlotte, the Barons had come to the plate in the bottom of the ninth with a chance to pull the game out of the furnace... and three times they had failed.

The lead was now down to three... with Lynchburg due in tomorrow.

"I'm confident we can sweep Lynchburg," offered Sullivan.

CHAPTER 54

Haywood Sullivan

The Lying Bastard

Sullivan was steaming. He'd just gotten a call from Hank Peters, the KC general manager, informing him that Blue Moon, after pitching in the critical series opener against Lynchburg, was to leave first thing in the morning for Kansas City.

With ten games left in the Barons' season, Sully had charted his pitching rotation until the end of the season...and Blue Moon was penciled in for two more starts after this game, including the last game of the season against Lynchburg on the road. Calling up Moon now flew in the face of what Finley had promised...that Blue Moon would leave only after the Barons clinched the pennant.

Sullivan tried to compose himself. First Campy, then Sanders, and now Blue Moon. The heart of his team. These moves confirmed what Sullivan had suspected all along—that Finley had been lying when he pontificated about doing everything he could to help his beloved hometown. In the scale of disasters in the universe, Sullivan knew that this didn't rank in the top twelve million; nor would a Baron Southern League championship lead the news with Walter Cronkite. But the team had been a positive force in the community all summer long. They'd shown the possibilities of an integrated future in the most unlikely setting.

With no other choice, Sullivan broke the news to Blue Moon thirty minutes before he took the mound against Lynchburg.

Nightmare in the First

Heading to the mound, Blue Moon had the swagger of a young man knowing he was catching a plane to The Show in the morning. He hadn't lost a game in more than a month, and after a rocky start to his pro career, he was living up to the hype and Finley's big investment. He'd adjusted well to pro ball, a nineteen-year-old unwrapping the gift of a complex new world every day. His teammates had learned to enjoy his cocky demeanor, and he'd become an active participant in locker room banter, even though he was the richest guy on the team, and the possibility of resentment had been huge. But his "pleasant and refreshing personality," as a sportswriter put it, and his considerable gifts, helped ease his transition.

In the first inning, Blue Moon struck out the first hitter. And then the nightmare began. By the time Sully summoned Stanley Jones from the bullpen—still in the first inning—Blue Moon had been rocked for eight runs on six hits and two walks, his worst outing as a pro by a factor of many…an embarrassing way to be escorted to the big leagues.

The Barons never recovered, losing 12–6, their lead over Lynchburg now down to two.

Extra Security

Sullivan arrived at the ballpark the next day surprised to find two motorcycle police officers stationed in front of the Baron clubhouse. Belcher had ordered extra security for the team's final two games.

It wasn't because the Barons and Lynsox hated each other—which they did—but because an uneasy tension had settled over Birmingham and the rest of the South. With the opening of school scheduled in a few days, school integration loomed as the big civil rights battleground, and Belcher was taking no chances on anything spilling over to Rickwood and spoiling what had been a historic five months.

During the game, the two police officers would be stationed at the ends of the Barons' dugout.

For the start of the 1964–65 school year, as resistance to school desegregation slowly, painfully began to weaken across the South, it was anticipated that as many as five thousand blacks would attend previously segregated schools in Alabama, Mississippi, Georgia, Florida, Arkansas, Louisiana, North and South Carolina, Tennessee, and Virginia. But in Birmingham, despite court orders to accelerate the inclusion of black students, only a dozen were expected to enroll in previously all-white schools. These court orders had rekindled fears around the city of a repeat of last year's ugly school integration battles that included KKK cross burnings, Governor Wallace calling out state troopers to prevent black students from entering classes, angry white parents screaming insults and throwing rocks, white students boycotting classes, and—when all of that didn't satisfy the extremists—the dynamiting of the 16th Street church.

"Appreciate you being here," said Sullivan, walking between the two cops.

Sullivan's Gamble

Nervously, Sullivan watched Ron Tompkins complete his warm-up pitches prior to the start of the second game against Lynchburg. Tompkins's first pitch was lined up the middle for a single. After striking out the second hitter, he walked the next man on four pitches. Sullivan had an uneasy feeling—Tompkins was steering the ball again rather than cutting loose as he had when he was the most dominant pitcher in the league.

The Lynsox cleanup hitter, Deacon Jones, lifted a routine fly to center. But as Wayne Norton circled under it, he slipped, and the ball landed behind him. By the time he recovered, the two runners had scored. After retrieving the ball, he threw to third in an effort to get Jones, but his throw missed the mark by the length of twelve police motorcycles and Jones waltzed home, too.

As had been the case the night before, the Barons never regrouped, and lost 7–4. It was Lynchburg's eighth win in a row. The momentum was all on their side.

The Baron lead was now down to one . . . and the Lynchburg starting pitcher tomorrow night would be Manly Johnston, gunning for his nineteenth win.

"We sure need to win this last home game," observed Sullivan, offering a managerial glimpse into the obvious.

The Last Home Game

The headline the next morning read: HAVE THEY BLOWN IT? According to Van Hoose, "The most popular conversation around town this week is whether the Barons will continue their slide and disappoint the Birmingham fans."

The Barons had led the league since May 29—ninety-six days—and only ten days before had led by six games (with seventeen to go). Now they led by one (with eight to go). They'd lost seven of their last nine, their worst slump of the year, and the clubhouse, which had been loosey-goosey all year, now had the mood of a coffin sale at a nursing home.

"If they lose tonight," wrote Van Hoose, "Flagville would be nowhere but uphill, and on the cruel road, too."

For the final game, a crowd of 2,299 whooped, hollered, and cajoled as the Barons took a 2–0 lead over Johnston into the fifth inning. Rich Allen, the team's hottest pitcher over the last three weeks, was tossing a nifty one-hitter. Hope lived.

After a leadoff single to start the fifth, Lynsox centerfielder Danny Murphy hit a high pop-up back of second.

"I got it," yelled Hoss.

It was the proverbial can of corn, but as he circled under it, his feet got tangled—or exhaustion finally won out—and down he went, the ball landing a few feet away for a base hit, reminiscent of the ball that Norton had missed the previous night.

Unnerved, Allen walked the next hitter to load the bases. That brought up Manly Johnston, the pride of Auburn University, the winningest pitcher in the minor leagues, and the best-hitting pitcher since Babe Ruth.

He drilled a two-run single to tie the score.

And then Allen came completely unraveled. By the time Sullivan signaled for Shaky Joe in the bullpen, Allen had given up six runs on six hits. Grzenda arrived on the mound carrying a couple of cans of high-octane ugly, giving up four more runs in a third of an inning.

Hope died.

The pennant race was tied.

In the clubhouse, Sullivan reminded his downcast players that there was still a week left, and with their final three games against Lynchburg, the season was far from over.

"But it's uphill from here," he admitted, the first time all season that he had expressed anything but optimism.

The Incline

It was 4 a.m. as Iron Lung chugged up an incline east of Spartanburg heading toward Charlotte and the final week of the season. The weary players were all curled up in their seats, asleep—no card games, no beer drinking, no visions of Hawaii dancing in their dreams. Also making this final trip was Albert Belcher. He, too, was asleep. But not Sullivan. Two weeks earlier he had been touted as a shoo-in for minor-league manager of the year. Now he was overseeing a sinking ship on the verge of one of the great collapses in minor-league history.

Prior to the series against Lynchburg, he'd predicted that if his team hit, they'd win. As it turned out, they did hit, averaging six runs and twelve hits in the three games. But the starting pitching that he'd counted on—Blue Moon, Tompkins, and Allen—had bombed miserably, giving up twenty-two runs and twenty-one hits in a combined total of only eleven innings.

He stared at the incline ahead.

This team has earned a special niche in local memory, chiefly that for three months they interrupted the clouds over Birmingham.

—Alf Van Hoose, *Birmingham News*

PART VIII

THE SEASON

September

League Standings, September 1

	W	L	GB
Birmingham	76	56	
Lynchburg	75	57	1
Macon	71	60	4½
Charlotte	71	61	5
Knoxville	64	68	12
Chattanooga	62	68	12
Columbus	58	71	17
Asheville	48	82	26½

CHAPTER 55

Haywood Sullivan

Telegram from Finley

The Barons lost the opening game to Charlotte, 2–1, wasting a strong pitching performance by Nicky Curtis. The loss, coupled with Lynchburg's tenth win in a row, dropped them out of first place for the first time since May.

In the morning, Sullivan received a telegram from Finley:

Dear Sully,
    Know you and the boys have been going through a bad storm of late. I'm sure the storm will pass and you will see the sunshine and the rainbow.
    Tell the boys when the going gets tough, the tough get going.
    Go out and play loosey-goosey baseball and have lots of fun. And regardless of whether you win or lose, I want you to take the boys out tonight and be my guests for two-inch steaks.
Regards,
Charlie Finley

Although the telegram struck Sullivan as a bit disingenuous, he read it to the team prior to the second game. They bounced back, winning 7–3, sparked by an RBI double by Reynolds, a homer by Rosario, and strong pitching from Lindblad (11–7). Coupled with Lynchburg's loss to Asheville (snapping their winning streak at ten), the race was now all even again, with five to play.

Blue Moon's Big-League Debut

In his first inning against the Yankees, Blue Moon gave up a single to Tony Kubek, a walk to Bobby Richardson, and then, after retiring Roger Maris, he threw a fastball down the pipe to Mickey Mantle...and the A's trailed 3–0.

Blue Moon was pulled after just two innings, yielding a total of six runs, six hits, and two walks.

"Not what we were hoping for," concluded Finley.

Learning of Blue Moon's disastrous debut, Sullivan paused to wonder. Why had Finley started him against the mighty Yankees instead of letting him open against an easier team, say, the Senators, especially after Blue Moon hadn't even gotten out of the first inning in his final start with Birmingham?

He shrugged.

Hottest Slugger on the Planet

In the fifth inning of the third game against Charlotte, Reynolds stepped to the plate with two runners on, the Barons trailing 2–1 despite solid pitching from Tompkins.

Charlotte starter Bill Whitby delivered a hanging slider, coming in over the plate big as a tetherball. Reynolds uncoiled, making perfect contact. The left fielder didn't even bother to move, the ball leaving the park at the 375 mark.

In the top of the seventh, with the Barons leading 5–2, Reynolds stepped up again, this time with a runner on first.

"Be alive up there," warned Sullivan.

Sure enough, the first pitch knocked him down. The second pitch left the yard at the 375 mark again, giving him five RBIs for the game.

Seated in the press box, Belcher marveled. "That boy's the best hitter on the planet right now," he declared.

In the eighth, Reynolds came up with the bases loaded and the Barons leading 13–2. With the count 3–0, Sullivan gave him the green light. It was a fastball, low and in. Reynolds golfed it high and deep to left center. As he dropped his bat and headed to first, the ball sailed over the fence—by a hundred feet—giving him a grand slam . . . and his third homer of the game and nine RBIs.

For the second time in two weeks, he'd hit three monster home runs in one game, all of them blasts that would've cleared any ballpark in America. His nine RBIs was a Southern League record.

And just as important, the victory kept the Barons tied with Lynchburg with four to play.

In the raucous Baron clubhouse, Belcher raised his arms and asked for quiet. "Steaks are on me tonight," he announced.

Lindblad nudged Hoss. "You gonna order another chicken-fried steak?"

Droopsy Delivers a Luau-Worthy Game

In the Sunday-afternoon finale against Charlotte, Reynolds led off the second inning with a deep drive to straightaway center. Gone—his fourth consecutive homer, an all-time Barons' record. Charlotte countered with two runs in their half of the inning, but in the bottom of the third Reynolds scorched a liner over short to drive in another run and put the Barons on top.

"Damn, they held him to a single," observed Belcher.

Sullivan had taken another gamble in starting Paul "Droopsy" Seitz in this crucial game. It was Blue Moon's turn in the rotation, but with him off getting pulverized by the Yankees, the start went to Seitz. Of all the pitchers on the staff, nobody puzzled Sullivan more than the laconic Seitz. He threw as hard as anyone on the team, and had a knuckle curve that broke so sharply when he threw it messing around in the outfield before games, nobody wanted to play catch with him. But ever since the disaster of opening night and his two weeks on the disabled list, he had been a base-on-balls machine... until the last couple of weeks, when he'd become Sullivan's most reliable man out of the bullpen.

Helped out with two double plays in the seventh and eighth innings, Seitz picked up the win in a 6–4 Baron victory.

"I think it's time to order the grass skirts," hollered Hoss in the rowdy post-game locker room.

With their three wins in a row against Charlotte, a confident group of Barons climbed aboard Iron Lung for the seven-hour trip to Lynchburg and the final three games of the season. Lynchburg had also won, so going into the final series, the teams remained tied, with all the aggies, steelies, and cats'-eyes on the line. Slated to pitch the opening game for the Lynsox was King Kong himself, Manly Johnston.

CHAPTER 56

Haywood Sullivan

Too Good Not to Have a Happy Ending

"We'll win this thing," boldly predicted Sullivan.

Back in Birmingham, *News* sports editor Benny Marshall was just as optimistic. In a column titled "A Vote for Sully and His Gang," he labeled the Barons "the team that will not die" and marveled at how the pennant race had knocked the season start of Bear Bryant and the Alabama football team's quest for a national championship out of the headlines:

> The weary Barons will board the bus after the final game and make the long, ten-hour drive back to Birmingham, arriving at Rickwood at 9 a.m. as the Southern League champions of 1964. This story has been too good not to have a happy ending.

A Targeted Man

In all his years in baseball, Sullivan had never seen a hitter on such a slugging rampage as Reynolds. He could only remember witnessing two three-homer games—one each by Mantle and Ted Williams—so to have Reynolds accomplish the feat twice in a two-week span was mind-boggling. He'd also never seen anybody collect nine RBIs in one game. But it wasn't just the numbers that impressed him...it was the way Reynolds had turned into a stone-cold fastball assassin, absolutely ripping the cover off the ball, and doing it when he knew there was a possibility that every pitch could be coming straight at his head.

Reynolds had quietly gone about his business all season—at least on the outside—but inside he'd felt the pressure, arriving in Birmingham with a steamer trunk full of high expectations. Not only was he supposed to be the

278

Barons' power hitter, but he was also supposed to be the model of how a black player was to comport himself in a hostile environment. The Latin players—Rosario, Huyke, and Campaneris—were instructed to stay calm, too, but they somehow didn't educe the same level of racist vitriol that the black Americans did.

During the course of the season, no black player in the league had been targeted for more verbal abuse than Reynolds, especially in Lynchburg. He heard it every game when he trotted out to take his position in left field or when he waited in the on-deck circle. But it wasn't just verbal abuse. He led the league in getting knocked down at the plate. It was as if the target that had been painted on the window of his Super Sport on his way to spring training had been a premonition of the season ahead.

"Get ready for one at your head, Monkey Man."

He hadn't heard those taunts in Birmingham. It wasn't that Rickwood didn't sell tickets to racists. It was just that the racists frequenting Rickwood took the attitude that the Barons' black players were—to borrow Bull Connor's phrase—"my nigguhs." It was okay to hurl racial insults at black demonstrators, or children trying to integrate their schools, or even players on opposing teams, but the Baron players were off-limits. If "my nigguhs" could bring a championship to Birmingham, then they would be tolerated...as long as they stayed in their own neighborhood when the game was over.

As the Barons got dressed before the first game in Lynchburg, Sullivan pulled Reynolds aside.

"Tommie, I've got good news for you," he said.

He'd just talked to farm director Hank Peters again, and the big-league team was calling up Reynolds and Larry Stahl.

"When?" asked Reynolds, knowing that the call-ups of Campy, Sanders, and Blue Moon had left a sour taste.

"As soon as the season is over," Sullivan replied. "You and Larry will be leaving directly from here and joining the A's in Baltimore."

"Good," replied Reynolds. "I want to stick around and beat these jerks."

Trotting out to the field, Reynolds wondered if Manly Johnston's first pitch would be at his rib cage.

"Hey, black boy," greeted a fan. "I gave my slave the day off. Go get me a beer."

Ninety-Nine Years Earlier

Sullivan had his pitching rotation set for the series—Rich Allen in the opener against Johnston, and then Nicky Don Curtis in game two, and Lindblad in the last game. His batting order, however, was still not settled. With so many of his players banged and bruised, he'd wait until after batting practice and see what players seemed least injured. The roster looked like a MASH unit.

As a bit of a history buff, Sullivan saw his situation as analogous to that of another commanding officer who found himself in a similar plight ninety-nine years earlier—General Robert E. Lee. In the closing days of the Civil War, Union forces had chased renegade remnants of Lee's army into Lynchburg, a city on the verge of chaos. Lee was running low on ammunition, and many among his combat ranks were lame and infirm. Seeing the end, he moved out of the town to a courthouse twenty miles down the road at Appomattox and surrendered.

But waving a white flag wasn't in Sullivan's character. He would stay and fight, despite his team's inventory of injuries, with its health resembling the hobbling legions of Lee's remnant army: Stahl with a sprained ankle; Norton at half speed with a puffed knee; Meyer limping with a pulled muscle; Frulio dizzy and throwing up with the flu; Stutz and Huyke hurt with jammed fingers; and Hoss with all the strength of a moth.

"Let's jump on Johnston early," he instructed.

Balk!

Leading off for the Barons in the first, Chavarria got on board when Johnston bobbled his slow roller back to the mound for an error.

"Choke!" screamed voices in the Barons' dugout.

Sullivan flashed the hit-and-run sign, Hoss's specialty. Johnston threw to first to keep Chavarria close.

"Balk!" hollered the ump.

"You're choking, Manly," screamed the dugout voices. "You can't handle the pressure."

Hoss lined the next pitch to right for a base hit. As Chavarria rounded third, Sullivan threw up the stop sign, not wanting him thrown out at the plate to kill a potential big first-inning explosion.

Thinking the throw was going home, Hoss put his head down and charged for second. But the first baseman cut off the relay and threw to second, hanging him out to dry, Chavarria anchored on third.

And then Johnston struck out Meyer and Huyke, ending Sullivan's hope of jumping on Johnston early. Lynchburg's biggest crowd of the year, 4,467, gave Johnston a standing ovation as he walked off the field.

In the Lynsox half of the first, Allen gave up two runs.

In the third, he gave up two more . . . and for the rest of the game the Barons anemically flailed away against Johnston. They lost, 8–1, Johnston picking up his twentieth victory.

The only Baron to do any damage was Reynolds, going 2 for 3 and driving in the Barons' only run despite getting knocked down every trip to the plate. His boiling point, which had been miraculously held in check all season, was finally reached on a force play at second when the throw to first from the Lynsox's shortstop clipped his jersey as he started his slide. He popped up and flung the shortstop to the ground as both benches sprinted onto the field, a seasonful of anger ready to explode. But somehow, in the shadow of Appomattox, flaring tempers surrendered to equanimity and no blows were struck, the teams retreating to their dugouts.

In a dispirited Barons' locker room, Sullivan did the math. "It's simple," he said. "We have to win the last two games."

"End Appears Near for Limping Barons"

For almost a month, the News had been tracking the Barons' magic number. 17...12...10 and finally down to 4. But the headline following the opening game drubbing told of a different number: JOHNSTON'S MANLY MOUND JOB PUTS TRAGIC NUMBER AT 1.

The subtitle summed it up: END APPEARS NEAR FOR LIMPING BARONS.

But Sullivan wasn't about to concede. In a brief pre-game meeting, he addressed the team. "No matter how this thing turns out, I'm proud of you," he said. "You've battled your butts off all year. That's all a manager can ask."

There was no battle cry from the team, no clasping of hands in the middle...just a quiet determination as they headed for the field.

"Hey, Reynolds," a fan hollered. "Bananas are on sale over at Piggly Wiggly. Better stock up."

After retiring the side in order in the first, Nicky Curtis gave up a leadoff homer in the second to Lynchburg first baseman Deacon Jones. And then the roof caved in. By the time the inning was over, the Lynsox had scored eight runs off Curtis, and then a ninth when Jones crushed his second homer of the inning, this one off Lindblad, whom Sullivan had summoned in desperation out of the bullpen.

For the next seven innings, the Lynchburg fans shouted and stomped their approval as every Baron out brought the Lynsox closer to the pennant. There was even a smattering of applause when Reynolds, after getting low-bridged once again, walloped a tape-measure home run in the seventh inning that traveled well over 475 feet. So impressive was the blast that the players in the

Lynchburg dugout, who'd been riding him unmercifully all season, stood and applauded as Reynolds circled the bases.

But it was too little, too late for the Barons, the Lynsox cruising to a 10–3 win . . . and the Southern League pennant.

The headline in the *News* the next day summed up the feelings of the Barons' faithful: SHUCKS!

CHAPTER 57

Albert Belcher

The Long Ride Home

As the Barons' bus neared the outskirts of Birmingham after the ten-hour ride home following the final game of the season (which they won, 8–5, sparked by another long Reynolds homer), the morning sun danced off the city's skyline. Beer cans littered the floor and bleary-eyed players stared out the windows. Up front, Sullivan turned to Belcher in the next seat.

"Sorry we couldn't win it for you," he said.

"A hell of a year anyway," replied Belcher.

In the distance, they could see the Vulcan, the iconic statue atop Red Mountain that paid homage to the city's industrial origins. A mile away, the 16th Street Baptist Church stood quiet but resolute. The one-year anniversary of the dynamite blast that shocked the nation was four days away. "Who knows?" said Sullivan. "Maybe I'll be back next year."

"I doubt it," said Belcher. "Mr. Finley has bigger plans for you."

They didn't need to say it, but they both believed that Mr. Finley had cost them the pennant. It didn't take Casey Stengel to understand that Campy, Sanders, and Blue Moon would've been worth a couple more wins.

Still, for Belcher, the millionaire lumber baron, the season had been a success. His team had turned a small profit, but—more important—he had defied the odds, the Big Mules, and the Ku Klux Klan in bringing professional baseball back to his hometown. "Sully, I think I can speak for Birmingham," said Belcher. "Thanks for a great ride."

The Unwitting Activist

As the bus turned onto 3rd Avenue near Rickwood, Belcher smiled. Sometimes, the course of events can change a person's heart. For the past week he had watched Tommie Reynolds put on one of the greatest hitting exhibitions in the history of the game, major or minor league. He'd seen his left fielder get knocked down almost every time he stepped to the plate, yet quietly pick himself up, dust off his uniform, and then hit a wicked line drive somewhere. He'd heard the witless insults hurled at the young man, and marveled at how Reynolds, in the manner of a Jackie Robinson, just kept doing his job, eyes straight ahead, carrying himself with dignity and pride when it would've been easy to charge into the stands. Having witnessed all that, Belcher's allegiance to the hard-core tenets of segregation was forever shaken.

He had never thought that returning Baron baseball to Birmingham made him a civil rights activist. But his 1964 Birmingham Barons had given a glimpse of what integration could accomplish. In terms of impact or courage, his efforts paled next to those of Martin Luther King Jr. or the Reverend Fred Shuttlesworth, two men he regularly disagreed with. Running an integrated baseball team wasn't on a scale of the significant deeds of the time—it didn't compare to the "I Have a Dream" speech, the Montgomery bus boycott, the lunch-counter sit-ins, the registering of black voters, or the confrontation with Bull Connor and his police dogs and fire hoses. Those were acts of courage and conviction. But Belcher's effort was a stepping-stone on the road to racial equality and, if not a knife to the heart, at least a head butt to the chest of Jim Crow.

The Barons had shown Birmingham what was possible. In the same way that a house needs someone to first lay the foundation and frame the walls, Albert Belcher helped set the groundwork for changes to come...for the city, for the Southern League, for himself.

Nobody had gotten shot or beaten up. Nobody had his house dynamited. Nobody caught a disease while sharing a Rickwood restroom. Instead, night after night at a baseball park older than any in America, players and fans of different shades gathered to enjoy a game as solidly rooted in Southern culture as the segregated schools and lunch counters of the city in which those games were played.

Albert Belcher was already planning for next year.

The Most Maligned City in America

Belcher had been the one to recruit Charlie Finley, a fellow Birmingham native, and despite Finley's meddling he and Belcher had set the tone and the design that lured the fans into coming out to Rickwood. And it was those fans in Birmingham—the most maligned city in America—who ignored the hatred and the violence and, for nine innings at least, did their best to root, root, root for the home team...and in their own little way, improve the city's image.

When the season started, the stench of dynamite still lingered. Five months later, as the Barons' bus turned into the Rickwood parking lot, Birmingham, at least on the surface, had made little progress: It still did not have a black policeman; the FBI still had not made any arrests in the church bombing; schools had admitted only a handful of black students; blacks could still not eat in most restaurants, stay at the Tutwiler Hotel, or live on the canopied streets of Mountain Brook or Homewood; blacks still made half as much for the same work as whites...if they could even get hired; blacks still drank from separate drinking fountains; and whenever a black committed a crime, the newspapers fanned the flames by always using the word NEGRO in the headline.

But at Rickwood, the blacks had cheered on the Barons just as loudly as the whites. The Checkers Rule had been demolished, and the chicken wire that separated the races had come down. Despite the fears of the hard-liners, there had been no rush on the Jefferson County Courthouse for applications for interracial marriages. The money that blacks had spent at the ticket windows and concession stands turned out to be as green as anybody's.

Albert Belcher had delivered a message to civic and business leaders that was clear—the old Jim Crow way of doing things had not only been bad for the city's image but bad for the economy, too, including the business of baseball.

Belcher's Experiment

In 1964, the people demanding an end to racial segregation were not focused on the Southern League experiment or the Birmingham Barons. Their primary battlefields were schools, lunch counters, buses, hotels, drinking fountains, and other forms of public accommodation. America's recreational fields seemed somehow less relevant, especially with cities all across the country erupting in violence.

Although the attendance figures at Rickwood were only slightly higher than they had been back in 1961, when the players were all white and the blacks sat on the other side of the chicken wire, a threatened boycott by white fans never materialized. People wanting to see quality minor-league baseball turned out, sometimes in large numbers, as they had for the Kansas City exhibition game. Across the country, minor-league attendance was falling—largely because of the rise of nationally televised major-league games and more competition for the entertainment dollar—but the Barons had held their own.

It was too soon, and perhaps too much of a reach, to proclaim that the Barons' experiment was a turning point in the march toward equal rights, but if it could happen at Rickwood, then maybe the same thing could happen at other venues around Birmingham—restaurants, hotels, department stores, schools, businesses. Although the Civil Rights Act had now been passed, nobody in the South, or anywhere else for that matter, believed the law was going to change what was in people's hearts. That would take years, or decades, if it happened at all. But Belcher's Barons had provided a living lab for how an integrated community could function successfully.

Discussions had begun in Birmingham to open an Alabama Sports Hall of Fame. There was no shortage of candidates—Hank Aaron, Mel Allen, Johnny Mack Brown, Bear Bryant, Willy Mays, Willie McCovey, Satchel Paige, Bart Starr. It didn't seem like a stretch to think that Haywood Sullivan and Albert Belcher would be added to that list.

CHAPTER 58

Paul Lindblad

Saying Good-Bye

Slowly, the players filed off the bus in the Rickwood parking lot. There were no parades or camera crews to greet them, just wives and small children. Lindblad's wife, Kathy, had already packed the Impala with all their earthly belongings crammed inside for the drive home to Chanute, Kansas. It had been seven months since they had loaded their two infant daughters into that same packed car and taken off for spring training in Daytona, uncertain whether his injured arm would be able to sustain the dream, or even if they would have enough money to buy groceries. Now, 187 innings, eleven wins, eight losses, and a $1,000 progressive bonus later, that dream and his arm were stronger than ever.

Like everyone else on the team, he was tired and disappointed. Leading the league for ninety-six days only to lose it at the end had left a sour taste. It was no consolation that Lynchburg had won fourteen out of fifteen to overtake them.

"No more road trips for five months," he whispered to Kathy as he lifted his younger daughter into his arms.

Lindblad's baseball career was still in front of him. Birmingham had been a stopover, not the destination. For as long as possible, he would hold on to his dream, forestalling any thought of a life and career after baseball. He was not a sure bet to make the big leagues, but he'd now had two winning years, and because he was a lefty, he figured to have a good shot. And he was pretty sure Sullivan liked him.

He would look back on this season and remember it fondly. It helped that it had been—until the end—a winning year. Winning silenced the petty bickering; winning made for happy bus trips and trading friendly insults with Hoss; winning made the daily grind of going to the park tolerable; winning relieved the monotony of endlessly shagging balls during batting practice; winning

287

eased the daily grind with rarely a day off; winning made the time away from Kathy and his daughters more tolerable.

After unloading his bag, he approached Sullivan. "Thanks for everything, Skip," he said, "especially for not giving up on me."

"Baseball needs more good people like you," replied Sullivan.

They shook hands. In 1964, that's what baseball men did—no hugs, high fives, or fist pumps—just a firm affirmation of mutual respect.

Something Special

Lindblad was not a complicated man, just pure Midwestern stock. But as he thought back on the season and his teammates, he knew it had been something special: the grace and speed of Bert Campaneris, who'd risked his life to flee Fidel Castro's Cuba...the power and determination of Tommie Reynolds, who two years earlier had filled out his last will and testament prior to hoisting his combat gear onto an army truck in Germany as the world waited on the precipice of ruin...the physical stamina of Hoss Bowlin, who grew up on an Arkansas tenant farm and spent much of the season hunched over in pain from having one of his testicles removed...the raw talent of Johnny Blue Moon Odom, who started the year washing dishes for the minimum wage at Macon's Dempsey Hotel, where he was expected to use only the rear entrance...and the calm leadership skills of Haywood Sullivan, who grew up down the road in Dothan and knew all about the South's history of lynchings and the hard-edged racial protocols but treated his players as equals.

Of course Lindblad hadn't come to Birmingham to study family trees. In a sense, he and the rest of the team were poorly paid mercenaries, bringing to Birmingham their arsenal of skills and talent. They had applied those skills to winning ball games, and now it was time to move on. Other than Stanley Jones, none of them would stay around. They would all retreat, hurrying back to their hometowns, families, friends, and jobs in the warehouse for a buck twenty an hour. A few would return to Florida for Instructional League. From his time in Birmingham, Lindblad would preserve some newspaper clippings and a few Kodak moments taken by the apartment pool, but little else.

He was proud to have been part of Birmingham's first integrated team. But sports had already provided a blueprint for breaking down barriers. For years black athletes had gotten white fans to suspend their prejudices in the name of team or national pride, as they had for Jackie Robinson, Jesse Owens, and Joe Louis. Although these black athletes couldn't belong to elite country clubs or send their children to the schools of their choice, their exploits on the playing fields and arenas had pulled down a few pickets of the fence guarding the house of bigotry. The Barons had just invited all the neighbors to join them in the backyard.

"See ya next spring," said Lindblad, shaking Hoss's hand.

"Now, don't you be going and drinking out of any strange toilets," replied Hoss.

"My biggest regret this whole year," said Lindblad, "is not getting to see you in that grass skirt."

"You can thank Mr. Finley for that."

For the second-sacker named Lois, it was back to Paragould, Arkansas. His wife, Madelyn, had a job teaching school, but he wasn't sure what he was going to do. Maybe take a few college classes. Maybe drive a school bus. In a few days, the disappointment of losing out to Lynchburg would subside. He would start thinking about where he would play next year. His slump at the end of the year had dropped his final average to .242, not exactly a punched ticket to move up, but he knew Sullivan liked the way he played the game. He led the team in games, at-bats, walks, and ugly scars. Maybe, if he was lucky, he'd get invited to the big-league training camp. That was the dream anyway.

Neither Lindblad nor Hoss, nor anyone else on the team, had volunteered to come to Birmingham—they'd been assigned by the baseball gods. Before the season started, none of them had said, *You know, I think it's deplorable what has happened in Birmingham this past year and I would like to go there and make a difference.*

They were not social activists. They didn't volunteer at soup kitchens or in school programs. Basically, they lived in their apartments, drove their Malibus, Bonnevilles, and Impalas to the ballpark, played the games, and then went home and watched Johnny Carson and got ready to do it all over again the next day. They did not carry signs to end Jim Crow. They did not march on City Hall. They did not speak out on the issues. Some of them didn't know Bull Connor from Strom Thurmond . . . or care about either one of them.

They just showed up and played integrated baseball, which, according to Alf Van Hoose, was the way baseball was supposed to be played, even in Birmingham.

In 1964, the culture of minor-league baseball—or for that matter, the ethos of all sports—didn't encourage the mixing of social justice and athletic competition.

It was supposed to be about what happened on the field. And Birmingham was better for it.

I like to believe that the negative extreme of Birmingham's past will resolve into positive and utopian extreme of her future, that the sins of a dark yesterday will be redeemed in the achievement of a bright tomorrow.

—Dr. Martin Luther King Jr.

PART IX

EXTRA INNINGS

Final Standings

	W	L	GB
Lynchburg	81	59	
Birmingham	80	60	1
Macon	75	65	6
Charlotte	73	67	8
Knoxville	67	73	14
Chattanooga	65	74	15½
Columbus	65	74	15½
Asheville	52	86	28

Epilogue

Whatever Happened To...

Haywood Sullivan

In 1965, Finley fired his manager Mel McGaha and named Sullivan the A's newest manager. At thirty-four, he was the youngest skipper in the big leagues. His meteoric ascension had taken only a year.

He didn't have any better luck than Finley's previous managers, however, either in winning games with his inept team or in curtailing Finley's constant meddling. When he got a call in the off-season from Tom Yawkey, the owner of the Boston Red Sox, offering him the position of vice president of player development, he said yes.

Over the next twenty-seven years, he would become the first person in the history of the major leagues to be a player, manager, general manager, and owner... and one of the most respected men in the game.

His time as general manager and owner, however, wasn't without controversy. For years, the Red Sox faced repeated charges of racism, and Yawkey's response to the team's lack of black players didn't help:

I have no feeling against colored people. I employ a lot of them in the South. But they are clannish, and when the story got around that we didn't want Negroes they all decided to sign with some other club.

As general manager, Sullivan incurred the ire of Red Sox Nation for letting go of popular players such as Luis Tiant, Bernie Carbo, Fred Lynn, Carlton Fisk, and Bill "Spaceman" Lee. And it was under his watch that the Red Sox blew a fourteen-game lead and lost in a one-game play-off to the evil Yankees on Bucky Dent's homer.

293

When Yawkey died in 1976, his widow loaned Sullivan a million dollars, and he became a third owner of the team. After he and Mrs. Yawkey survived an attempted coup by co-owner Buddy LeRoux, he took over running the team, and although the fans had grown increasingly impatient for a championship, he became one of the most respected owners in the game. He served on the Major League Executive Council, the committee that basically runs baseball. In 1981, he was named by the *Sporting News* as the top executive of the American League.

Around Fenway, Sullivan had a reputation for dignity and decency, treating the grounds crew and the ticket takers with the same respect he afforded his players and fellow American League owners. There was discussion among the other owners of naming him the league president.

Perhaps the criticism of Sullivan's tenure as general manager–owner that stung the most was regarding his older son, Marc, the little boy whom Hoss and Tommie Reynolds used to push around the Barons' locker room in a laundry cart. In 1980, the Red Sox selected him in the second round of the draft. Some said his skills didn't merit being drafted that high, and he'd been picked only because his father owned the team. Marc was good enough, however, to play parts of five years in the big leagues, mostly as a backup catcher, although his career .193 batting average did little to quiet the doubters.

In 1993, a year after the death of Mrs. Yawkey, Sullivan sold his share of the team and retired from baseball after five absorbing decades. He confessed to friends and family that as much as he loved the game, he no longer wanted to be part of the direction it was taking, with strikes, labor disputes, skyrocketing salaries, and agents and players who cared too little about the history and integrity of the game. According to the *New York Times*, he received $36 million for the sale.

Sullivan moved to Fort Myers, Florida, and went into real estate investment, developing among other properties a marina and hotel. Eventually, his son Marc, who had spent several years scouting for the Texas Rangers after injuries ended his playing career, came to work with him in Florida. (Sullivan had separated from his wife, Pat, years earlier, but they never divorced and he supported her financially. Their two other children, twins Kyle and Sharon, both stayed in the Boston area.)

One of the many projects that Sullivan became involved in was helping to lure a major-league expansion team to Florida. He formed an unlikely partnership with the legendary Russian ballet dancer Mikhail Baryshnikov to develop a combination sports-and-entertainment complex in Orlando.

The further Sullivan's days in Boston receded into the past, the more his critics, as well as his supporters, came to reassess his impact. Mostly, they focused on the content of his character. "He is one of the great executives of our generation," said Commissioner Bud Selig. "A decent and good person, professionally and personally. He was a credit to the game and to the Red Sox franchise."

ESPN analyst Peter Gammons, a former Boston journalist, credited him with transforming a chronically bad franchise into a perennial contender, keeping them there "from 1966 to the present."

USA *Today* sports columnist Bob Nightengale also had high praise: "It was the way he carried himself," he wrote. "Always with a lot of class, an elegant act. He didn't play political games or favorites.

"Everyone thought the world of him. In baseball, it's tough not to have some enemies, even a lot of enemies. In his case, I'm not sure he had any. Everybody treated him with respect, and he did the same to them. He was one of the last great men in baseball."

On February 12, 2003, a brilliantly sunny day in Fort Myers, Sullivan was with his son Marc and a friend as they unloaded some building supplies from the back of a pickup. He sat down on a strip of grass, and when Marc turned around, his father was lying on his back. Rushing to his side, Marc knelt down next to him, calling his name. But Sullivan was unresponsive, his arms extended, his eyes rolled back in his head. Marc felt a faint pulse and began CPR while the friend called 911. The medics arrived quickly and applied the shock paddles, but to no avail. Haywood Cooper Sullivan, a baseball icon, was dead at the age of seventy-two, his last breath taken in his son's arms.

Sullivan was buried, not in Boston, but in a plot next to his parents in Dothan, not far from the house he'd bought for them with his bonus money back in 1952. At the service, his son Marc summed up his father's legacy with eloquent simplicity: "Dad always knew where he came from and where he wanted to end up."

John Blue Moon Odom

Blue Moon's life after the Barons has been marked by more twists and turns than a kayak in white water. In 1965, after having been demoted to Lewiston in A ball, he married Perrie and had a son. In 1968, after four mediocre years in the minors, his big-league career finally took off after Finley moved the team to Oakland. In his first full year in the major leagues, he posted a 16–10 record, with a 2.45 ERA, pitching 231 innings, giving up only 179 hits, while striking out 143 and walking just 98. He hit his first big-league home run and was named to the American League All-Star team, pitching two scoreless innings.

He did great again in '69, winning fifteen and losing six, with a 2.92 ERA. Named again to the All-Star team, he was a cover boy on the *Sporting News*. To top it off, he hit five home runs, tops among any major-league pitcher that season.

Life was good for the pride of Macon. But then the waters started churning.

In 1970, although he was 9–8, he developed elbow problems and had to have surgery. He returned in 1971, but some of the zip was gone from his fastball, and his record fell to 10–12, with a 4.20 ERA and only 69 strikeouts in 149 innings. In 1972, however, he bounced back, achieving a 15–6 record, with a 2.5 ERA, as the A's began a three-year run as the world champions.

Through his farm system, Finley had assembled a lineup that included Reggie Jackson, Joe Rudi, Sal Bando, Rick Monday, Bert Campaneris, and Gene Tenace. He also had, arguably, the best pitching staff in the majors— Catfish Hunter, Ken Holtzman, Vida Blue, and Blue Moon, with great support out of the bullpen by Paul Lindblad and Rollie Fingers.

As they were winning championships, they also gained a reputation for arguing and fighting among themselves, and Blue Moon was often at the center of it. He was involved in publicized clubhouse altercations with Vida Blue and Rollie Fingers, as well as scrapes with Reggie Jackson and his former Baron teammate Tommie Reynolds.

His scariest episode, however, happened the night of January 6, 1972. Because the days of multimillion-dollar salaries and player agents were still a decade away, Blue Moon was working as a clerk in a liquor store. He got a call from Perrie telling him that she'd seen three young men trying to break into the house next to his mom's home (which Blue Moon had purchased); they were now fleeing on foot. As he was talking to her, he spotted the three youths running past his store.

Grabbing a gun, he took off in pursuit. Often used as a pinch runner, he quickly caught them. One spun around, and before Blue Moon could react, the boy fired three shots from a .38, two of them hitting Blue Moon, one in the neck, the other in the side of the chest. Gushing blood, he fell to the sidewalk.

Perrie was the first to arrive on the scene. She loaded Blue Moon into the car and rushed him to the hospital.

Luckily, the bullets had not hit any organs, and after three days in the hospital, he was released. He reported to spring training that season throwing as hard as ever, and would go on to have his best year. The three youths were caught and convicted.

In 1975 he was traded, bouncing from Cleveland to Atlanta and finally ending up with the Chicago White Sox. His last major-league victory was a no-hitter against his old team, the A's. The attendance that night in Oakland was

3,367, less than half the crowd that had showed up to see his pro debut eleven years earlier in Macon.

Blue Moon finished with a career big-league record of 84–85 and a 3.70 ERA. He set several A's records, including most strikeouts in a game (thirteen) and most wild pitches in a season (seventeen). He hit an impressive total of twelve home runs, and was used as a pinch runner over a hundred times. His post-season record was 3–1, with a 1.07 ERA. He also set an unofficial A's club record for participating in the most altercations with teammates.

His adjustment to life after baseball initially did not go well. He divorced Perrie and remarried, eventually settling in Fountain Valley in Southern California. In 1985, at the age of forty, he was arrested and charged with selling a small amount of cocaine to a co-worker at his job in maintenance with Xerox. While waiting for the case to drag its way through the courts, he was unemployed and fell deep into debt and depression.

One day while drinking heavily, he flew into a rage at his wife. She called the Fountain Valley police. When they arrived at his apartment, he was holding a shotgun to her head and threatening to kill her. A SWAT squad quickly surrounded the place. After being reached on the phone by a hostage negotiator, he released his wife but refused to come out, cutting off talks with the negotiator. Finally, after several tense hours without any movement, the police lobbed in four tear-gas canisters. Blue Moon surrendered immediately. Eventually, he spent six weeks in court-ordered rehab and fifty-five days in jail on the drug conviction.

It has been over twenty years since that episode, and Blue Moon has remained clean and sober and out of trouble, his "pleasing and pleasant personality" returning. In 2004, after initially being rejected because of his post-baseball problems, he was inducted into the Georgia Hall of Fame. He still lives in Fountain Valley, now with his third wife, Maureen. They live a quiet life, supported by Blue Moon's major-league pension and Social Security. He regularly attends baseball alumni golf tournaments and autograph signings.

He has nothing but good things to say about Charlie Finley. "He treated me great," he said.

Would he do anything differently? "Oh, I've made lots of mistakes, especially with women," he admitted. "But you know, I married a black, a Jew, and now I'm married to an Irish lady. She keeps me in line, and that's just fine with me."

Lois Weldon Hoss Bowlin

For a guy who grew up picking cotton on a tenant farm in Arkansas, Hoss's life turned out well... or at least it did until 2012.

After the 1964 season, he played seven more years in the minors (a total of twelve) before retiring. In his last year, 1971, he was a player-manager at Wisconsin Rapids in the Class A Midwest League. He didn't exactly set the league on fire in either department, hitting only .239 and managing the team to a last-place finish. He retired with a career .260 lifetime batting average in the minors. He did, however, get called up by the A's in 1967, and in his one and only game, he went 1 for 5.

But that wasn't the biggest thing that happened to him in 1967. He was leaving the ballpark after a game in Montgomery when he heard someone call his name. He turned around, startled to see legendary coach Bear Bryant motioning him over, and even more surprised when Bryant invited him to join him for a late-night supper at the Elite, a downtown restaurant in Montgomery frequented by politicians and Alabama's movers and shakers. Bryant had watched Hoss play numerous times, and liked his hustle and spirit.

The two men hit it off, and within twenty-four hours Bryant, who was also the athletic director at Alabama, had gotten Hoss's transcripts transferred from Arkansas State, hired him as a graduate assistant for the baseball team (even though he hadn't graduated), set him up in married-student housing, arranged for meals in the athletes' cafeteria, and lined up a full-time teaching position for Madelyn at a local junior high.

For the next four years, Hoss and Madelyn lived in Tuscaloosa, coaching, teaching, taking classes, and raising their son Parrish. Each spring, Hoss would resume his pro career. In 1971 he earned a degree in physical education from the University of Alabama, and got hired the next year as the head coach at Livingston University (later renamed the University of Western Alabama), a small liberal arts school in Livingston, fifty miles west of Tuscaloosa. Madelyn also got a job there, teaching sixth grade.

He remained cancer-free. After being told he couldn't have any more children, he and Madelyn had another son, Lance, born seventeen years after Parrish.

He coached at Western Alabama for thirteen years, leading his team to three league championships and a fourth-place finish at the Division II World Series in 1976. He put in long hours, not only coaching the game he loved but also helping build a new baseball field, as well as modern locker rooms and practice facilities. He also earned a master's degree and taught undergraduate health classes.

"Not bad for an ol' country boy," he said. "I'm sure if the Barons had taken a poll back in 1964 on the most likely to get a master's degree, I would've come in last."

After hanging up his whistle, he worked as the city's park director, as well as the greenskeeper at the local golf course. He played more than he mowed. To this hail-fellow-well-met man, nobody in Livingston was a stranger. At

Diamond Jim's, a popular café, he held court every morning, eating pastries, drinking coffee, and bullshitting about his playing days. Two pictures of him in his Kansas City uniform still adorn the wall.

After twenty-seven years of marriage, he and Madelyn divorced. "I think she finally just outgrew me," he explained. They remained good friends, however, often stopping at each other's houses for lunch, even after they both remarried.

In retirement, Hoss and his second wife, Yvonne Moody, helped raise her granddaughters from her first marriage. He grew especially close with the youngest granddaughter, Summer, a beautiful blue-eyed blonde and talented high school volleyball player. She called him Papa, and they ate family suppers together on Sundays.

But in April 2012, Summer accompanied her boyfriend and two other boys on a late-night outing in Mobile Bay. Using a small motorboat, they made their way to Gravine Island, a remote fishing village. The boys' plan was to burglarize a vacated fishing camp. But three men, all convicted felons, were lying in wait for them. There had been previous break-ins, and according to the felons, a police officer had told them to "take matters into their own hands" because of the remoteness of the island and the difficulty the police had patrolling it. When the men spotted the teens in the darkness, they fired a couple of "warning shots." The boys took off running, but Summer stopped and sat down near a tree by a dock. One of the "warning shots" struck her in the head from close range. She died ten days later, and her death quickly became one of the most publicized cases in Mobile history.

In a controversial decision that angered many and brought comparisons to the Trayvon Martin case in Florida—where the defendant who shot an unarmed teenager pleaded self-defense, claiming he feared for his personal safety—the district attorney charged the three boys who'd brought Summer to the island with burglary but filed no charges against the three men involved in the shooting, not even for being felons in possession of firearms. The family has filed a civil suit.

"Nothing in my life can compare to this," said Hoss, choking back tears as he sat in his den under his framed Big A certificate with Bear Bryant's signature. "Even if they arrest these guys, which they probably never will, there is a hole in my heart that can never be filled. Summer was a beautiful child, who unfortunately made a bad decision to tag along with those boys and paid with her life."

Tommie Reynolds

Reynolds was a career baseball man, spending fifteen years as a player and another dozen as a minor-league manager and major-league coach. And through all the years, and all the teams, and all the packing up and moving again, he stayed married to Penny, the woman he met in 1963 spring training and married at the Jefferson County Courthouse in Birmingham in 1964. In 2014, they will celebrate their fiftieth anniversary.

Although his playing career included parts of eight years in the big leagues, he never matched the blistering last month of his season in Birmingham. But who could?

His big-league career included three years in Kansas City, a year with the Mets, a year in Oakland, two with the California Angels, and one with the Milwaukee Brewers. He played a total of 513 games, with 265 hits, twelve home runs, and a batting average of .226. Twice he had four-hit games, and eight times he got three hits. His best big-league season was 1969, when he hit .257 for Oakland. The nadir of that year was his fight with Blue Moon.

If his major-league career didn't reach star status, his minor-league career did. Playing mostly in AAA, he hit a career .302, with 187 homers. Eight times he hit over .300, including .303 for Spokane in the Pacific Coast League in his last full season at the age of thirty-six. He also hit twenty homers and led the league with forty-five doubles that year.

His work ethic, knowledge of the game, and temperament led him to the coaching profession. In 1986, he was the only black to manage a whole season in the minors.

In 1989, he was tapped by his old teammate, A's manager Tony La Russa, and for the next seven years he served as a third-base and bench coach for the Oakland A's during the era of the Bash Brothers—Mark McGwire and Jose Canseco. (Ironically, it was Canseco who broke Reynolds's single-game RBI record [9] when he was a minor leaguer in the Southern League.) When La Russa moved to St. Louis in 1996, he took Reynolds with him.

During all of the years that Reynolds was chasing all over the country with his baseball career—a total of thirty-three different assignments, not counting spring training and winter ball—Penny was, according to him, the rock of the family. After going back to college following their marriage in '64, she graduated from Bethune-Cookman in 1966.

"I was lucky," she said. "Tommie paid for my schooling."

When they moved to San Diego following the 1966 season, she got her California teaching credential, and for the next thirty-two years taught English full-time in the San Diego Unified School District, the first twenty years at Samuel Gompers junior high, the last twelve at Kearney High. She also provided the primary care for their two children as Tommie pursued his baseball career.

"We were apart a lot," said Tommie. "Maybe that's why the marriage has lasted so long."

Following Penny's retirement, she wanted to move back to Chattahoochee to help care for her ailing mother, the woman who had worked three jobs to send Penny to college. Tommie didn't hesitate, stepping away from baseball to move to Georgia. After all, he reasoned, she'd let him chase his dreams for four decades.

Despite the abuse he took during his year in the Southern League, Reynolds had positive memories of his season in Birmingham. "The main reason I enjoyed that year can be summed up in two words: Haywood Sullivan," he said. "I loved playing for that man. He treated all of us with respect. When I became a manager, I tried to do the same thing with my players."

Tommie and Penny Reynolds settled in southwest Georgia, a few miles from Chattahoochee, near the Florida line. It takes a Hernando de Soto to find their house...a visitor has to pass Bradley's Hometown Proud grocery store, around the recruiting billboard for the Sons of the Confederacy with its tattered American flag flapping in the breeze. After that, it's a sharp turn at Jinx Crossing, past the penitentiary and the state mental institute, then a few miles through a canopy of trees and swampy underbrush that provides cover for deer and snakes, and then finally down a dirt road that leads to their sixty acres and two-story wood-and-brick house.

Tommie spends his days fixing roof leaks, riding his lawn mower, watching MSNBC, clearing brush, killing snakes, and fixing meals.

"I'm a good cook," he claimed. "Living alone all those years during baseball, I had to learn how."

Penny's main job became caring for her mom's "bed-to-chair" existence.

Financially, they live very comfortably on her pension from thirty-two years of teaching in San Diego, and his pension from fifteen years of playing and coaching in the big leagues...two people who worked hard and earned their retirement.

"We're blessed," concluded Penny. "God has provided well for us. And the older I get, the more I appreciate my husband. I struck gold with this man."

Alabama Sports Hall of Fame

Alf Van Hoose, Benny Marshall, and Bob Phillips, three journalists who covered the Barons in 1964, are all members of the Alabama Sports Hall of Fame.

Haywood Sullivan, Charlie Finley, and Albert Belcher, all natives of Alabama, are not.

Paul Aaron Lindblad

Kathy Lindblad sat in the living room of her three-bedroom brick house on a cul-de-sac in Arlington, Texas, remembering her husband. Tears filled her eyes. So many great memories...at least until the end.

Commanding her living room were two very large, gold-plated trophies celebrating Paul's two world championships with the A's in '73 and '74. A hallway was decorated with pictures of her and Paul and their three children, Cindy, Paula, and Troy. Hanging next to them were pictures of Paul in the uniforms of the five teams he played for in his fourteen-year major-league career—the Kansas City and Oakland A's, Washington Senators, Texas Rangers, and New York Yankees. But the picture that catches the eye is the one of him in his A's uniform sitting on a bullpen bench next to the legendary Joe DiMaggio, who was a part-time hitting instructor for the A's at the time.

"I got a call from a memorabilia collector recently," said Kathy, speaking in a soft Texas drawl that belies her Kansas roots. "He wanted to know if I wanted to sell any of the stuff I have. I'm sure it would fetch a pretty penny—three World Series rings, two big trophies, uniforms, and lots of other stuff. But there's no way I would sell any of it. It means too much to me."

Paul's climb to the big leagues followed the perfect arc—a year in A ball (Burlington), a year in AA (Birmingham), and a year in AAA (Vancouver). He got called up at the end of the '65 season when Sullivan was managing the A's; he got into four games and basically stunk it up, giving up nine runs in only seven innings for an inglorious 11.05 ERA and an 0–1 record. He did, however, strike out twelve in those seven innings.

That inauspicious start belied the big-league career he would go on to have. Over the span of fourteen years in The Show, he compiled a winning career record of 68–63, with a 3.20 era. His best year was 1975, when he went 9–1, with a 2.72 ERA, combining with Rollie Fingers as the best lefty-righty closing duo in the majors. As it was in Birmingham, nobody outworked him. Unofficially, he put in more miles of running than any pitcher of the time. Along the way, he accomplished several noteworthy feats:

- seventh on the all-time list of appearances by a left-hander
- 385 games (1966–74) without an error, a major-league record
- the last pitcher ever to face Willie Mays (in the tenth inning of game three of the 1973 World Series—Mays grounded out, and Paul was the winning pitcher)

After the A's first World Series victory, he finally made it to Hawaii, he and Kathy vacationing there with his best friend and hunting buddy on the team, Catfish Hunter and his wife, Helen.

In addition to his likable personality, he was also known around the league for one of his pre-game routines. At home and on the road, he was usually the first player at the ballpark, and when the other players arrived they would find

Paul either out in the outfield or up in the stands, searching for coins or other things of value with his metal detector. At the end of each road trip, he would proudly show his discoveries to Kathy.

After his playing days were over, he and Kathy settled in Arlington and he started a construction business, building houses. He built their home, including a workshop in the back, where he spent endless hours tinkering and fixing.

"He could fix anything," recalled Kathy. "Once when we were playing winter ball in Venezuela, he bought an old wreck of a junker and completely rebuilt it. We drove it everywhere, and then sold it for four times as much as we paid for it."

As she recalled stories about Paul, Kathy kept a box of Kleenex nearby. She never told him about the abuse she suffered as a child, although she and her sisters did finally share their stories.

"We had different attitudes back then about that kind of abuse," she said. "I know Paul could have dealt with it, but it just seemed the easier way to go."

Despite experiencing success in his contracting business, in the early 1990s Paul started to get the itch to get back into pro ball. He accepted a job as a minor-league pitching coach for the Mariners. It was during his second season in El Paso that Kathy first noticed something wasn't quite right. For most of the season she stayed in Arlington to be near their kids and the new grandchild, but in June she flew to El Paso to spend time with him. When she arrived at the airport, he wasn't there to greet her. She waited…and waited…and when he still didn't show, she called and reached him at his apartment. He had totally spaced out.

Over the course of the next year, she noticed other small things that caused her to raise her eyebrows, such as him getting confused filling out simple forms, or forgetting where he'd left a tool. Eventually, they went to the doctor in 1993, and at the age of fifty-two he was diagnosed with early-onset Alzheimer's.

"It didn't make any sense," said Kathy. "He'd done all the right things— exercising, vitamin E, crossword puzzles. He was in perfect shape. But if you have the gene—his mom and brother died from it at a young age—it doesn't make any difference."

For the first few years, Kathy cared for him at home as he slowly deteriorated. He forgot the children's names. He could no longer do math or read. He would walk into a room, and if something was out of place, he would get totally befuddled. On a couple of occasions, he gathered up all his fishing gear and waited in the driveway all day for someone to pick him up. Another time, he put on an old A's uniform and went outside to wait for a ride.

He created an imaginary friend named "Fly Guy," and would spend endless hours sitting in the driveway, scanning the skies and the planes passing overhead, waiting for Fly Guy to swoop down and pick him up. Sometimes Kathy would have to go out late at night and try to convince him to come inside and go to bed.

"He would get so upset," she recalled, "and then he'd cry like a baby. It was heartbreaking."

Eventually, the disease took a ghastly turn, and Paul began to get progressively more upset at the smallest of things, turning his flailing anger on Kathy, sometimes even growing violent. This was so out of character—he had been the kindest, most considerate man she'd ever met. She began to live in fear.

In a family meeting, she recommended putting him into a special care facility. Not all of her children were willing. Their son Troy couldn't stand the thought of his father, who'd always been such a tower of strength, not living at home. But everyone eventually agreed that Kathy's health was at risk, too. She looked as if she was about to go over the edge. So they put him into Peach Tree Place in Arlington, a care facility with cats, birds, and a dog on the premises. He was the youngest patient by ten years. Most of the residents were in their eighties, while Paul was still in his fifties.

Kathy would visit on a regular basis, but it was hard for her to watch him deteriorating. He would often get upset when she'd leave, convinced she was never coming back. For months he thought an eighty-four-year-old patient was his wife. And almost every day he would go out into the courtyard and stare up into the sky, waiting for Fly Guy to land and take him away.

His physical appearance also began to slide. He'd practically run his way to the big leagues, and then had been a jogger for years, but now he couldn't exercise regularly. The lean muscles he'd developed baling hay as a boy were gone. So was his trim stomach. T-shirts no longer fit over his belly, and his face grew puffy.

"The beautiful man I married wasn't there anymore," said Kathy.

All his memories of the World Series victories were gone. He had no idea that he'd once played on the first-ever integrated team in Birmingham and had been part of something special that helped change the city's culture forever. And yet somewhere in a far corner of his brain, he knew that baseball was a big part of who he was, because some afternoons he would take a baseball and glove that Kathy had brought him and go out into the courtyard to either bounce the ball against a wall or to play a game of toss with anybody who would say yes.

Paul died on New Year's Day of 2006. He was sixty-four. At his funeral in Arlington, his casket was flanked by his two large World Series trophies.

"Watching his decline was horrible," said Kathy. "He was such a good man, a wonderful husband and father. But the disease turned him into something else. Once it became full-blown, I didn't feel safe in the same house."

She reached for the Kleenex again. "But I choose to remember all the good memories. I loved the baseball life. Oh, it was hard at times, all the travel and moves. Every year we had to pack up and move several times. But I wouldn't trade it for anything, including Birmingham. I was stuck in our apartment most of that season with two babies under the age of two. Looking back, I think we were pretty oblivious to all the civil rights turmoil that was going on. We lived in our own little cocoon."

In the years that have passed since Paul passed away, Kathy has not remarried or even dated. He was her high school sweetheart to the end. "I could never find anyone that could measure up to him," she said. "Sometimes, it gets lonely without him, but I have all these wonderful memories."

Like so many widows of ex-players, Kathy is thankful for the major-league players' pension fund. Not only were his expenses covered during his years at Peach Tree Place, but she continues to receive the pension he accrued during his fourteen-year big-league career, a pension plan as generous as that in any industry. She is also thankful for all the friends she made in the game, reuniting annually with five wives from their years with the A's, including Helen Hunter, the widow of Catfish, Paul's best friend with the A's. Catfish, who passed away in 1999, named his son Paul Aaron Hunter.

Paul had no shortage of admirers. "I don't think he ever got enough credit for what he did," recalled ex–A's teammate Darold Knowles. "He worked harder and was probably in better shape than anyone on the club. He was a jogger, and nobody had more energy than he did."

A fan from Kansas City shared a memory. "Paul and my dad played baseball in the KC area growing up," he said. "I had the opportunity to meet him when the Oakland A's came to town to play the Royals in the early '70s. I was on cloud nine when my dad hollered to him in a sea of autograph seekers and it was like Moses parted the Red Sea when he yelled back and had us come to the railing by the A's dugout. He was the nicest professional athlete I ever met. He made a comment to me that has always stuck . . . it was about what a good ballplayer my dad was growing up. I had a friend with me at the game and I was BMOC at our grade school the next day as the word spread of our encounter. Paulie, as my dad called him, and his family will always be in our prayers. Thanks, Paulie, for the memories. I will always remember your kindness."

His next-door neighbor in Arlington, Harold Phillips, also spoke fondly. "He was like a brother," he said. "We were so close. The guy would do anything for anybody. If you came walking down the street and needed something, needed help, Paul Lindblad would be the first guy out there. There wasn't a bad bone in the rascal."

The city of Arlington named a street in his honor—Lindblad Court. He was voted as one of Kansas's all-time 150 greatest athletes. And the baseball park in Chanute, which was built as a WPA project in 1939, was renamed Paul Lindblad Stadium. At the dedication ceremony, a city commissioner and high school classmate of Paul had this to say: "There was nobody in the school who didn't like him."

Including all the cute girls who used to drive Kathy crazy.

In 2012, Kathy was dealt another blow when Cindy, her oldest daughter, was diagnosed with early-onset Alzheimer's at age fifty. Despite the sadness, Kathy finds comfort through her church, family, and friends, as well as the fond memories shared by Paul's old teammates, including some Barons.

"He was as decent a man as anybody I met in the game," recalled Tommie Reynolds.

"The perfect teammate," added Blue Moon.

ACKNOWLEDGMENTS

Rick Wolff, my editor and favorite banjo hitter, for all the help and encouragement along the way.

Richard Pine, my agent, for first believing in this project, and being in my corner for three decades.

John Strawn, my great friend and literary guru.

Stacy Bartley, for many reasons.

Wendy and Sarah Colton, my beautiful daughters; and Cole, Aiden, and Rylan, my wild and woolly grandsons.

The staff, board, and volunteers at Wordstock, for putting together such a great book festival.

The goat brothers, boys of Bandon, and Week 10 campers at the Lair of the Bear.

Hoss Bowlin, Madelyn Mack, Ron Tompkins, Joe Grzenda, Marc Sullivan, Rene Lachemann, and Gene Tenace for all the help.

Art Black and the helpful folks at the Birmingham Library.

Johnny Blue Moon Odom, for being my golf partner.

Tommie and Penny Reynolds, for class and dignity.

Paul Seitz, for being my main man in Birmingham.

Tim Boyle, Arlene Schnitzer, Greg Dufault, and Don and Wendy Cobleigh for long-standing friendships. And to the outstanding journalist Richard Ben Cramer.

Kathy Lindblad, for opening her heart.

Many thanks to David Brewer, Clarence Watkins, and the Friends of Rickwood.

And to Amy Soverow and John Archibald at the *Birmingham News*.

APPENDIX

Baron Final Stats

Hitting	BA	HR	RBI
Hoss Bowlin	.242	6	57
Bert Campaneris	.325	6	40
Ossie Chavarria	.242	5	14
Tony Frulio	.267	6	65
Dan Greenfield	.000	0	0
Elwood Huyke	.289	10	47
Rene Lachemann	.667	0	1
Mike Maloney	.200	0	4
Bill Meyer	.231	14	54
Wayne Norton	.238	17	56
Rolland Petranovich	.217	0	5
Tommie Reynolds	.313	19	78
Luis Rodriguez	.303	1	12
Santiago Rosario	.273	14	64
Eusebio Rosas	.182	0	0
Brice Smith	.125	0	2
Larry Stahl	.286	10	47
John Stutz	.257	10	37
Federico Velazquez	.476	0	1
Stan Wojcik	.482	2	7

Pitching	*W–L*	*ERA*
Dick (Rich) Allen	7–8	3.03
Nicky Curtis	12–10	4.08
Joe Grzenda	4–1	5.52
Lou Hemauer	3–4	4.12
Stanley Jones	9–7	3.30
Ken Knight	1–3	3.98
Paul Lindblad	11–8	3.32
Jim Nash	0–0	6.00
Blue Moon Odom	6–5	4.14
Ken Sanders	9–1	2.28
Gary Sanossian	0–4	5.36
Paul Seitz	5–5	4.01
Ron Tompkins	13–6	3.83

AUTHOR'S NOTE

Because this is a nonacademic narration, I don't feel it is necessary to footnote or provide a comprehensive bibliography of resources. But I do want to include the names of authors who were essential in my research:

Allen Barra, *Rickwood Field*; Glenn T. Eskew, *But for Birmingham*; John Lewis, *Walking with the Wind*; Clarence Watkins, *Baseball in Birmingham*; Michael Winslow, *The Chile Cone Chronicles*; Bill O'Neal, *The Southern League*; Marjorie L. White, *A Walk to Freedom*; Bruce Adelson, *Brushing Back Jim Crow*; William A. Nunnelley, *Bull Connor*; James S. Hirsch, *Willie Mays: The Life, the Legend*; Steve Travers, *A's Essential*; G. Michael Green and Roger D. Launius, *Charlie Finley*; John E. Peterson, *The Kansas City Athletics*; Bruce Markusen, *A Baseball Dynasty*; Steve Jacobson, *Carrying Jackie's Torch*; David Halberstam, *October 1964*; Roberto Gonzalez Echevarria, *The Pride of Havana*; Diane McWhorter, *Carry Me Home*; The Birmingham Civil Rights Institute, *March to Justice*; Larry Moffi and Jonathon Kronstadt, *Crossing the Line*; David Falkner, *Great Time Coming*; Juan Williams, *Eyes on the Prize*; Roger Kahn, *The Boys of Summer*; Taylor Branch, *Parting the Waters, Pillar of Fire*, and *At Canaan's Edge*

With the exception of two minor characters, the names in this book are real.

To read more about the players and stories covered in Southern League, *please go to* www.larrycolton.com/southernleague/extrainnings.

311

INDEX

ABOUT THE AUTHOR

Since his days as a ballplayer, Larry Colton has taught high school, worked for Nike, and written four books. Between 1976 and 2000, his magazine articles appeared in publications such as *Esquire*, the *New York Times Magazine*, *Sports Illustrated*, and *Ladies' Home Journal*. He is the author of *No Ordinary Joes*, *Counting Coup* (2000 winner of the Frankfurt eBook Award for nonfiction), *Goat Brothers* (a main selection for Book-of-the-Month Club), and *Idol Time*. Additionally, he is the founder and former executive director of two nonprofit programs: Community of Writers, a nonprofit program to improve writing instruction and student achievement in Oregon schools; and Wordstock, the acclaimed Portland Book Festival.